‖‖ ‖ ‖‖‖‖‖‖ ‖ ‖ ‖ ‖‖ ‖‖‖‖‖‖‖‖‖‖‖‖‖‖

◁ **W9-BDJ-454**

SPORT EDUCATION

EDUCATION LIBRARY
UNIVERSITY OF KENTUCKY

Sport Education: international perspectives presents a series of studies of the innovative pedagogical model that has taken the physical education (PE) world by storm. Since the emergence of the Sport Education (SE) model in the mid-1990s, it has been adopted and adapted in PE programs around the world and a new research literature has followed in its wake. This book offers a review of international SE schemes and projects, and documents what it takes to run a successful SE program.

Exploring SE across all levels of education, from the elementary school to the university, the book provides answers to key questions such as:

- What models have been developed to teach SE?
- What do successful SE programs look like?
- What do teachers think about SE and how to make it work?
- What are the implications for professional development across the range of human movement studies?

With contributions from leading international scholars and practitioners from the United States, Europe, and Asia, this book offers a more thoughtful and critical set of perspectives on SE than any other. It is essential reading for any student, pre-service teacher, classroom teacher or university instructor working in SE, PE, youth sport, sports coaching or related disciplines.

Peter Hastie is a Professor in the Department of Kinesiology at Auburn University, USA. His research interests focus on examining various aspects of Sport Education in the attempt to find ways in which the model can be most effective in school and sports settings.

ROUTLEDGE STUDIES IN PHYSICAL EDUCATION AND YOUTH SPORT

Series Editor: David Kirk, University of Bedfordshire, UK

The *Routledge Studies in Physical Education and Youth Sport* series is a forum for the discussion of the latest and most important ideas and issues in physical education, sport, and active leisure for young people across school, club, and recreational settings. The series presents the work of the best well-established and emerging scholars from around the world, offering a truly international perspective on policy and practice. It aims to enhance our understanding of key challenges, to inform academic debate, and to have a high impact on both policy and practice, and is thus an essential resource for all serious students of physical education and youth sport.

Also available in this series:

Children, Obesity and Exercise
A practical approach to prevention, treatment and management of childhood and adolescent obesity
Edited by Andrew P. Hills, Neil A. King and Nuala M. Byrne

Disability and Youth Sport
Edited by Hayley Fitzgerald

Rethinking Gender and Youth Sport
Edited by Ian Wellard

Pedagogy and Human Movement
Richard Tinning

Positive Youth Development Through Sport
Edited by Nicholas Holt

Young People's Voices in PE and Youth Sport
Edited by Mary O'Sullivan and Ann Macphail

Physical Literacy
Throughout the lifecourse
Edited by Margaret Whitehead

Physical Education Futures
David Kirk

Young People, Physical Activity and the Everyday
Living physical activity
Edited by Jan Wright and Doune Macdonald

Muslim Women and Sport
Edited by Tansin Benn, Gertrud Pfister and Haifaa Jawad

Inclusion and Exclusion Through Youth Sport
Edited by Symeon Dagkas and Kathleen Armour

Sport Education
International perspectives
Edited by Peter Hastie

SPORT EDUCATION

International perspectives

Edited by Peter Hastie

Routledge
Taylor & Francis Group

LONDON AND NEW YORK

EDUC
GV
709.2
.S662
2011

First published 2012
by Routledge
2 Park Square, Milton Park, Abingdon, Oxon OX14 4RN

Simultaneously published in the USA and Canada
by Routledge
711 Third Avenue, New York, NY 10017

Routledge is an imprint of the Taylor & Francis Group, an informa business

© 2012 Peter Hastie selection and editorial material; individual chapters,
the contributors

The right of the editor to be identified as the author of the editorial
material, and of the authors for their individual chapters, has been asserted
in accordance with sections 77 and 78 of the Copyright, Designs and
Patents Act 1988.

All rights reserved. No part of this book may be reprinted or reproduced or
utilized in any form or by any electronic, mechanical, or other means, now
known or hereafter invented, including photocopying and recording, or in
any information storage or retrieval system, without permission in writing
from the publishers.

Trademark notice: Product or corporate names may be trademarks or
registered trademarks, and are used only for identification and explanation
without intent to infringe.

British Library Cataloguing in Publication Data
A catalogue record for this book is available from the British Library

Library of Congress Cataloging-in-Publication Data
Sport Education: International Perspectives/edited by Peter Hastie.
  p. cm.—(Routledge studies in physical education and youth sport)
  Includes bibliographical references and index.
  1. Sports for children—Study and teaching. 2. Physical education and
  training—Study and teaching. I. Hastie, Peter A., 1959–
  GV709.2.S662 2011
  613.7′042—dc22
  2011011390

ISBN: 978-0-415-78159-6 (hbk)
ISBN: 978-0-415-78160-2 (pbk)
ISBN: 978-0-203-80715-6 (ebk)

Typeset in Bembo
by Book Now Ltd

Printed and bound in Great Britain by
TJ International Ltd, Padstow, Cornwall

This text is dedicated to Daryl Siedentop, whose vision for an alternate physical education has provided thousands of teachers and students throughout the world with a renewed vigor and level of excitement for their engagement in a subject we all value.

CONTENTS

ILLUSTRATIONS

Tables

Figures

CONTRIBUTORS

Swee Chong Ang is Head of the Physical Education and Co-Curricular Activities Department at Elias Park Primary School, Singapore. His research interests include physical education curriculum development, affective aspects of physical education, and physical education and sport pedagogy.

Matthew Atencio is an Assistant Professor in the Department of Curriculum, Teaching and Learning at the National Institute of Education, Singapore. His research focuses on physical education curriculum development, pedagogy, and continuing professional development, as well as the sociology of sport, health, physical activity, and education.

Sean Bulger is an Assistant Professor in the School of Physical Education at West Virginia University, USA. His research focuses on children's physical activity promotion in school, family, and community-based settings.

Antonio Calderón Luquin is a Professor in the Department of Physical Activity and Sport at the Universidad Católica San Antonio de Murcia, Spain. His research interests include teaching effectiveness, task organization, teaching models including Sport Education, and student achievement in secondary physical education.

Nicola Carse is a doctoral student in the Institute for Sport, Physical Education & Health Sciences at the University of Edinburgh, Scotland. Her thesis is investigating the complex process of curriculum change within Scottish primary physical education.

Ashley Casey is a Senior Lecturer/Course Leader in Sport and Physical Education in the Faculty of Education, Sport and Tourism at the University of Bedfordshire, England. He undertook his PhD as a full-time teacher and his research is informed by his dual role of teacher-as-researcher. He is predominantly interested in how teachers learn about and implement pedagogical models (such as Sport Education) in their classrooms, under the unique milieux that exist within these spaces.

Matthew D. Curtner-Smith is Professor and Department Head of Kinesiology in the Department of Kinesiology at the University of Alabama, USA. His research interests include physical education teaching, teacher education, teachers, and curriculum.

Peter Hastie is a Professor in the Department of Kinesiology at Auburn University, USA. His research focuses on all dimensions of Sport Education, and is now focusing on the introduction and development of the model in new settings and countries.

Andrew Hawkins is a Professor in the College of Physical Activity and Sport Sciences at West Virginia University, USA. His research focuses on behavior analysis of teaching expertise and fluency in performance; epistemology and its bearing on research methods and professional fragmentation; and technology effects of social relationships and instructional effectiveness.

Lynn Housner is Associate Dean and Professor of Physical Education Teacher Education in the School of Physical Education at West Virginia University, USA. His research interests focus on teacher and coach cognition and teaching physical education.

Mike Jess is a Senior Lecturer in the Institute for Sport, Physical Education & Health Sciences at the University of Edinburgh, Scotland. His research interests include the antecedents underpinning young people's involvement in physical activity at participation and performance levels, as well as young people's motor development.

Jinhee Kim is an Assistant Professor in Physical Education in the School of Art and Physical Education at Andong National University, Korea. Her research focuses on the process of learning to teach, and she is also interested in reflective pedagogy, and self-study of teacher education and coach education practices.

Gary D. Kinchin is a Senior Lecturer in the School of Education at the University of Southampton, England. His research focuses on implementation of Sport Education within physical education and physical education teacher education.

David Kirk is the Alexander Chair in Physical Education and Sport at the University of Bedfordshire, England. He has published widely on physical education and curriculum change, and on youth sport. His interests lie in the social construction of physical education and sustainable curriculum renewal in physical education through models-based practice.

Paul McMillan is a teaching fellow in the Institute for Sport, Physical Education & Health Sciences at the University of Edinburgh, Scotland. His research interests include Sport Education as well as the influence of teachers' beliefs and values on practice. He has successfully passed his master's thesis entitled: "The influence of socialisation and physical education teachers' value orientation".

Ann MacPhail is a Senior Lecturer in the Department of Physical Education and Sport Sciences at the University of Limerick, Ireland. Her research interests include physical education teacher education, young people in sport, curriculum development in physical education, teaching, learning, and assessment issues within school physical education, and methodological issues in working with young people.

Diego Martínez de Ojeda is a teacher at Mediterranean High School in Cartagena, Spain. As a PhD student, he is interested in teaching models, Sport Education professional development, and Sport Education in elementary schools.

Wesley Meeteer II is an Assistant Professor in the Department of Human Performance at Concord University, USA. His research interests include the use of the Sport Education model in university and community settings, and the use of reflective practices in coaching education programs.

Toni M. O'Donovan is a Senior Lecturer with the University of Bedfordshire, England. Her research interests are in the area of pedagogy in physical education, focusing particularly on models-based instruction.

Dawn Penney is Professor of Physical Education and Sport Pedagogy in the Faculty of Education at the University of Waikato, New Zealand. Dawn's research focuses on policy, curriculum, and pedagogy in physical education.

Oleg Sinelnikov is an Assistant Professor in the Department of Kinesiology at the University of Alabama, USA. In addition to research interests in professional development and motivational climate in physical education, his research focuses on models-based instructions, specifically Sport Education and its efficacy and ecology.

Karen Swabey is the Academic Coordinator in the Faculty of Education at the University of Tasmania, Australia. Karen's research focuses on curriculum in health and physical education as well as aspects of social and emotional well-being.

Deborah Tannehill is a Senior Lecturer in the Department of Physical Education and Sport Sciences at the University of Limerick, Ireland. Her research interests focus on teaching and teacher education in physical education and sport, in particular those issues related to continuing professional development and communities of practice, as well as curricular initiatives, assessment, instructional strategies, and supervision and mentoring.

Niki Tsangaridou is an Associate Professor in the Department of Education at the University of Cyprus. Her research interests revolve around instructional and curriculum analysis, teachers' reflection, knowledge, and beliefs, and learning to teach.

Tristan Wallhead is an Associate Professor in the Department of Kinesiology and Health at the University of Wyoming, USA. His research interests include examining sport-based physical education curricular models and their influence on student learning and motivation to participate in physical activity.

Robert Wiegand is a Professor in the PETE Program at West Virginia University, USA. His research focuses on physical education and PETE curricula, as well as supervision.

PREFACE

In 1994, Daryl Siedentop presented the first text formally outlining his vision of Sport Education, a pedagogical model aimed at promoting positive sport experiences for all students through simulating the key contextual features of authentic sport. Sport Education's rationale is that the presentation of sport units in physical education has been typically decontextualized, where skills are taught in isolation rather than as part of the natural context of executing strategy in game-like situations, and where the rituals, values, and traditions of a sport that give it meaning are seldom even mentioned. Furthermore, in typical sport units, students rarely experience the affiliation with a team or group that provides the context for personal growth and responsibility in sport. Consequently, Sport Education (with its philosophy of greater depth of coverage of content and an expanded set of content goals) was designed to integrate skills, strategies, and aspects of sport culture in a context in which students participate in an environment emphasizing fair play, equity, and inclusiveness.

Since the initial appearance of Sport Education, teachers and researchers have expanded the degree of sophistication of the model, and the creativity of its implementation, in ways even beyond the scope of its original intent. This book presents a number of stories that celebrate the expansion of Sport Education from one elementary school in the American mid-west to schools in the United Kingdom and Ireland, in east and west Europe, the Korean peninsula, and the island state of Tasmania in Australia. The authors who have contributed to this text are the pre-eminent writers on Sport Education, with a combination of over 40 academic papers and book chapters between them.

This book fits with the *Routledge Studies in Physical Education and Youth Sport* series in two ways. First, it provides a number of international perspectives on Sport Education implementation, but second, and perhaps more significant, the chapters within the book demonstrate the diversity of contexts in which Sport Education seasons have been carried out. The book includes examples from as young as third grade through to university students, and reports on seasons conducted by classroom teachers, physical education specialists, and preservice teachers.

While readers can begin to read anywhere within the book, it is suggested that Chapter 1 is particularly foundational, and provides a new way of summarizing the research on Sport Education beyond those reviews currently in academic journals.

Following the first chapter, the book is then presented in three parts. The first examines various sites of adoption of Sport Education. The model is now used by classroom teachers, specialist physical educators in elementary and secondary schools, and in universities that offer physical education courses for students of all academic majors. Part II provides examples of students' and teachers' responses to Sport Education, culminating with an eloquent explanation for the attractiveness of the model. The third and final part of this book describes the various contexts in which preservice and practicing teachers have been introduced to and trained in the implementation of the model. Here we see that substantive and on-going interaction with the elements of Sport Education is the key to the most successful realization of the model's objectives.

Sport Education: international perspectives is therefore a text that will provide valuable reading for both students and researchers with a particular interest in providing quality sporting experiences in schools for instructors and pupils alike.

1

THE NATURE AND PURPOSE OF SPORT EDUCATION AS AN EDUCATIONAL EXPERIENCE

Peter Hastie

Sport Education is a pedagogical model designed to provide authentic, educationally rich sport experiences for girls and boys in the context of school physical education. Essentially, a pedagogical model provides a "design specification" which can lead to the development of a specific program in schools for their own local purposes. This design specification consists of the essential components that identify the model, which Metzler (2005) refers to as benchmarks. It is important to note Metzler's key point that some aspects of a pedagogical model cannot be modified, for to do so would be to fail to implement the particular model. In other words, if the design specification is changed sufficiently that it does not remain true to the original intent of the model, then it becomes something else. Examples of models that have taken some aspects of Sport Education and changed them to create new models include *Sport for Peace* (Ennis *et al.*, 1999) and *Empowering Sport* (Hastie and Buchanan, 2000).

While it is true there are numerous ways in which Sport Education seasons can be configured, and many of the chapters in this book show creative iterations in many different contexts, there are five immutable aspects which cannot be compromised if one is to correctly describe a particular unit within physical education as Sport Education. These include (i) an extended period of time over which the unit takes place, (ii) that students remain on the same team for the duration of the unit, (iii) the inclusion of developmentally appropriate competition, (iv) the taking of various roles and responsibilities by students other than that of player, and (v) that the entire experience takes place in an atmosphere of festivity.

The genesis of Sport Education came in the 1980s when its founder Daryl Siedentop became disenchanted with the fact that many physical education programs, even when taught effectively, were not interesting or challenging enough to inspire students. To that end, Siedentop developed the format, features, and pedagogies of the model. This was followed by in-school application by teachers in Columbus, Ohio (USA), and the subsequent teacher and student responses confirmed the model has significant potential to engage students utterly and intently in their physical education experiences.

Siedentop's criticism of the way in which sport was presented to students within physical education was that he considered those experiences to be inauthentic. That is, they did not resemble the exciting and engaging experiences that students either participated in outside of school, or watched on television. Rather, sport within physical education was characterized by a smorgasbord curriculum of short units in which any competition was *ad hoc*, team membership changed within lessons, and students often would not know what would transpire in a class when they entered the teaching space. Furthermore, he noted that the total experience is lacking in festivity.

Consequently, Sport Education's six key features were designed to mimic the authentic form of sport within the larger culture, as these were considered as essential in preserving the primary features of sport. These were listed as seasons, affiliation, formal competition, record keeping, culminating events, and festivity. A season of sport occupies an extended period of time in one activity. By consequence, a season of Sport Education (a term preferred to "unit") is often two to three times longer than usual, with the operational assumption being that less is more, and that this extended time promotes more in-depth understanding of the material. With regard to affiliation in Sport Education, students quickly become members of teams, and remain on the same team throughout the competition. Sport seasons are also characterized by formal competition. That is, the games that are played count toward a ranking system in which teams are categorized according to their performance. In addition, these competitions are typically interspersed with practices. Most sporting events also have some form of culminating event. These festive events (swimming carnivals, basketball championships, etc.) create the opportunity for a festival and celebration of accomplishments, a significant characteristic of play and sport. Records in sport help to define particular standards and can also serve to define local sport traditions. Finally, the festive atmosphere of sport enhances its meaning and adds an important social element for participants.

Recognizing how interscholastic and elite sport can be particularly exclusionary, together with a potential for a "win at all costs" mentality, Siedentop designed Sport Education not as a direct replication of interscholastic sport, but with three significant modifications that fit the purposes of an educational setting. These included (i) participation requirements, whereby through the use of small-sided teams everyone plays all the time, (ii) developmentally appropriate involvement, in which the secondary rules of games are modified and matched developmentally to the abilities of students, and (iii) students taking roles other than player, whereby students learn to be coaches, referees, trainers, safety officials, scorekeepers, managers, publicists, and broadcasters, thereby leading to a more complete understanding of sport.

The rationale for these changes was not only to give students a more equitable experience, and eliminate some of the traditional ways in which sport in physical education has served to alienate students (see Ennis, 1996), but also to provide an expanded set of curriculum goals so that students would become competent, literate, and enthusiastic sports players. By "competent" we mean a student has sufficient skill to participate in games satisfactorily, understands and can execute strategies appropriate to the complexity of the game, and is a knowledgeable games player. By "literate," we mean a student understands and values the rules, rituals, and traditions of sport and can distinguish between good and bad sport practices as either participant or spectator. Finally, by "enthusiastic" we mean a student participates and behaves in ways that preserve, protect, and enhance the sport culture within the class, school, and community (Siedentop *et al.*, 2004).

To date, responses to Sport Education throughout the world have been particularly positive, particularly when one considers that many of the pedagogies adopted within Sport Education are particularly emancipating for both teachers and students. That is, much of the decision-making is turned over to students, with the teacher becoming less of a ring master and more an overseer of class events. Siedentop (1998) notes that Sport Education is best achieved through pedagogical combinations of direct instruction, cooperative small-group work, and peer teaching, rather than by total reliance on directive, drill-oriented teaching. To use a sport metaphor, the teacher becomes the commissioner of a league in which the students are both the subsidiary administrators and players, and are responsible for much of the day-to-day operations of that league.

If we were to make an executive summary of the responses of teachers and students, it could be described as follows. For students, Sport Education is a more attractive form of physical education than their previous experiences, as they perceive there is a level of curriculum ownership, with roles and responsibilities as part of a persisting team. For teachers, the model is also seen as attractive, particularly as they see students with greater interest in the subject. Teachers also appreciate the release from a direct instructional role which allows for more individual attention to students and the ability to achieve other pedagogical tasks such as assessment (Kinchin, 2006). The model has also been significantly evaluated by researchers who have produced over 60 empirical publications examining various aspects of the model.

It is the purpose of this chapter to consolidate those research findings and to relate them to the extent to which the model has been validated in achieving its goal of producing competent, literate, and enthusiastic sports players. We will begin, however, with a vignette of a Sport Education lesson in order to show the varying responsibilities of students and teachers within.

> We are guests in Ms. Brown's fifth-grade class in which the students are participating in a Sport Education season of badminton. As the students enter the gym, they go immediately to their home court and begin a warm-up led by one of their peers. Another student has collected the racquets and shuttles from the equipment area and distributes these to the team after the warm-up. Ms. Brown is completing last-minute preparations and interacting with the "Strikers" team about some challenges they faced in their games the day before. A third student now leads the team in a short practice period prior to the upcoming competition.

At some point, a signal is given to begin the day's first competition, which is a mixed-doubles format. Each team will have decided which team members make up the two-person teams that compete in the name of the larger team. These competitions are often "graded" in the sense that students of comparable skill levels compete against each other. Members of two of the three teams are sent by their managers and coaches to one of the four or five small courts where games take place. Members of the third team, called a duty team, are organized to referee and keep score and statistics at the various courts.

All the games start on the same signal. The game itself is a modified version of badminton, emphasizing basic tactics and skills relevant to the game. All games end at the same time and there is a short transition to allow students from the duty team to move to courts to compete in the second game, and for members of one of the initial competing teams to transition to duty team responsibilities. Scorekeepers and statisticians leave their sheets in an assigned place so that they can all be collected at the end of the class by the students from each team that had the ongoing role of team statistician.

You will notice that an attractive bulletin board not only has the seasonal schedule and the day's schedule, but also up-to-date team standings and statistics for all players. A third game is played to ensure that all students both play and do duty team chores that day. A brief reflective period ends the class, with the teacher recognizing students and teams that show tactical improvement as well as examples of fair play. This two-versus-two competition eventually yields a team winner (all individual games count toward overall team points) and the class will then move to a single competition where more advanced tactics and skills will be introduced. The season culminates with a further team competition, with an overall class winner determined by participation, competition results, and fair play points.

(Adapted from Siedentop, 2002)

The development of competence

As noted above, competence encompasses the elements of skill execution, the execution of strategies, and knowledge of games.

Skill improvements

Reports of skill improvement in Sport Education come in two forms. The first, characteristic of the earliest studies, relates to student self-perception of skill development, while the second relates to pre-test/post-test scores on skill and game play tests. With regard to perceptions of skill improvement, there are numerous studies in which students comment on how they believe their skills improved during a particular season. These include Carlson (1995) with eighth- and ninth-grade girls playing touch rugby, Pope and Grant (1996) with fifth-grade students also during touch rugby, Browne *et al.* (2004) with eighth-grade students playing rugby, and

Kinchin *et al.* (2004) with ninth-grade students in soccer, rugby, and basketball. In the recent Australian study of Spittle and Byrne (2009), significant differences for perceived confidence were found between eighth-grade students who completed seasons of Sport Education or more traditional approaches on changes in perceived competence. Of interest in that study was that, while students in Sport Education showed no significant difference between pre- and post-test scores on perceived competence, there was a significant decrease on perceived competence scores for the traditional group. The general trend of students reporting skill improvements is not limited to English-speaking settings. The sixth-grade Russian students in the study of Hastie and Sinelnikov (2006) confirmed that they believed they had made significant gains in their skill and understanding of basketball. In Hong Kong, Ka and Cruz (2006) investigated soccer seasons with high-school students and teachers and reported positive effects on students' learning interests.

Teachers have also suggested improvements in skill. In both the New Zealand (Grant, 1992) and Australian (Alexander *et al.*, 1996) trials, teachers stated that students' skills and game play improved more with Sport Education than with previous curricular approaches used. Nonetheless, in other studies, teachers seem more skeptical, with only 54 percent of teachers in the Alexander and Luckman (2001) survey agreeing or strongly agreeing that motor skill development was more achievable under Sport Education than their previous approaches.

More recent investigations of skill competence in Sport Education have focused on empirical measurement. The first came in 1998 when Hastie used Gréhaigne *et al.*'s (1997) game-play efficiency index to quantitatively examine sixth-grade students' passing and catching competencies through a 30-lesson season of Ultimate Frisbee. In this study, team game-play efficiency performance improved as the season progressed, although there were no significant improvements in individual player passing or catching competencies. A second study in 1998 demonstrated that fifth- and sixth-grade students increased their success rates (in terms of controlling the puck and making accurate passes) during a season of floor hockey (Hastie, 1998b). In a second hockey study (with seventh-grade students), Hastie and Trost (2002) found that students of differing entering skill levels performed better on related discrete skill tests at the end of the season. Later, in a badminton study in which eighth-grade Russian students were the participants, Hastie *et al.* (2009) found improvements in both the selection (what shot to make) and execution (ability to produce the desired shot) dimensions of their game play. In that study, however, students also made significant improvements on badminton skills tests that measured their ability to control the shuttle and hit it more aggressively.

Even more recently, studies of competence in Sport Education have used comparative designs. In these cases, students participating in seasons are weighed against those who undertake units of work that follow a more traditional, skills–drills format. Pritchard *et al.* (2008) adopted a 2 (group) × 3 (time) research design in which 47 secondary school students were tested pre-, mid-, and postintervention through the 20-lesson volleyball unit. The purpose of the study was to investigate how participation in both units would affect skill development, knowledge, and game performance. While results revealed no difference between models for discrete skills, the Sport Education group was significantly superior in game play throughout. In particular, students in Sport Education improved in their ability to make correct decisions of using the right type of shot and executing that shot correctly, which in turn improved skill execution.

Tactical development

Research on tactical development follows a similar trend as that of skill execution. In the earliest studies, anecdotal evidence from New Zealand teachers suggested that "students were more interested in tactics as well as a desire for self-improvement and personal success as the season progressed" (Grant, 1992, p. 311). Australian teachers also believed that students had better student understanding of rules and strategies (Alexander *et al.*, 1996). Furthermore, according to Wallhead and O'Sullivan (2005, p. 196),

> Observations of 5th grade (Pope and Grant, 1996), 6th grade (Hastie and Buchanan, 2000), and 9th grade students (Carlson and Hastie, 1997) during extended seasons of SE have provided evidence that increases in student knowledge of strategy concepts manifests within improved game-play performance.

Students, too, provided evidence that their tactical understanding had increased (see Clarke and Quill's [2003] study of multiple seasons with eighth-grade students).

Within empirical studies, Hastie (1998a) showed that students in the Frisbee study made positive tactical adjustments as their season progressed. Teams used shorter, more efficient passes (in contrast to long uncontrolled passes) and improved their percentage of interceptions, suggesting an improved ability to read the flow of play. Hastie *et al.*'s (2009) study also formally tested students' tactical awareness. This was achieved in two ways. First, using the assessment instrument developed by Blomqvist *et al.* (2000), these authors found that the students demonstrated significant improvements in their ability to select tactical solutions and make arguments for those decisions when watching videotaped performances of badminton games. Second, as noted above, the students were able to improve their ability to make appropriate shot selections during play, a claim supported by pre–post analysis of Game Performance Assessment Instrument (Oslin *et al.*, 1998) scores.

An earlier study (Hastie and Curtner-Smith, 2006) also examined the development of tactical understanding. During a hybrid season in which the organizational structure followed Sport Education principles, but adopted a pedagogical style using problem-solving and guided discovery approaches, it was found that, by the unit's conclusion, the students were able to understand, appreciate, and execute a number of rudimentary batting, bowling/pitching, and fielding tactics and strategies. They also understood the overarching principles, rules, and structures of batting/fielding games; appreciated their importance; and were able to transfer them from one game to another.

Game knowledge

Two studies (Browne *et al.*, 2004; Pritchard *et al.*, 2008) have offered comparisons between seasons of Sport Education and units best referred to as "traditional" (i.e., ones taking a more skills–drills, teacher-directed approach). In both these studies, significant improvements in game knowledge were achieved by all students, irrespective of curriculum format. In a more recent study focusing on students' ability to provide instructional leadership during Sport Education, Wallhead and O'Sullivan (2007) used a defined didactic research methodology to examine the problematic episodes in the teaching–learning process during the peer teaching tasks during an eighth-grade tag rugby season. In that study, the authors report that the instructional approach of peer teaching could be effective in developing participants' knowledge of many of the lower complexity tag rugby content learning goals of the unit, even if ineffective in achieving higher order content.

A significant component embedded in Sport Education is the taking of roles other than player. As part of being competent participants, students are expected to be knowledgeable of the rules and protocols of the sport, and to be able to carry out their designated team tasks (such as manager, statistician, or fitness leader). While few studies have empirically examined student achievement of this knowledge, Hastie (1996) as well as Hastie and Sinelnikov (2006) used event and duration of recording to measure the extent and accuracy of student work in the tasks of scorekeeper, referee, and statistician. In both cases, students demonstrated high levels of compliance with the attentional requirements of these roles, but also improved in the accuracy of their decisions when officiating during the unit. From questionnaires, students commented that they enjoyed taking these roles and took them seriously. During interviews, students commented on how they felt challenged, with comments such as "Yeah, I really liked it. It's pretty amazing when you get down to it" (Toby [a scorer]) and "You had to know what was going on" (Jake [a statistician] being representative of the American students (Hastie, 1996, p. 96). For the Russian students, the concern was doing a good job: "You have to look and pay attention to the game. The games are so interesting to watch that sometimes you forget to make a call because you were watching the game. So that was hard" (Hastie and Sinelnikov, 2006, p. 141).

The development of literacy

A literate sports player is one who appreciates the notion of fair play, and who can differentiate between good and bad sport practices whether in children's or professional sport. One of the structural features of Sport Education that sets it apart from out-of-school sport is the opportunity for teachers to include a formal accountability system for fair play. By having season champions being decided by factors other than just a win/loss record helps to reinforce the educative values of the sport experience (Siedentop *et al.*, 2004).

The idea that fair play needs to be specifically foregrounded in a season is supported by the findings of two studies. In the first instance, Mowling *et al.* (2006)

examined a season where sportsmanship points weighed more heavily than points for winning the game. In fact, in this season design, it was possible that the team losing a game could actually have more points, depending on the fair play of the other team. Despite this feature, the fourth-grade students participating in this season still had "winning through competition" as their primary agenda as the unit progressed into the later phases of the season. Similar findings were reported by Brock and Hastie (2007) when they discussed fair play with sixth-grade students. In that instance, students initially described fair play as being polite to other teams and not arguing with the officials or with their own team. However, as the season progressed, and winning games became more important, the captains believed that they could only justify equal amounts of playing time for all team members during low-risk situations when the game was not in jeopardy. Particularly it appeared that students perceived as lower skilled could only be goalkeeper during practice or in a game when the team had a big lead. Furthermore, although there was initial resistance by the players to the captain's choices of some students playing more than others, by the postseason they also justified more playing time for higher skilled students if winning the game was in question.

Based on the conception that fair play and other social skills need to be explicitly taught, two studies set out to determine the extent to which Sport Education encourages fair play behaviors and to examine the extent to which specific interventions could influence the occurrences of fair play behaviors during a season. First, Hastie and Sharpe (1999) put in place a formalized fair play accountability system in a season of modified Australian football with a cohort of at-risk seventh-grade boys. By taking a specific focus on positive and negative interpersonal interactions, the students showed significant increases in their level of compliance within the fair play system, increasing their positive interactions, and reducing their derogatory and negative comments to classmates. In the second case, Vidoni and Ward (2009) adopted an applied behavior analysis methodology to study the effectiveness of an intervention called Fair Play Instruction. The results of this study demonstrated that fair play instruction was consistently effective in increasing students' active participation, and in decreasing waiting time for all participants. There was, however, little difference between baseline and intervention for helpful behaviors, but on a positive side, there was a decrease in the number of harmful behaviors.

The expression of enthusiasm

From a review of the research, it is clear that student responses to Sport Education have been overwhelmingly enthusiastic. Siedentop (1994) suggested that enthusiasm would be shown in particular by high levels of student participation in classes. Across various levels of schooling, both teachers and students suggest that there are greater efforts in both team practices and in game play. Sample studies include Strikwerda-Brown and Taggart (2001) and Pope and Grant (1996) in primary school grades, Hastie (2000) in middle schools, Alexander et al. (1996) and Wallhead and Ntoumanis (2004) in high schools, and Bennett and Hastie (1997) in university classes. These claims have also been empirically validated in studies that adopted systematic observations of student engagement during a number of seasons (e.g., Carlson, 1995; Hastie, 1996, 1998b). The enthusiastic response to Sport Education is not limited to those in English-speaking countries. Students in Russia (Hastie and Sinelnikov, 2006), Hong Kong (Ka and Cruz, 2006), and Korea (Kim *et al.*, 2006) all have reported that their attraction toward physical education taught using the model. These results provide evidence for the assertion that, no matter the location, students enjoy participating in classes that they consider to be "more organized and serious" than regular physical education (Sinelnikov and Hastie, 2010a, p. 175).

Two features of the model seem to be the most influential factors in promoting this enthusiasm. These are team affiliation and the idea of formal competition. With respect to team affiliation, students report not only a sense of connection with their teammates (and a subsequent investment toward group identity; MacPhail *et al.*, 2004), but that this leads to greater levels of inclusion (see Alexander *et al.*, 1993; Clarke and Quill, 2003; O'Donovan, 2003), particularly by lower skilled students (Carlson, 1995; Hastie, 1998a; Hastie and Sinelnikov, 2006). The idea of formal competition was a particular attractive feature of Sport Education for students in the upper grades (Alexander *et al.*, 1993; Carlson and Hastie, 1997; Grant, 1992; Grant *et al.*, 1992) and in university courses (Bennett and Hastie, 1997).

Of significant interest with respect to affiliation and competition were the responses of students participating in a sports camp for young people with visual impairments (Fittipaldi-Wert *et al.*, 2009). In that camp, students took membership on teams, developed mascots and posters, participated in games, and, with the assistance of their sighted counselor, took part in some of the officiating and record keeping aspects of the season. What was particularly notable was that many campers appreciated the opportunity to get "the whole sport experience." That is, many of these students had not even played a full-length (in terms of time and player numbers) game of any team sport before, and certainly not one where the scores counted toward a season competition, or one that had designated officials.

While early research on Sport Education unearthed this enthusiastic response by students, more recent research has turned to motivational research theories in attempts to explain these findings. It was Wallhead and Ntoumanis (2004) who first suggested one of the reasons for the attractiveness of Sport Education is that it provides a task-involving class climate that serves to promote intrinsic motivation. That is, the autonomy-supportive social factors of Sport Education result in high levels of students' self-determined behavior and hence high levels of motivation (see MacPhail *et al.*, 2008; Sinelnikov *et al.*, 2007). Consequently, a number of papers have begun to empirically test motivational aspects of Sport Education. Roughly grouped, these studies focus on measuring the perceived and objective climates of Sport Education seasons, comparing student motivation between Sport Education and more traditional units, and motivational changes that take place over a season (Perlman, 2010; Perlman and Goc Karp, 2010; Sinelnikov and Hastie, 2010b; Spittle and Byrne, 2009). More specific details of these studies are presented in Tristan Wallhead's paper in Chapter 10 of this volume.

Summary

In Daryl Siedentop's words, he believes that the Sport Education model will primarily define his legacy in the world of physical education. Indeed, even he is amazed at the extent to which the near-70 studies that have been completed to date show such amazing positive similarities for different grade levels, activities, and countries. If we were to make a summary of the literature concerning the goals of the model, it could be suggested that evidence for competency is "burgeoning and developing," support for literacy is "emerging," and that enthusiastic responses by students have been "significantly substantiated." The chapters that follow in this book will provide further evidence of their achievement of those goals.

References

Alexander, K. and Luckman, J. (2001) "Australian teachers' perceptions and uses of the Sport Education curriculum model," *European Physical Education Review*, 7: 243–267. doi:10. 1177/1356336X010073002

Alexander, K., Taggart, A., and Medland, A. (1993) "Sport Education in physical education: Try before you buy," *Australian Council for Health, Physical Education, and Recreation National Journal*, 40(4): 16–23.

Alexander, K., Taggart, A., and Thorpe, S.T. (1996) "A spring in their steps? Possibilities for professional renewal through Sport Education in Australian schools," *Sport, Education and Society*, 1: 23–46. doi:10.1080/1357332960010102

Bennett, R.G. and Hastie, P.A. (1997) "A Sport Education curriculum model for a collegiate physical activity course," *Journal of Physical Education, Recreation and Dance*, 68(1): 39–44.

Blomqvist, M.T., Luhtanen, P., Laakso, L., and Keskinen, E. (2000) "Validation of a video-based game-understanding test procedure in badminton," *Journal of Teaching in Physical Education*, 19: 325–337.

Brock, S.J. and Hastie, P.A. (2007) "Students' conceptions of fair play in Sport Education," *ACHPER Healthy Lifestyles Journal*, 54(1): 11–15.

Browne, T.B.J., Carlson, T.B., and Hastie, P.A. (2004) "A comparison of rugby seasons presented in traditional and Sport Education formats," *European Physical Education Review*, 10: 199–214. doi:10.1177/1356336X04044071

Carlson, T.B. (1995) "'Now I think I can': The reaction of eight low-skilled students to Sport Education," *Australian Council for Health, Physical Education, and Recreation Healthy Lifestyles Journal*, 42(4): 6–8.

Carlson, T.B. and Hastie, P.A. (1997) "The student social system within Sport Education," *Journal of Teaching in Physical Education*, 17: 176–195.

Clarke, G. and Quill, M. (2003) "Researching Sport Education in action: A case study," *European Physical Education Review*, 9: 253–266. doi:10.1177/1356336X030093004

Ennis, C.D. (1996) "Students' experiences in sport-based physical education: (More than) apologies are necessary," *Quest*, 48: 453–456.

Ennis, C.D., Solmon, M.A., Satina, B., Loftus, S.J., Mensch, J., and McCauley, M.T. (1999) "Creating a sense of family in urban schools using the 'sport for peace' curriculum," *Research Quarterly for Exercise and Sport*, 70: 273–285.

Fittipaldi-Wert, J., Brock, S.J., Hastie, P.H., Arnold, J.B., and Guarino, A. (2009) "Effects of a Sport Education curriculum model on the experiences of students with visual impairments," *Palaestra*, 24(3): 6–10.

Grant, B.C. (1992) "Integrating sport into the physical education curriculum in New Zealand secondary schools," *Quest*, 44: 304–316.

Grant, B.C., Treddinick, P., and Hodge, K. (1992) "Sport Education in physical education," *New Zealand Journal of Health, Physical Education and Recreation*, 25: 3–6.

Gréhaigne, J.-F., Godbout, P., and Bouthier, D. (1997) "Performance assessment in team sports," *Journal of Teaching in Physical Education*, 16: 500–516.

Hastie, P.A. (1996) "Student role involvement during a unit of Sport Education," *Journal of Teaching in Physical Education*, 16: 88–103.

Hastie, P.A. (1998a) "Skill and tactical development during a Sport Education season," *Research Quarterly for Exercise and Sport*, 69: 368–379.

Hastie, P.A. (1998b) "The participation and perception of girls during a unit of Sport Education," *Journal of Teaching in Physical Education*, 18: 157–171.

Hastie, P.A. (2000) "An ecological analysis of a Sport Education season," *Journal of Teaching in Physical Education*, 19: 355–373.

Hastie, P.A. and Buchanan, A.M. (2000) "Teaching responsibility through Sport Education: Prospects of a coalition," *Research Quarterly for Exercise and Sport*, 71: 25–35.

Hastie, P.A. and Curtner-Smith, M.D. (2006) "Influence of a hybrid Sport Education–teaching games for understanding unit on one teacher and his students," *Physical Education and Sport Pedagogy*, 11: 1–27. doi:10.1080/17408980500466813

Hastie, P.A. and Sharpe, T. (1999) "Effects of a Sport Education curriculum on the positive social behaviour of at-risk rural adolescent boys," *Journal of Education for Students Placed at Risk*, 4: 417–430. doi:10.1207/s15327671espr0404_4

Hastie, P.A. and Sinelnikov, O.A. (2006) "Russian students' participation in and perceptions of a season of Sport Education," *European Physical Education Review*, 12: 131–150. doi:10.1177/1356336X06065166

Hastie, P.A., Sinelnikov, O.A., and Guarino, A.J. (2009) "The development of skill and tactical competencies during a season of badminton," *European Journal of Sport Science*, 9: 133–140. doi:10.1080/17461390802542564

Hastie, P.A. and Trost, S.G. (2002) "Student physical activity levels during a Sport Education season," *Pediatric Exercise Science*, 14: 64–74.

Ka, L.C. and Cruz, A. (2006) "The effect of Sport Education on secondary six students' learning interest and collaboration in football lessons," *Journal of Physical Education and Recreation (HK)*, 12(2): 13–22.

Kim, J., Penney, D., Cho, M., and Choi, H. (2006) "'Not business as usual': Sport Education pedagogy in practice," *European Physical Education Review*, 12: 361–379. doi:10.1177/1356336X06071469

Kinchin, G.D. (2006) "Sport Education: A review of the research," in D. Kirk, M. O'Sullivan, and D. Macdonald (eds.) *Handbook of research in physical education*, London, UK: Sage.

Kinchin, G.D., Wardle, C., Roderick, S., and Sprosen, A. (2004) "A survey of year 9 boys' perceptions of Sport Education in one English secondary school," *Bulletin of Physical Education*, 40(1): 27–40.

MacPhail, A., Gorely, T., Kirk, D., and Kinchin, G. (2008) "Children's experiences of fun and enjoyment during a season of Sport Education," *Research Quarterly for Exercise and Sport*, 79: 344–355.

MacPhail, A., Kirk, D., and Kinchin, G.D. (2004) "Sport Education: Promoting team affiliation through physical education," *Journal of Teaching in Physical Education*, 23: 106–122.

Metzler, M.W. (2005) *Instructional models for physical education 2*, Scottsdale, AZ: Halcomb Hathaway.

Mowling, C.M., Brock, S.J., and Hastie, P.A. (2006) "Fourth grade students' drawing interpretations of a Sport Education soccer unit," *Journal of Teaching in Physical Education*, 25: 9–35.

O'Donovan, T.M. (2003) "A changing culture? Interrogating the dynamics of peer affiliations over the course of a Sport Education season," *European Physical Education Review*, 9: 237–251. doi:10.1177/1356336X030093003

Oslin, J.L., Mitchell, S.A., and Griffin, L.L. (1998) "The Game Performance Assessment Instrument (GPAI): Development and preliminary validation," *Journal of Teaching in Physical Education*, 17: 231–243.

Perlman, D.J. (2010) "Change in affect and needs satisfaction for amotivated students within the Sport Education model," *Journal of Teaching in Physical Education*, 29: 433–445.

Perlman, D.J. and Goc Karp, G. (2010) "A self-determined perspective of the Sport Education model," *Physical Education and Sport Pedagogy*, 15(4): 401–418. doi:10.1080/17408980903535800

Pope, C. and Grant, B.C. (1996) "Student experiences in Sport Education," *Waikato Journal of Education*, 2: 103–118.

Pritchard, T., Hawkins, A., Wiegand, R., and Metzler, J.N. (2008) "Effects of two instructional approaches on skill development, knowledge, and game performance," *Measurement in Physical Education and Exercise Science*, 12: 219–236. doi:10.1080/10913670802349774

Siedentop, D. (1994) *Sport Education: Quality PE through positive sport experiences*, Champaign, IL: Human Kinetics.

Siedentop, D. (1998) "What is Sport Education and how does it work?" *Journal of Physical Education, Recreation, and Dance*, 69(4): 18–20.

Siedentop, D. (2002) "Sport Education: A retrospective," *Journal of Teaching in Physical Education*, 21: 409–418.

Siedentop, D., Hastie, P.A., and van der Mars, H. (2004) *Complete guide to Sport Education*, Champaign, IL: Human Kinetics.

Sinelnikov, O.A. and Hastie, P.A. (2010a) "Students' autobiographical memory of participation in multiple Sport Education seasons," *Journal of Teaching in Physical Education*, 29: 167–183.

Sinelnikov, O.A. and Hastie, P.A. (2010b) "A motivational analysis of a season of Sport Education," *Physical Education and Sport Pedagogy*, 15: 55–69. doi: 10.1080/17408980902729362

Sinelnikov, O.A., Hastie, P.A., and Prusak, K. (2007) "Situational motivation in a season of Sport Education," *ICHPER-SD Research Journal*, 2(1): 43–47.

Spittle, M. and Byrne, K. (2009) "The influence of Sport Education on student motivation in physical education," *Physical Education and Sport Pedagogy*, 14: 253–266. doi:10.1080/17408980801995239

Strikwerda-Brown, J. and Taggart, A. (2001) "No longer voiceless and exhausted: Sport Education and the primary generalist," *Australian Council for Health, Physical Education, and Recreation Healthy Lifestyles Journal*, 48(4): 14–17.

Vidoni, C. and Ward, P. (2009) "Effects of fair play instruction on student social skills during a middle school Sport Education unit," *Physical Education and Sport Pedagogy*, 14: 285–310. doi:10.1080/17408980802225818

Wallhead, T. and Ntoumanis, N. (2004) "Effects of a Sport Education intervention on students' motivational responses in physical education," *Journal of Teaching in Physical Education*, 23: 4–18.

Wallhead, T. and O'Sullivan, M. (2005) "Sport Education: Physical education for the new millennium?" *Physical Education and Sport Pedagogy*, 10: 181–210. doi:10.1080/17408980500105098

Wallhead, T. and O'Sullivan, M. (2007) "A didactic analysis of content development during the peer teaching tasks of a Sport Education season," *Physical Education and Sport Pedagogy*, 12: 225–243. doi:10.1080/174089807016101

PART I

Contexts of adoption of Sport Education

2

SUSTAINABLE SPORT EDUCATION IN PRIMARY EDUCATION

An English case study

Toni M. O'Donovan, Ann MacPhail, and David Kirk

Research has shown that many primary teachers lack confidence in physical education, perceive that they do not have the skills to teach physical education well and that often physical education lessons are cancelled, prioritising other curriculum areas (Caldecott *et al.*, 2006; Hardman and Marshall, 2000). Yet in Forest Gate Primary, the school has succeeded in establishing a new curriculum which is being embraced by generalist teachers and physical education specialists alike, those with plenty of confidence in their ability and those who describe themselves as definitely not sporty. The community of teachers is increasing in size as the programme continues to spread across the school with years 4, 5 and 6 embracing the approach. What factors have influenced the sustainability of the programme? Why have teachers across the spectrum of age, experience, confidence and seniority bought into this particular curriculum innovation?

This chapter presents the story of how a community of practice (Lave and Wenger, 1991) formed to introduce Sport Education to year 5 in an English Midlands primary school in 2000 and became an ingrained and integrated part of the upper-school experience for pupils and teachers alike. The story outlines the fluid nature of a teaching community in a busy primary school, with staff leaving and joining the Sport Education teacher group and the growth of the community as the initiative expanded to other year groups. The analysis considers what features particular to Sport Education have been influential in the sustainability of this curricular initiative where others may flounder and lose momentum. In particular, we consider the impact of Sport Education on the professional lives of the teachers involved: the extent to which the teachers 'bought into' Sport Education and what impact they thought it had on their pupils' lives and the extent to which these teachers took ownership of the programme, adapted it to the needs of their own pupils and integrated it with the ethos of the school.

Prior to examining the specific school context and the specifics of Sport Education in this school, it is necessary to consider the broader physical education context in English primary schools as it underpins why some physical education initiatives may fail and why Sport Education may have been particularly successful in this context.

Primary physical education in the United Kingdom

In England, there is a National Curriculum for pupils aged 5–16 years, presented in four key stages: key stage 1 for pupils aged 5–7 years, key stage 2 for pupils 7–11 years (the primary phase), key stage 3 for pupils 11–14 years and key stage 4 for pupils 14–16 years (the secondary phase). Traditionally key stages 1 and 2 are taught by primary school teachers who are responsible for implementing the entire National Curriculum even though they might have a subject specialism other than physical education. The very nature of the English system requires primary school teachers to be generalists and thereby responsible for teaching all areas of the National Curriculum with their own class, including physical education. Little use is made of specialist teachers in individual subject areas and thus the onus is on all teachers reaching a required level of subject expertise. Where teachers lack the required expertise, a recent trend is that, although specialist teachers do not typically teach in primary schools in England, there are an increasing number of sports coaches that are now being used to deliver physical education lessons (Griggs, 2010; Talbot, 2006).

Downey (1979) suggested that the reason primary school physical education was so problematic was due to primary teachers' lack of accomplishment in the area. In 2003, Ofsted (Office for Standards in Education, Children's Services and Skills) inspectors pointed out that primary school physical education teaching effectiveness is reduced by weaknesses in teachers' subject knowledge. The limited time allocated to initial teacher training in physical education has been an ongoing concern of the professional associations in England. Research by Carney and Armstrong (1996) and Ofsted (1998) has revealed that few trainees experience the minimum 60 hours of training related to physical education that has been recommended since the 1970s by the Physical Education Association of the United Kingdom (PEAUK, the former organisation to the Association for Physical Education). Carney and Armstrong (1996) noted a reduction in time allocation for physical education since the studies conducted by the Physical Education Association (1984) and Williams (1985). The findings of Caldecott et al. (2006) suggest that the situation has, since the 1970s, deteriorated still further. Warburton (2001) is of the view that far too many teachers will have had little more than an introduction to physical education during their initial teacher training, a 'token gesture' towards the teaching of physical education.

Inevitably concerns about the quality of physical education that children receive now, and in the future, are readily apparent (Hardman and Marshall, 2000). Evans et al. (1996), Gilbert (1998), Oxley (1998), Davies (1999), Speednet (2000), Warburton (2001) and Wright (2004) all highlight the same concern that the National Curriculum for Physical Education in England and Wales is being taught ineffectively in primary schools. Speednet (2000) claimed that more than half a million hours of physical education had been lost in primary schools to make way for literacy and numeracy work as a result of government initiatives. In a survey carried out by Warburton (2001), in 228 primary schools in the north-east of England, it was found that over half of the schools offered only one lesson of physical education a week, with many lessons being only of half an hour in duration.

Within this broader context, Sport Education was introduced to one state-run primary school based in the Midlands of England in 2000.

School context

Forest Gate Primary School is a state-run, co-educational, predominantly middle-class nursery and primary school based in the Midlands of England and caters for over 540 children between the ages of 3 and 12 years. Approximately 10 per cent of children are on the school's register of special educational needs and approximately 8 per cent of children come from ethnic minority backgrounds and have English as an additional language. The attainment of 11-year-old children in national tests for English, mathematics and science in 2001 was close to or above national averages when compared to all schools. The 2002 Ofsted report for Forest Gate notes that the school makes very good provision for sport. Children's standards in physical education at the end of years 2 and 6 are in line with national expectations. The school is involved in national and local initiatives, for example the Sport England 'Active Sports' project, to increase the range and quality of the sporting activities available to children.

Until 2006, Forest Gate's physical education provision was directed and supported by two classroom primary generalist teachers who took on the shared role (one responsible for key stage 1 and the other for key stage 2) of 'Physical Education Coordinator'. Following this a newly qualified physical education specialist was employed part-time to take on some of their responsibilities. The roles of these three teachers included organising sport in and out of school, maintaining physical education resources, health and safety, updating the school physical education policy, liaison with the community and monitoring innovative ideas related to the delivery of sport and physical education. All the teachers in the school teach physical education and primarily rely on the physical education content input they received while training to be a teacher. Some had attended in-service courses to update their knowledge and ideas. Key stages 1 and 2 physical education lesson plans and related support materials were available for all teachers to collect from the staff room. All physical education lessons at Forest Gate were grouped by class. Year 4, 5 and 6 children received two timetabled sessions of physical education broken into one hour and one half-hour. Prior to Sport Education, the hour session tended to be provided by people external to the school, that is, coaches and Sport Development Officers, who concentrated on particular games.

Within games activities presented in physical education in the National Curriculum, children at key stage 2 were expected to be taught to play and make up small-sided and modified games, use skills and tactics and apply basic attacking and defending principles and work with others to organise and maintain game play (Department for Education and Employment and Qualifications and Curriculum Authority, 1999). The half-hour slot was taught by the classroom teachers who promoted dance, gymnastics and athletics. When the school made the decision to introduce Sport Education to year 5, the established hour that was staffed by external people became the Sport Education unit time. The younger key stage 2 children in lower years took part in a physical education environment centred on mini games and swimming, with a target of one 40-minute class a week. Prior to the implementation of Sport Education, the teachers explained that physical education lessons, like art, were occasionally squeezed for time.

The curricular innovation

The research project reported here has been ongoing within Forest Gate since 2001 when Sport Education was introduced to the school. Originally introduced as a year 5 activity the programme was introduced to year 6 in 2005/2006 and to year 4 in 2007/2008, with Sport Education features being gradually developed throughout the pupils' upper-school experience. The teachers in the school have retained, refined and developed a number of features of Sport Education.

Forest Gate had previously worked with two of the researchers in relation to an earlier physical education-related study and were approached and asked if they would be interested in introducing Sport Education as part of their ongoing collaborative project. The introduction of Sport Education in 2001 resulted in the key stage 2 Physical Education Coordinator, another female primary generalist teacher and the male head teacher restructuring the physical education programme to accommodate the introduction of Sport Education. This resulted in very little disturbance to the physical education timetable, and teachers appreciated the possibility and benefit of introducing pupil-centred learning into the existing structure of the primary school physical education programme. The same three teachers were also responsible for planning and teaching the unit. None of the teachers had heard of, or had any experience of, Sport Education and it was very much the key stage 2 Physical Education Coordinator who drove the Sport Education initiative. Initially they chose to introduce Sport Education to year 5 pupils with a modified generic invasion game (see MacPhail et al., 2004).

The school chose to run a Sport Education unit from January to July including pre-season, a round-robin league and a culminating festival. A generic game was chosen in order to reduce the pupils' pre-conceptions about the game rather than playing a popular, recognised game with an established culture (MacPhail et al., 2003). The chosen game was an invasion game adapted from netball for year 5 and, later, floorball for year 6. Each team was selected by the teachers across all classes and was coeducational and mixed ability.

Following team announcement, the pupils in each team then selected players to act, for example, as team manager, captain, coach, portfolio manager and equipment manager. All pupils held at least one role in addition to that as a player and the roles developed each year to give the pupils additional responsibility. In all years, the games were officiated by a non-playing team. However, this ranged in complexity from providing timekeepers and reporters to a full-officiating team including referees, assistant referees, score keepers and statisticians. In 2006, the teachers introduced a Sports Panel for year 6 for the first time, which allowed a referee to refer a player to the Panel if they were particularly concerned about the conduct of play. The Sports Panel adjudicated on a player's conduct and a referee's decision and, where necessary, penalised the offending player and awarded points to other teams.

The school had a dedicated notice board for Sport Education outside the year 5/6 classrooms which included information on the league, team performance and organisational responsibilities. It formed the focal point for information related to Sport Education between sessions.

Table 2.1 outlines the key development features of Sport Education in the school, along with the staff involved and the associated research components.

Research generation

The far-right column in Table 2.1 provides a brief outline of the range of methodologies used at various stages over the duration in which Sport Education has been implemented at Forest Gate.[1] The data presented in this chapter were generated during the 2006/2007 Sport Education season, and focus on interviews with the head teacher, classroom teachers and the physical education specialist. Using participant observation, pupil and teacher interviews, focus groups, questionnaires and pupil drawings, the aim was to explore the factors that have influenced the sustainability of the programme, and why a relatively diverse group of teachers have bought into this particular curriculum innovation.

From the interviews, the researchers identified text segments, attached category labels to the segments and sorted all text segments that related to a specific category or theme. Similar to the constant comparative method of analysing the data (Glaser and Strauss, 1967; Lincoln and Guba, 1985), the data were manually reviewed repeatedly and continually coded, during which time the researchers looked for similarities and differences, groupings, patterns and items of particular significance (Mason, 1996). The interview questions were exploratory in nature as Sport Education was implemented with a view to allowing themes to be generated from the data analysis rather than seeking to determine the extent of particular attributes of Sport Education.

Discussion

From their studies of change, Hord (1992) identified seven developmental stages of concern related to the introduction of innovations in schools. These stages provide

TABLE 2.1 Development of Sport Education since 2000

Year	Teachers involved	Year groups	Focus/nature of SE season with yearly developments	Research data generation activities
2000	Amelie, Lesley, head teacher	Year 5	Introduction of Sport Education to year 5 with a generic netball game. Teaching Games for Understanding (TGfU) unit preceded Sport Education	Participant observation. Pupil and teacher interviews. Questionnaires (see MacPhail et al., 2003)
2001–2002	Amelie, Lesley, head teacher	Year 5		
2002–2003	Amelie, Sarah	Year 5	Modification of generic netball game to accommodate visually impaired and cerebral palsy students	Pupil drawings and follow-up interviews. Teacher interviews (see MacPhail and Kinchin, 2004)
2003–2004	Sarah, Andy	Year 5	Introduction of new scoring protocols to generic game	
2004–2005	Sarah, Andy	Year 5		
2005–2006	Sarah, Jon, Andy, Hannah, Danielle, Lesley	Years 5 and 6 (previous year 5 group from 2004 to 2005)	Introduction of year 6 Sport Education with the inclusion of student referees and a Sports Panel. Pre-season introduction to tactics using kabaddi and teaching games for understanding for years 5 and 6	Participant observation. Pupil and teacher interviews. Questionnaires (see O'Donovan et al., 2010)
2006–2007	Sarah, Jon, Andy, Hannah, Lesley, Lynn	Years 5 and 6	Increasing cross-curricular links. Jon, a physical education specialist working part-time in the school, joins the Sport Education team	
2007–2008	Sarah, Jon, Andy, Hannah, Danielle, Lesley, Lynn, Karen	Years 4, 5 and 6	Introduction of year 4 Sport Education. Introduced to and implemented in other local schools	

insights into teachers' attitudes that contribute to their willingness to engage in the school improvement effort. Individuals progress from the 'self' stage of concern, which occurs during the early stages of change effort, through concerns about completing the task, concerns about the innovations' impact on pupils and, finally, concerns about finding even better ways to reach and teach students.

The analysis of the interview data from Forest Gate is organised around three key issues closely related to the stages identified by Hord (1992) in order to understand why Sport Education has had such longevity in this school. First, we examine the impact of Sport Education on the professional lives of the teachers involved. Second, we consider the extent to which the teachers 'bought into' Sport Education and what impact they thought it had on their pupils' lives. Finally, we analyse the extent to which these teachers have taken ownership of the programme and adapted it to the needs of their own pupils and integrated it with the ethos of the school.

Impact on teachers' personal and professional lives

Welch (1989) reports that teachers assess advantages and disadvantages of collaborative consultation primarily in terms of how implementation will impact them personally, rather than how it might impact student growth. He states that, 'for innovative change in school settings to be meaningful, its effectiveness must be proven in terms of the personal and professional growth of all involved, not just student growth' (p. 538; cited in Boyd, 1992). Inevitably there is some additional work in the implementation of any new programme but many of the teachers described the work associated with Sport Education as short term in nature and ultimately facilitating their teaching. As Danielle, a classroom teacher, noted:

> Just from a very practical point of view of the work–life balance, it takes a load off, once it is up and running. It takes a load off the staff as well . . . Because you know from the word go where you're going, what you're aiming for, what you're doing and you are working together as a team, you're not going out with just your class. It's very tangible, it's meant to me that on a Wednesday evening I am not sitting planning, because it's already there, it's been planned and the beginning of every year I know that it has to be reconsidered according to what you want for the children.

Another teacher, Hannah, suggests that it is the logistics of Sport Education rather than the teaching of sport that takes the time and as a primary generalist teacher she is more comfortable with this work. She states: 'I think it's perhaps it's just like bringing it all together, the total thing, just the logistics of it, because you do have to carefully map out what time of year and things like that.'

In Forest Gate, two key teachers (Sarah and Jon) have taken the lead in this area. The initial time commitment of the model is not seen as problematic as both Sarah and Jon perceive ownership of the curriculum and want the community to continue to grow.

> The thing with the other teachers is they don't take an active role in any of the planning, or the work that Jon and I have done, and quite rightly so, because I have actually said to them don't bother if they don't want.
>
> *(Sarah)*

As a physical education specialist, Jon took joint leadership of the year 6 programme with Sarah in his first year working at the school. Although as a physical education specialist he remains sceptical about the physical activity levels of the pupils during each lesson, he appreciates that the diverse experience of the generalist teachers means that many pupils participate in significantly more physical education as a result of the initiative. He commented: 'I think it makes life a lot easier for teachers that don't understand sport.'

Echoing Jon's thoughts, Danielle suggests that her insecurities about her ability to plan physical education lessons have been dissipated by Sport Education when she stated:

> I feel that I enjoy doing games but I'm not the most confident person, because I think 'I've got to get this series of lessons and where am I going with this?' and it [Sport Education] has just taken a lot away.

The head teacher identified that the implementation of Sport Education had been a stimulating but challenging experience, not only for those who had little perceived expertise in teaching games, but also for those who excelled at teaching games. He explained that 'purist' games teachers have sometimes struggled with Sport Education as the goals of the programme are significantly broader than those of traditional games units which are dominated by skill development. This perhaps explains Jon's concerns that this model would not replicate the physical activity levels a specialist physical educator 'teaching' the pupils could achieve. In comparison for the generalist teachers, he felt that Sport Education brought a purpose to teaching games. These perceptions were mirrored by some of the classroom teachers who commented that they could see the outcomes they were working towards from the beginning, and the unit felt very purposeful.

It was Hannah again who suggested that:

> it makes games so much more meaningful for me than it was before, because I never thought they were learning anything. They were, however, just not as much. Before it was quite hard to write their reports because everything was so bitty, the children who were really good would shine and that would be it, and the rest would be medium standard and I didn't really feel they were improving and now it's much more pared down, and you keep going through the whole year on the same things [so] you can actually tell that the children have improved a lot . . . I like the fact that [we] could see the outcomes we were working towards before I started. Quite often when you're

teaching games you think that by the end of this unit these skills will have been taught, but I could see the larger picture.

Likewise Sarah recognises the diverse experiences of the teachers in the school and their confidence in teaching physical education and identifies that the real strength of Sport Education is that it can engage such teachers in a meaningful way.

> There are lots who don't like outdoor teaching, because you are away from the confines of the walls, and a lot of people find that hard, especially primary teachers who have not had a great experience, it's often the first thing to go: 'Oh it's raining, I'll not go, etc.' That and art get sidelined straightaway as areas in the curriculum . . . I think it [Sport Education] gives people who are not particularly interested in teaching games and sport an end insight and it covers everything, so you know by the end of the year you have taught them teaching skills, you're teaching attitude, there's all different skills and attitudes in all areas of learning that we work in, so we know we have definitely covered that in Sport Education, because they have learned a specific skill and they have been faced with choosing their own attitude towards behaviours.

Lesley, Danielle and Hannah are all generalist teachers who would previously have considered themselves as outside any community involved with sport or physical education. Sport Education has modified their view of this community as one which includes an ethos they value and draws on skills they possess, and although they are not core members of the planning team they each contribute to the community in a variety of ways. Lesley's comment provides an example of this change of sentiment:

> Just by seeing sport in a different way, I'm not an outside games person at all, not a fear of it, just not being too confident, but here teaching them the socialising skills, integrating with other areas of the curriculum other than just sport. I feel more confident with that side of it . . . I have been working with the portfolio group or skills group and I've been developing questioning skills to help them develop in these areas. This is what I would follow on with in class anyway.

Although a number of the teachers may not have been receptive to physical education innovation because of their perceived lack of ability in this area, the positioning of Sport Education as a cross-curricular educational innovation drawing on skills such as general organisation and management, which many generalist teachers are confident in, overcame this barrier. Hannah noted:

> I think that my interest has been maintained not necessarily because of the sporty things but because of the other aspects that have been really

important. We're going to include it in all our literacy planning as well as part of our speaking and listening, because it will be an ongoing thing that we're doing and we're supposed to be doing a lot more speaking and listening in school and it's something that happens every week. So it will be put in all of our planning. We've started doing some different PSHE [*personal, social and health education*] work as well and it would link in with that. So though it is a lot of work you cover a lot of things within it, and you know when you're strapped for time within the curriculum to do everything.

The teachers identified numerous cross-curricular links with PSHE, literacy, art and maths. The head teacher explained that curriculum overcrowding has pushed the staff to look for more creative solutions to covering the key stage 2 targets. For example, two of the six speaking and listening targets have been embedded in Sport Education for year 5 and 6 pupils as the teachers quickly became aware that they knew 'it effectively covers them anyway' (Hannah). Given the key stage 2 target of preparing pupils for an active role as citizens in the national framework for PSHE and citizenship, it is perhaps unsurprising that the head teacher values the opportunity Sport Education offers for active participation. According to the head teacher Sport Education compares favourably with other school experiences as the children 'are very much participants'. He suggested that the overcrowded curriculum means that often 'in the school system generally we have moved from a very much an active participation. Lots of children in primary school are receivers rather than participants in lots of their day's education.' Furthermore, he suggests that, as Sport Education lessens, rather than increases, pressure on the curriculum, it offers a 'creative solution' to the overcrowded primary curriculum and for this reason, among others, Sport Education has been supported by the management at the school.

Although Welch (1989) identified the importance of the innovation impact on teachers' personal and professional lives, the teachers recognised that their 'buy in' to the ethos of Sport Education was central to the longevity of Sport Education, given the numerous staffing changes over the course of this project and competing initiatives vying for their time.

The ethos of Sport Education

Initially the head teacher was at the core of the Sport Education community in the school. As a head teacher who valued Sport Education and wanted to see it established he came to all of the lessons in the first year. Confirmation of this valuing came from Sarah, who noted:

I think the fact that he had initially been involved in Sport Education because he used to go down and teach the unit with Amelie and me, so the fact that he actually had a hands-on approach to the game was really good.

His support lent a certain inevitability to the teachers' involvement with Sport Education in the early stages, which Sarah endorsed when she said that 'it wasn't so much an attraction to being involved in it, it was part of your role teaching that age group of children, so it came with the job'.

In contrast, the head teacher suggested that Sport Education was sustainable because the staff were particularly invested.

> We have been lucky really in that we've had staff who really value it, but everyone who had participated in it, even people who come in new to it like Jon this year, I mean once he's involved now he's really very much into it.

For Andy, who was confident in teaching physical education and did not feel teaching physical education burdensome, buying into the programme was focused on the value to the pupils.

> I think it's more than understanding, it's understanding it and appreciating its worth, because if you don't see the value of it then obviously it will be the type of thing you don't do unless you are forced to do. I think particularly at Forest Gate teachers have identified that it really does help the children, and the children themselves will tell you that they have progressed throughout the year and their attitude to sport has improved as the year has gone on.

The head teacher's initial support for the programme was based on a similar premise. What he really appreciated was

> the ethos that you were building up the team spirit, there was a lot of citizenship, all the other aspects of team games, the roles and responsibilities come into it so that the children were developing not just their skills but themselves as well – the holistic approach. The fact that you're building up to this gala where the children get a chance to share everything they have achieved with their parents, so then you have the home–school involvement as well. It just seems really purposeful and the children have found that as well. It has really brought them together.

Sarah identified that the value the head teacher placed on teaching Sport Education further enforced the sustainability of the programme when she suggested that 'his genuine liking for the whole concept through his own work has maintained a good profile of it, because it's something he has always spoken about to people when they have come in'.

Sport Education for Forest Gate students

The impact of Sport Education on teacher and pupil lives was keenly observed by all teachers but tailoring the initiative to the needs of their own pupils has been a central part of the sustainability of this programme. Furthermore, adapting the programme for their own specific context and pupils has also given teachers significantly more ownership of the physical education curriculum. As Sarah noted:

> When I felt much more in control was when we had to revamp the year 5 unit to accommodate the two children who had disabilities, that's where [a researcher] came down and actually checked the game out. Because Amelie and I had to revamp the game then I suppose we had ownership of the game, and I felt much more confident with the game, because it was a game that I had actually understood; up until then I was using someone else's rules and it's easy to take on someone else's rules, that's fine, just but I think you get more because you design it.

Sarah highlighted a key issue in her comment 'I was using someone else's rules . . . but I think you get more because you design it'. Sport Education was developed to educate competent, literate and enthusiastic sports people and to provide pupils with an authentic experience of sport (Siedentop, 1994) rather than to merely teach skills specific to one sport. The centrality of pupils' experiences rather than the particular game in Sport Education resulted in the teachers being more comfortable with modifying the experience. The teachers' first experience of modifying the game for their specific students gave them the confidence to begin a process of game development and adaptation and, since then, Sport Education has undergone sustained development. Given the longevity of Sport Education in Forest Gate and despite the changes in staffing and management during the lifetime of this programme, it may be surprising that Sarah commented that 'every year you adapt and change it'.

> Andy and me, we've got the second and third hoop in, because there wasn't enough scoring, so we thought, right, we'll bring that in for the year 5 game, because we only had the one central hoop before, so we put in a hoop up very close, so if a kid gets a ball well how does she get a point, it should be as fast as that, so we put a hoop fairly near the shooter now.
>
> *(Sarah)*

Gradually the programme has been extended to reintroduce an introductory unit on tactical games prior to the Sport Education season, which was part of the original design of the intervention when first introduced to the school in the 1999–2000 academic year, and to include pupils in years 4 and 6. The development of cross-curricular targets within physical education has also allowed the teachers to redesign aspects of the programme. In 2006/2007, the introduction of a Sports Panel for year 6 pupils to adjudicate on players' conduct was greeted with much enthusiasm from the teachers who were amazed by the maturity shown by the pupils in reaching fair decisions. In 2007/2008, a year 4 unit was introduced with modified roles and responsibilities. This allowed the teachers to extend the leadership responsibilities of pupils in years 5 and 6 to allow progression through the curriculum. The alignment of the goals of Sport Education with the whole school ethos and its gradual integration with the whole curriculum has been central to the success of the programme, which Danielle particularly valued 'because it fits well within our whole school ethos of integrating curriculum and looking at the more holistic approach'.

The integrated nature of the programme has resulted in Sport Education becoming an unavoidable element of the school curriculum. Both the teachers and management referred to pupil enjoyment as another important factor in the sustainability of Sport Education. Indeed, the head teacher commented that both parents and pupils found Sport Education as one of the most memorable experiences of their time at Forest Gate. The parent and pupil responses to Sport Education has meant that it has become so ingrained in the curriculum, there is an inevitability about it. There is now an expectation from Forest Gate upper-school pupils that they will be given the opportunity to experience Sport Education and for this reason it would be difficult not to offer it. In an already crowded curriculum, the inevitability of Sport Education has helped cement physical education's place in the curriculum where it may otherwise have slipped. From an administrative perspective, the head teacher noted that

> it's so easy if you've got the crowded timetable to say well we're operating in this little box, therefore such another part of life is more important. With this [Sport Education] there's an unavoidability about it, it's what happens in years 5 and 6 and the kids have come to expect it I think.

Instead of fizzling out, Sport Education has become a valued, integrated and unavoidable element of the upper-school calendar at Forest Gate.

Conclusion

This chapter has outlined the key features of Sport Education that engaged primary generalist and specialist teachers and allowed the programme to flourish despite the many staff changes over the duration of the programme. In a world of educational research where almost all educational change efforts and explanations are based on snapshot views of change, the longitudinal nature of the study in Forest Gate allows the opportunity to examine what has allowed such a sustained programme of educational change. All too often curriculum innovations flounder and lose direction after the initial momentum, particularly when key agents withdraw from the setting (Hargreaves and Goodson, 2006). This has not been the case at Forest Gate.

For those teachers who lack confidence, the clear structure of Sport Education facilitated their teaching of physical education, thus easing the impact on their workload. The broader goals of the model resulted in a need for skill sets where primary generalist teachers perceived they have more ability, such as general management and organisational skills. Subsequently, improved self-confidence in teaching physical education was noted by many teachers and this cemented the role of physical education in the curriculum. Furthermore, the support from the head teacher, the commitment of the staff leading the programme and the teachers' willingness to renew their approach to physical education facilitated the sustainability of the programme. Simultaneously, the pupil-centred nature of Sport Education and the alignment of the goals and ethos of the school and that of the model facilitated the teachers taking ownership of the experience and integrating the programme with the broader school curriculum and the creation of a range of cross-curricular links. This helped some generalist teachers to 'buy into' the programme as they could clearly see the pupil-centred nature of the model. The success of the programme is evident in the reputation of the unit with parents and younger pupils that has resulted in an inevitability about the structure of upper-school physical education.

Note

1   Ethical approval was gained from Loughborough University for this research.

References

Boyd, V. (1992) *School context: Bridge or barrier to change*, Austin, TX: Southwest Educational Development Laboratory. Available HTTP: http://www.sedl.org/change/school (accessed 9 January 2011).

Caldecott, S., Warburton, P. and Waring, M. (2006) 'A survey of the time devoted to the preparation of primary and junior school trainee teachers to teach physical education in England (Part one)', *British Journal of Teaching Physical Education*, 37(1): 45–48.

Carney, C. and Armstrong, N. (1996) 'The provision of physical education in primary initial training courses in England and Wales', *European Physical Education Review*, 2: 64–74. doi: 10.1177/1356336X9600200107

Davies, H.J. (1999) 'Standards in physical education in England at key stage 1 and key stage 2: Past, present and future', *European Journal of Physical Education*, 4: 173–190. doi:10.1080/1740898990040206

Department for Education and Employment and Qualifications and Curriculum Authority (1999) *Physical education: The national curriculum for England*, London: Her Majesty's Stationery Office (HMSO) and Qualifications and Curriculum Authority.

Downey, J. (1979) 'The training in physical education of the non-specialist primary school teacher', *Bulletin of Physical Education*, 15(1): 5–10.

Evans, J., Penney, D. and Davies, B. (1996) 'Back to the future policy and physical education', in N. Armstrong (ed.) *New directions in physical education – Change and innovation* (pp. 1–18), London: Cassell.

Gilbert, R. (1998) 'Physical education: The key partner', *The British Journal of Physical Education*, 29(1): 18–22.

Glaser, B.G. and Strauss, A.L. (1967) *The discovery of grounded theory*, Chicago, IL: Aldine Publishing Company.

Griggs, G. (2010) 'For sale – Primary physical education: £20 per hour or nearest offer', *Education 3–13: International Journal of Primary, Elementary and Early Years Education*, 38(1): 39–46. doi:10.1080/03004270903099793

Hardman, K. and Marshall, J. (2000) 'The state and status of physical education in schools in international context', *European Physical Education Review*, 6: 203–229. doi:10.1177/1356336X000063001

Hargreaves, A. and Goodson, I. (2006) 'Educational change over time? The sustainability and nonsustainability of three decades of secondary school change and continuity', *Educational Administration Quarterly*, 42: 3–41. doi:10.1177/0013161X05277975

Hord, S.M. (1992) *Facilitative leadership: The imperative for change*, Austin, TX: Southwest Educational Development Laboratory. Available HTTP: http://www.sedl.org/change/school (accessed 9 January 2011).

Lave, J. and Wenger, E. (1991) *Situated learning: Legitimate peripheral participation in communities of practice*, New York: Cambridge University Press.

Lincoln, Y.S. and Guba, E.G. (1985) *Naturalistic inquiry*, Beverly Hills, CA: Sage.

MacPhail, A. and Kinchin, G. (2004) 'The use of drawings as an evaluative tool: Students' experiences of Sport Education', *Physical Education and Sport Pedagogy*, 9: 87–108. doi:10.1080/1740898042000208142

MacPhail, A., Kinchin, G. and Kirk, D. (2003) 'Students' conceptions of sport and Sport Education', *European Physical Education Review*, 9: 285–299. doi:10.1177/1356336X030093006

MacPhail, A., Kirk, D. and Kinchin, G. (2004) 'Sport Education: Promoting team affiliation through physical education', *Journal of Teaching in Physical Education*, 23: 106–122.

Mason, J. (1996) *Qualitative researching*, London: Sage.

O'Donovan, T.M., MacPhail, A. and Kirk, D. (2010) 'Active citizenship through Sport Education', *Education 3–13: International Journal of Primary, Elementary and Early Years Education*, 38: 203–215. doi:10.1080/03004270903153947

Office for Standards in Education, Children's Services and Skills (Ofsted) (1998) *Teaching physical education in the primary school: The initial training of teachers. A report from the office of Her Majesty's Chief Inspector of Schools*, London: Ofsted.

Office for Standards in Education, Children's Services and Skills (Ofsted) (2003) *Physical education in primary schools: Ofsted subject reports series 2001/02*, London: Ofsted.

Oxley, J. (1998) 'Never mind literacy and numeracy, what about physical education?', *Bulletin of Physical Education*, 34(1): 55–57.

Physical Education Association (1984) *Professional courses in physical education for non-specialist primary and middle school teachers 1977–1983*, London: PEA.

Siedentop, D. (1994) *Sport Education: Quality PE through positive sport experiences*, Champaign, IL: Human Kinetics.

Speednet (2000) 'Primary school physical education – Speednet survey makes for depressing reading', *British Journal of Physical Education*, 30(3): 19–20.

Talbot, M. (2006) 'AfPE news: Progress and challenges for the association', *Physical Education Matters*, 1(1): 30.

Warburton, P. (2001) 'Initial teaching training: The preparation of primary teachers in physical education', *British Journal of Teaching Physical Education*, 31(1): 6–9.

Welch, M. (1989) 'A cultural perspective and the second wave of educational reform', *Journal of Learning Disabilities*, 22: 537–540. doi:10.1177/002221948902200903

Williams, A. (1985) 'Perspectives on initial teacher training in physical education', in *28th ICHPER World Congress Proceedings* (pp. 726–734), London: West London Institute of Higher Education.

Wright, L. (2004) 'Preserving the value of happiness in primary school physical education', *Physical Education and Sport Pedagogy*, 9: 149–163. doi:10.1080/1740898042000294967

3

SPORT EDUCATION IN KOREAN SCHOOLS

Jinhee Kim

This chapter is presented in three sections, the sum of which is to better understand the context of Sport Education as it has been implemented in Korean schools. The first section introduces the current role and status of physical education and physical education teachers within Korean education. Second, by reviewing the research on Sport Education in Korea, links are made between the pedagogical and cultural perspectives of this research and that from other countries. Finally, the third section discusses pedagogical perspectives of school Sport Education through operating cases in Korean schools.

Understanding of Korean school physical education

Physical education in Korea faces a huge transformation as the national curriculum has been drastically changed in recent years. Throughout the 2007 and 2009 curriculum revision, the Korean government emphasized "education for creativity and humanity" in order to foster competent people required by a rapidly changing society. However, this emphasis has been seen as essentially just a political catchphrase. The government's policy is such that the major subjects including Korean, English, and math account for an even greater part of the curriculum than previously. For example, according to the 2011 curriculum plan of the Korean Ministry of Education, 70 percent and 57 percent of middle schools have increased English and math classes, respectively. This phenomenon appeared because the government gave each school the autonomy of increasing or decreasing 20 percent of class hours based on the 2009 curriculum revision (*The Hankyorea* newspaper, September 11, 2010). Consequently, class hours spent in ethics, arts, and physical education are expected to be greatly reduced. Ironically, these subjects which are considered essential for humanity education to "enhance national competitiveness and to teach how to lead an abundant life" are in reality likely to remain marginalized. As a case in point, while the existing school physical education requires 3 hours a week until K-10, the new curriculum is mandatory only from K-8. To compound this, a student's grade for a physical education class is not considered for entry into high schools or colleges, further alienating the subject.

When one examines the new curriculum for physical education, with respect to the question "What is the subject of physical education?" the new curriculum defines physical education as a subject establishing the value of physical activity through school education. With respect to the goal of human education, students in physical education are expected to participate in class and demonstrate responsible behaviors. The new physical education curriculum establishes the content with six physical activity values: health activity, challenge activity, competition activity, value activity, expression activity, and leisure activity. With respect to these, primary schools (grades 1–6) are expected to focus on the basics of physical activity values, whereas secondary schools are responsible for the intensified education for physical activity values (Ministry of Education, Science and Technology, 2007).

Essentially, then, the purpose of this new physical education is to "understand and experience physical activity." Whereas physical education to date has been mostly limited to promoting physical fitness and improving health, from now on teachers must present content that emphasizes challenge, competence, expression, and leisure. For example, with regard to challenge, when learning movement challenges in a gymnastics class, students must learn the rationale or purpose for why they roll forward or backward. It is not enough for students to understand and master how to roll forward two times. Rather, they must also recognize why they roll forward through the brain, body, and mind, and second, what kind of benefits they could get by performing the movement. Furthermore, some esthetic appreciation of forward rolling is also expected.

The physical education teacher as a curriculum developer

In the past, subject curricula were developed at the national level by "experts," and on dissemination to schools, they were expected to be implemented in a uniform way. However, in order to keep pace with the international trend of giving responsibility for curriculum development and initiatives to local communities and schools, Korea has begun to follow suit. This change reflected the idea that, since the curriculum at the national level was based on abstract and general criteria, it had difficulties not only containing local specialty and students' individuality, but also employing a curriculum which considered local community and students. This paradigm shift resulted in a transfer of the authority for organizing and operating the curriculum to each school in 2007. This localization of curriculum has been attained at city, county, and town levels to the extent that local education offices at city, county, and school levels have reconstituted the curriculum and developed diverse materials (Park, 2003).

One manifestation of this new policy, however, has been a change in the role of teachers. While previously the agents of curriculum practitioner (where teachers were expected to accept and carry out the national curriculum passively developed by textbook experts), they are now expected to be curriculum developers. Not only do teachers now discuss the content of their yearly teaching–learning plans, they also create and implement their teaching and learning process plan in which they are asked to reflect directly on the school context as well as learners' needs. In addition, the 2007 revised curriculum extended the range of the content from exercise knowledge and skills to the "spirit and meaning of exercise." For this, physical education teachers are held responsible for extending content knowledge. They are no longer expected to focus on the acquisition of exercise skills and scientific knowledge as knowledge exclusive and particular to physical education, but to integrate these within a more holistic notion of physical activity.

The physical education teacher as an expert practitioner

The revised curriculum imposes more autonomy and responsibility on its practice at the teacher level, demanding a level of teacher expertise with respect to adopting a new perspective. While it requires not only an understanding and conveying of the new content, it does recognize the teacher's situational expertise and practical knowledge to the extent that it allows teachers to select and organize the educational content, and plan and operate their classes considering each school, classroom environment, and students' characteristics. Nonetheless, such expertise varies among teachers, and not all physical education teachers have achieved this status. Indeed, research across a number of sites has revealed that, to reach the level of an "expert," teachers need many years of experience and extensive teaching knowledge (Griffin *et al.*, 1996; Schempp, 2003).

Sport Education in Korea: fashion and passion

It was in 1997 when Moon and Yu introduced Sport Education to Korea. Following this, many curriculum materials were developed which included the translation and publication of the texts by Siedentop (1994; see Cho, 2002) and Siedentop *et al.* (2004; see Cho *et al.*, 2010), and home-based initiatives such as the Korea–Australia collaborative study sponsored by the government (Choi *et al.*, 2004) and the project for developing instructional materials related to the Sport Education model. This resulted in the *Handbook of Korean Sport Education* (Kim *et al.*, 2011).

From the Korean perspective, there are a number of reasons why Sport Education has been recognized for its value and usefulness. First, unlike other education models, Sport Education has been widely recognized as providing an understanding of sport itself, and through its educational value of allowing learners to experience various aspects of sport through diverse activities as a player, coach, captain, trainer, manager, referee, and so on. Second, Sport Education has a basis of systematic field research which has examined its organization and application as an appropriate instructional model for physical education. Third, in terms of application to school fields, it is believed that Sport Education is a useful instructional model because it can realize the educational value of sport by enabling learners with a lack of physical fitness and performance ability to participate in and perform various roles.

This section aims to share details about research on Korean Sport Education with Western scholars by not only listing research accomplishments, but also suggesting problems in conducting that research as it has applied to school physical education.

1997–2003: Introduction and application of Sport Education

Moon's (1998) doctoral dissertation that examined the application of Sport Education to a secondary baseball class was the first study completed after the introduction of Sport Education to Korea in 1997. According to the findings, the major roles and authority were frequently delegated to students with outstanding game ability, rather than equitably across all students. In the cognitive domain, students felt considerable responsibility in the process of role performance, which had a direct effect on their performance as referee and/or supervisor. In the psychomotor domain, students improved their game appreciation through various role performances which in turn enhanced their game performance. Finally, in the affective domain, as students' knowledge of roles increased, they understood deeply various aspects of the sport, in particular their ability to see the game of baseball from multiple perspectives.

Following this dissertation, most studies on Sport Education were conducted by school teachers for their master's and doctoral degrees (Choi et al., 2004; Han, 2000; Min, 2003; Park, 2003). Consistent with the main paradigm of Korean research on sport pedagogy which was predominantly quantitative based, research on Sport Education has consisted mainly of experimental applications comparing implementation with control groups. While evaluation was conducted in psychomotor, cognitive, and affective domains, the predominant concentration (43.2 percent) of total research was concentrated in the affective domain until 2006 (Yu et al., 2006).

The early research on the model can be summarized into several characteristics which are now described. First, research was concentrated on verifying the affective outcomes of Sport Education, in particular changes in students' attitudes toward class. The genesis for these studies were the results of previous studies (Carlson, 1995; Grant, 1992; Sport Physical Activity Research Centre, 1995) which revealed that Sport Education participation had positive responses in terms of engagement in lessons, interest in learning, the motivation of lower skilled students, and improvements in gender equality in physical education classes.

The second feature of early research related to methodology. The primary form of data collection was the questionnaire, with most research investigating the pre- and postdifferences of the experimental group (Sport Education) and comparison groups. However, since 2000, more research has begun to use qualitative techniques, resulting in more diverse perspectives and research questions.

The third feature, which came to pass after the model was introduced and as graduate schools and teacher educators have become more interested in this model, was an increase in published research relating to in-school applications. Considering the number of studies of Sport Education (51), we can guess the popularity of this model in Korea. However, despite this quantitative growth, the model is criticized because Sport Education in Korea still sticks with the content originally proposed by Siedentop without pausing to ponder over how the cultural context of Korea might be better represented in the model (Kim *et al.*, 2010). Consequently, there is a pressing need for study of the characteristics of Korean Sport Education and the kind of image it ought to have in the field.

2004–2010: The development of Sport Education research

By the mid-2000s, research on Sport Education in Korea was characterized by considerable variety, due to a qualitative change in the research environment such as the acceptance of diverse research logic, the development of new research methods, and a changing philosophical paradigm of physical education. The trigger for this research diversity was the special issue published in the *Korean Journal of Sports Pedagogy* titled as "Integrated Approach to Physical Education: Practice of Sport Education" produced by the Korea–Australia collaborative study. In this study, Korean and Australian scholars participated in teaching Sport Education classes in elementary, middle, and high schools with teachers for an entire academic year. In this study, Kim *et al.* (2004) offered meaningful implications for the practical operation of Sport Education. These focused on the school-centered curriculum of physical education operation, understanding teacher–student experiences, and on knowledge acquirement through instruction by applying Sport Education to Korean and Australian school physical education.

The authors also pointed out a lack of specific research of practical applications suitable to Korean Sport Education. They emphasized the necessity of methodological study which can systematize and generalize if we want to carry out Sport Education within the context of learner-centered physical education which the seventh curriculum stressed. In the collaborative study, Kim *et al.* (2004) provided in-depth cases of Sport Education programs suitable to Korea. In addition, Penney and Taggart (2004), as participants in the collaborative study, emphasized the need for the introduction of Sport Education into teacher education programs. They also emphasized the specific structure and support of all the schools as important sources for the successful change of Sport Education.

Moon and Jo (2004) conducted the first narrative research on the evaluation of the psychomotor domain in a physical education class using Sport Education. In this study, two teachers explained the possibility of the application of the Game Performance Assessment Instrument as an alternative to a more skills-testing focus for the purposes of assessing students. Following this, other in-depth studies (e.g., Choi and Kim, 2007; Kim and Kim, 2007; No, 2007) described diverse cases in the process of evaluating Sport Education in context.

Other qualitative research focused on individual students. Choi and Kim (2004) reported the process of how a female student with low skills participated in a physical education class. The study described the process through which Hyun-a moved from a resistant participant in physical education to one who enjoyed participating in various sport activities through Sport Education classes. This case indicated that the student-centered physical education class must be continuously attempted with diverse perspectives and contents, and that the teacher–researcher's persistent reflection and practice has been demanded within the sport domain. On that theme, Kim (2007) criticized the existing boy-centered physical education class that still appeared in Sport Education. Kim contended that comments like "girls with low skills had better participation" came from teachers who tried to distort Sport Education with positive images, whereas in-class observations showed that girls were in charge of only those roles hated by boys (Kim, 2007). Consequently, the potential for Sport Education to provide an alternative which can realize true gender equality in physical education was questioned.

In a move away from students' experiences, other studies investigated factors related to teachers and teaching. Lim (2004) examined the instructional planning, practice, and reflection of teachers who conducted Sport Education through an analysis of teachers' thinking. This study revealed that teachers who execute Sport Education had some difficulties in getting help from their colleagues and school principal. These teachers also need greater support in terms of materials of tools and methods for model application at the beginning stage. More specifically, these teachers experienced stress due to their perceived practical difficulty of application, due in the most part to the competitive culture of students and the difficulty of persuading them to take differing responsibilities. Nonetheless, Lim does describe that, after the teachers experienced students' positive change and went through the process of reflective deliberation, they came to have confidence not as simple and passive curriculum appliers but as active practitioners.

In another study focusing on teachers, Kim (2006) divided teachers into two groups (novice and experienced), and examined how they applied, evaluated, and dealt with their classes. Using an affective-psychological perspective, results showed that novice teachers were interested in implementing the model as is, whereas the experienced teachers changed and extended certain aspects of the model to satisfy specific class situations. The outcomes of this study provided school teachers and instructional researchers with implications of better model application and practice by describing various strategies derived from practicing teachers' thoughts and actions.

A general summary

As mentioned above, studies on Sport Education have been conducted using diverse views and methods since the model was introduced to Korea. We can summarize the research characteristics of Sport Education into two categories from the mid-2000s to the present as follows. First, compared with early research, recent research has employed diverse qualitative paradigms such as hermeneutical views and feministic views as a tool of research logic. Thus, the research has shown interest in fundamental matters such as students' and teachers' experience, its meaning, philosophical features, and the curriculum characteristics of Sport Education and how individuals respond to these. Second, teachers have started to have an interest in the fundamental method of using Sport Education in schools in a meaningful way. Recent research focuses on how fundamental features of Sport Education work in the Korean physical education situation, how teachers use Sport Education, and how students accept this.

Visions and reflectivity

While this chapter has discussed the achievements of Korean Sport Education, there are still problems left to consider for further research. The first concerns research design. Given that the method and extent of students' participation varies depending on each iteration of the model, research designs which are created in order to compare two different instruction models must be reexamined. That is, it seems meaningless to compare two totally different models with one criterion because they have different goals, participation methods, and student–teacher interactions. Each model is meaningful only if it appropriately reflects the teacher's value orientation and class objectives. In this regard, it is almost impossible to define what the best class model is, or "the model" which can be well applied in every single situation. Essentially, then, the design of hierarchical comparative research between the Sport Education model class and other class models needs to be rejected. Rather, we need to put in more effort to find out the necessary factors for the Sport Education model to be successfully applied in different and various situations and the reasons why such factors are fostered.

The second issue concerns how the outcome of Sport Education research can be applied in school settings. Researchers have created classroom environments to observe and describe specific effects and functions which Sport Education can produce. Consequently, this has caused teachers to run artificial classes to fit the agenda intended by the researchers. While this artificial and empirical method might be inevitable in the quest to get more refined results with the specific time and labor, what is needed for Sport Education to be successful is "practical effort." To do this, action research is a more appropriate methodology. The narrative inquiry of the teacher in self-study may be a good starting point. If teachers from the field write in the autographical way and reinterpret it with researchers, the Sport Education class for both teachers and students could be more practical. To achieve this, a close relationship with the school authorities and the researcher's understanding of the field is necessary along with the teacher's effort.

The last problem is about understanding who puts Sport Education into practice and who participates in it. The existing research on Sport Education has largely focused on Siedentop's theories. When teachers apply the theories to the field, they are only concerned about whether they use them correctly. As a result, Sport

Education can be limited in the extent to which it can provide practical information for the teachers who want to apply the model in various class situations. In other words, research on Sport Education has focused heavily on the fidelity of reproducing "textbook" Sport Education. This suggests that future research may have to focus more on pedagogical action research. Pedagogical action research helps physical education teachers use and develop philosophical and methodological aspects intrinsic to the Sport Education model. Moreover, teachers as action researchers have to pay more attention to the situational and contextual effects intrinsic to the model. To put this another way, they need to pay attention to how the pedagogical model can be efficiently used in the actual Korean class settings (Kim *et al.*, 2010). Using the pedagogical model effectively does not require physical education teachers to have a perfect understanding and application of the Sport Education model. This is because physical education teachers do not apply the model theories mechanically. They use their practical and mixed knowledge obtained through their experiences. This means that various model theories can be interpreted in new ways and modified through the personal experience of physical education teachers. In addition, we need to put in an effort to understand how Sport Education is interpreted and formed from the student's perspectives and what factors are needed for the class to be more significant to the students who take the class.

Locating Sport Education within the Korean cultural context

This section outlines one example of how the local context of Korean society was incorporated into a season of badminton. Referred to as "the unforgettable badminton festival," it outlines ways in which the festivity objective of Sport Education was enhanced through involving students and other adults from outside the class.

The season began with the usual teaching of techniques and a number of different strokes, and then followed a team-based competition. As doubles or singles, the team that gained the first three points won the game. Captains had to submit a piece of paper in advance with the name of the designated player for the next game. The key to engagement, however, was making badminton available at times other than during formally scheduled classes.

During lunchtimes and after school was over, the badminton court began to buzz with students. Students' previous understanding and experience with badminton was limited to hitting shuttlecocks in parks, but with increasing opportunities to play and practice (and play on a real court with a real net), clear levels of enjoyment became evident. During both class and out-of-class sessions, the focus was on the correct etiquette toward fellow players. Challenge matches sometimes involved the teacher playing against the students after school with bets on ice cream. Team matches were carried out in a tournament style. After class, the list of matches following the random drawing of teams was put up and the entire school began to be interested in badminton.

As the end of the year approached, a badminton festival was planned. It fell on a Saturday before Christmas and after the end of final exams. The students were notified in advance, and the matches were to be in the individual division. Instead of the games being between classes, the students were to participate in individual doubles with a partner of their choice. The prizes were either sponsored by the local badminton association or prepared with help from friends, including racquets, socks, gloves, hair bands, food vouchers from local shops, and so on.

While originally planned to be held in a public gymnasium outside the school grounds, due to the administrator's opposition, six courts had to be made on the school field using strings held in place by fixing with a hammer and chisel. This would have been impossible without the help of my fellow colleagues. The situation was notified to the parents and teachers' association (PTA), who were quick to lend a helping hand having seen what was being done for the students by the staff on their days off. Tents were put up, mats were rolled out onto the ground, and mobile heaters were made with barrels. Parents prepared noodles and kim-bap for the players.

While not all students chose to participate (even after having submitted an entry form), most came out on their day off to enjoy badminton, snack away, and become a true sport person along with their friends. In the middle of the tournament, coaches who had taken badminton lessons at "Sport for All Coaches" were invited for a demonstration match. The students, who by this stage had begun to think that they were the best, watched their brilliance in awe. The parents who had prepared the food were also invited to play, escalating the mood of the festival. Students experienced the everyday sport culture firsthandedly at this event. The badminton festival will be remembered even when these middle-school-aged students have become adults. As a physical education teacher, I could not wish for anything more than to see the students go on from this experience to enjoy sports for the rest of their lives.

Conclusion

The chapter has introduced the key changes that have been required for the Korean national curriculum. In particular, the greatest difference has been the teacher's role in curriculum development and class management. Since Sport Education gives teachers total authority to develop the curriculum which best fits the students, whether students enjoy the class or not is totally up to the teachers.

Despite these increases in autonomy, however, to fully realize the potential of Sport Education, Korean teachers must overcome several obstacles such as poor facilities, inflexible administrators, and students' attitudes. No matter how great the class model is, if it is not implemented well in the field, it is nothing. Then how can we solve this problem? Teacher training is the answer. We must change teachers' negative attitudes about Sport Education through various educational programs. The government must provide teachers with abundant resources or materials for diverse classes to acquire new knowledge and skills easily. Through regular teacher training, teachers must encounter best-application cases of Sport Education, and exchange their successful experiences as curriculum developers and class experts.

References

Carlson, T. (1995) "'Now I think I can': The reaction of eight low-skilled students to Sport Education," *The ACHPER Healthy Lifestyles Journal*, 42(4): 6–8.

Cho, M.H. (2002) "Sport Education," Seoul, Korea Daehan media, translation from D. Siedentop (1994) *Sport Education: Quality physical education through positive sport experiences*, Champaign, IL: Human Kinetics.

Cho, M.H., Kim, M.Y., Ryu, C.O., Park, G.J., Bang, M.H., Lee, S.H., Lee, S.H., Jo, Y.I., and Hong, H.J. (2010) "Sport Education," Seoul, Korea: Daehan media, translation from D. Siedentop, P.A. Hastie, and H. van der Mars (2004) *Complete guide to Sport Education*, Champaign, IL: Human Kinetics.

Choi, H.J., Cho, M.H., Kim, J.H., Taggart, A., Penney, D., Han, M.S., Nam, G.Y., and Choi, W.J. (2004) "Applications of Sport Education in school: Developing physical education curricular through the Korea and Australia collaboration project," *Korean Journal of Sports Pedagogy*, 11(3): 7–28.

Choi, W.J. and Kim, J.H. (2004) "(An) analysis of participation in physical education of low skilled girls on Sport Education," *The Korean Journal of Physical Education*, 43(5): 217–227.

Choi, W.J. and Kim, J.H. (2007) "Students, embodied experiences in Sport Education," *The Korean Journal of Physical Education*, 46(3): 135–148.

Grant, B.C. (1992) "Integrating sport into the physical education curriculum in New Zealand secondary schools," *Quest*, 44: 304–316.

Griffin, L., Dodds, P., and Rovegno, I. (1996) "Pedagogical content knowledge for teachers: Integrate everything you know to help students learn." *Journal of Physical Education, Recreation & Dance*, 67(9): 58–61.

Han, K.H. (2000) *A study on teaching strategies of volleyball through the Sport Education curriculum model*, South Korea: Korea National University of Education.

Kim, J.H. (2004) "Developing student-centred pedagogies through international collaborative research," *Korean Journal of Sports Pedagogy*, 11(3): 1–5.

Kim, J.H. (2007) "Gender perspectives in the Sport Education model," *The Korean Journal of Physical Education*, 46(1): 377–390.

Kim, J.H., Choi, H.J., Cho, M.H., and Kim, T.C. (2004) "Action research for the application of Sport Education programs in Korea," *Korean Journal of Sports Pedagogy*, 11(3): 29–54.

Kim, J.H., Nam, G.Y., and Choi, W.J. (2011) *Handbook of Korean Sport Education*, Seoul: Kyoyookbook.

Kim, M.Y. (2006) *Understanding of experienced Sport Education teachers' thinking processes*, South Korea: INHA University.

Kim, S.J. and Kim, J.H. (2007) "Gender perspectives in Sport Education," *The Korean Journal of Physical Education*, 46(1): 377–390.

Lim, H.J. (2004) "Perceptions and experiences of physical education teacher related to Sports Education," *Korean Journal of Sports Pedagogy*, 11(3): 85–102.

Min, H.G. (2003) *Effects of the Sports Education model on achievement of physical education in high school students*, South Korea: Korea National University of Education.

Ministry of Education, Science and Technology (2007) *Revised physical education in national curriculum 2007*, Seoul, Korea: Ministry of Education, Science and Technology.

Moon, H.J. (1998) *A case study of the Sport Education curriculum model in teaching physical education at a selected secondary school*, Seoul, Korea: Seoul National University.

Moon, H.J. and Jo, N.Y. (2004) "A narrative study of using GPAI for teaching the Sport Education model," *Korean Journal of Sports Pedagogy*, 11(3): 67–83.

Moon, H.J. and Yu, T.H. (1997) "Sport Education as an effective model in teaching physical education," *Korean Journal of Sports Pedagogy*, 4(2): 76–90.

No, S.S. (2007) *A case study of assessment in the physical education class applied Sport Education model*, South Korea: INHA University.

Park, T.J. (2003) *Effects of PE with the sports educational model on affective domain development*, Gongju, Korea: Gongju National University.

Penney, D. and Taggart, A. (2004) "Key challenges in the development of Sport Education: Primary and middle school teachers' experience," *Korean Journal of Sports Pedagogy*, 11(3): 117–134.

Schempp, P. (2003) *Teaching sport and physical activity insights on the road to excellence*, Champaign, IL: Human Kinetics.

Sport Physical Activity Research Centre (1995) *Report on the 1994 National Trial of Sport Education*, Perth, Australia: Edith Cowan University.

Yu, T.H., Lee, B.J., and Park, J.G. (2006) "Accomplishments and future directions of researches in instructional models for physical education," *Korean Journal of Sports Pedagogy*, 13(3): 1–26.

4

THE EMERGENCE OF SPORT EDUCATION IN SCOTTISH PRIMARY SCHOOLS

Mike Jess, Nicola Carse, Paul McMillan, and Matthew Atencio

Over the last decade, there has been an upsurge in the fortunes of primary school physical education in Scotland. While physical education in Scottish secondary schools remains largely focused on the more performance-oriented national certificates for senior secondary students (Thorburn, 2004), primary school physical education has been engaging with numerous curriculum and professional learning developments. This chapter discusses how the Developmental Physical Education Group (DPEG) at the University of Edinburgh has promoted a revised conception of the primary school physical education curriculum based on developmental principles. In particular, the chapter considers how this project has seen Sport Education emerge across many parts of Scotland as a key component of this revised primary school physical education curriculum. The chapter will present the conditions which have brought about the recent emergence of primary school physical education in Scotland, will discuss how Sport Education has become a significant feature of these primary school developments and will conclude by considering the impact Sport Education has had on primary teachers and their schools.

The emergence of primary physical education in Scotland

Scotland is a small country with a population of 5.1 million people and occupies the northern third of Great Britain. While it has shared a parliament with England since 1707, Scotland elected its first devolved parliament in three centuries in 1999. Early in this post-devolution period, the Scottish Executive set out to create educational policies with a collective emphasis on improving equality and inclusion (Humes, 2003) and also to use a lifelong learning agenda as the driver for educational improvement (Scottish Executive, 2003a). In addition, an innovative approach to curriculum development was taken with the introduction of 'Curriculum for Excellence' (CfE) (Scottish Executive, 2004a) which focused on curriculum coherence and greater teacher autonomy in curriculum developments. Policy moved from the 'traditional' subject-based secondary school curriculum with its associated narrow pedagogy (Bryce and Humes, 1999) towards an all-through 3–18 curriculum framed by learning goals concentrating on 'successful learners', 'confident individuals', 'effective contributors' and 'responsible citizens' (Scottish Executive, 2004a). Teachers in Scotland are now being challenged to actively engage with curriculum innovation and to use more active learning approaches to become 'the creative, adaptable professional who can develop the ideas that arise when children are immersed in their learning' (Scottish Executive, 2007, p. 19).

Alongside these education developments, physical activity (Scottish Executive, 2003b) and physical education (Scottish Executive, 2004b) emerged as areas of increased political interest. The Physical Education Review Group (PERG), comprising a wide range of professionals, was set up in 2002 to formulate recommendations to move physical education forward in the twenty-first century (Scottish Executive, 2004b). Supported by the Scottish Executive, these recommendations included two hours of curriculum physical education for all children, specialist physical education support for every primary school and continuous staff development in primary schools. In addition, the PERG proposed the biggest impact would come from improvements in the physical education curriculum with primary school physical education focusing on the development of movement skills and connections between physical activity, health and well-being. Subsequently, the emergence of lifelong physical activity and lifelong learning agendas aligned to the PERG recommendations presented primary school physical education with an opportunity to play a more central role both in the primary school and also as part of contemporary physical education (Scottish Executive, 2004b).

The DPEG

Within this emerging national context, the DPEG at the University of Edinburgh set out to provide a revised conception of physical education. Originally developed as a reaction to the perceived flaws with the traditional watered-down 'multi-activity' physical education curriculum model (see Kirk, 2004), the DPEG's initial innovation attempts were informed by developmentally appropriate principles (Gallahue and Ozmun, 1999) and focused on Basic Moves, an early years physical education programme for young children aged 5–7 years (Jess et al., 2004). Basic Moves aimed to help all children develop core basic movements and the cognitive, social and emotional learning that would underpin participation in most physical activities (Bailey et al., 2009). As such, Basic Moves moved beyond the isolated learning of movement technique and included aspects of adaptability and creativity. By 2005, the DPEG began to extend its curriculum agenda in two related ways: by creating curriculum experiences covering the age range of 3–14 years and expanding its theoretical basis by engaging with key principles from ecological (Newell, 1986), dynamical systems (Thelen and Smith, 1994), social constructivist (Vygotsky, 1978), situated learning (Lave and Wenger, 1991) and complexity

(Davis and Samara, 2006) perspectives. Consequently, notions of self-organisation, emergence, collaboration and authentic learning have had a significant impact on the group's thinking about curriculum in the upper primary and early secondary (UPES) years (Jess *et al.*, 2011). These new concepts challenged the predictability of the traditional physical education curriculum and its accompanying behaviourist-inclined pedagogy and led the DPEG to present a UPES curriculum structured around core learning, developmental applications and authentic applications (Jess *et al.*, 2007) (see Figure 4.1).

UPES core learning builds on the holistic learning of Basic Moves by focusing on the key knowledge, skills and understanding that helps older children success-fully participate in the more complex physical activities they encounter (see Table 4.1). Developmental applications have similarities to traditional multi-activity 'blocks' as they are taught for short periods of time and focus on specific activity contexts, for example games, gymnastics and dance. The key to these developmen-tal applications, however, is that they are specifically designed to connect core learning with the more 'real-life' learning experiences of the authentic applica-tions. Based on ideas from situated learning theory (Lave and Wenger, 1991), authentic applications take place for longer periods of time (e.g. term or semester), and set out to further develop core learning and developmental applications by contextualising them in 'real-life' situations across and beyond the school curricu-lum (Kirk and Kinchin, 2003). Examples of authentic applications include Sport Education (Siedentop, 1994), outdoor journeys (Beames *et al.*, 2009) and dance education (Irvine, 2009).

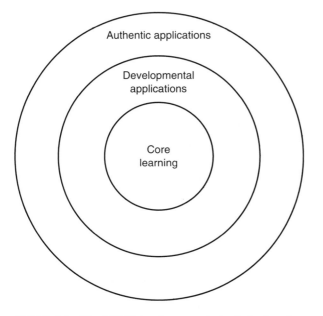

FIGURE 4.1 The UPES developmental physical education curriculum

TABLE 4.1 Examples of core learning in the developmental UPES Physical Education curriculum

Psychomotor	Basic movement combinations
	Health and performance-related components
	Physical activity lifestyle tracking
Cognitive	Critical thinking and decision-making skills
	Principles of performance and practice
	Health and recreational issues
	Etiquette
Social	Social learning skills
	Individual and team behaviours
	Roles and responsibilities
	Cooperation, inclusion and competition
Emotional	Task and ego behaviours
	Self-determination
	Physical identity
	Emotional intelligence
	Coping strategies

These DPEG innovations are also being disseminated throughout Scotland via its ongoing professional learning project. Since 2001, this project has passed through two overlapping phases beginning with Basic Moves and then the Scottish Primary Physical Education Project (SPPEP), which has enabled the DPEG to extend its professional learning efforts to the age range of 3–14 years. A collaborative venture with the University of Glasgow, the government-supported SPPEP was developed in response to the PERG recommendations and has focused on creating a national primary school physical education professional learning programme based on interlinked award and non-award bearing continuing professional development (CPD) programmes. Postgraduate certificates (PgCerts)[1] involving up to two years' part-time study are the foundation for SPPEP, and to date, almost 400 teachers, mostly primary class teachers, have enrolled on the PgCert in 3–14 physical education at the University of Edinburgh. Critically, the PgCerts have created the platform for the national primary school physical education-CPD programme which has recently seen over 200 primary school physical education tutors trained to help deliver professional learning programmes in their local contexts. From a DPEG perspective, these primary school physical education tutors are the catalysts for the on-going dissemination of the 3–14 curriculum innovations which, as will now be discussed, has placed Sport Education as a key feature of primary school physical education developments in many Scottish primary schools.

Introducing Sport Education into Scottish primary schools

Until recently, there have been few examples of Sport Education operating in Scotland. In secondary schools, largely due to the domination of the multi-activity curriculum model, Sport Education rarely appears on timetables. Professional learning opportunities for teachers to engage with Sport Education have been almost non-existent, although, for many years, Sport Education has been presented as an alternative curriculum approach to final-year student teachers on the United Kingdom's largest secondary Initial Teacher Education (ITE) physical education programme at the University of Edinburgh. In the few schools where Sport Education has been attempted, it has usually been in contexts where teachers are experimenting and, as one secondary teacher has reported, 'trying something different'. Unfortunately, these teachers have often met scepticism from colleagues who are generally unwilling to deviate from the traditional physical education curriculum, citing the marginalising of 'skill development' as a likely offshoot. In addition, there has been even less evidence of Sport Education in Scottish primary schools because of a lack of professional learning opportunities. However, the introduction of the PgCert in 3–14 physical education has, since 2008, resulted in hundreds of primary class teachers being directly introduced to Sport Education.

Methodology

In this chapter, we provide both practical and empirically based examples that illustrate the emerging role of Sport Education in Scottish primary school physical education. As PgCert graduates have started to teach Sport Education in their schools, many have provided compelling examples of the complex process of implementing Sport Education. To capture the details of these stories, semi-structured interviews were conducted with eight PgCert graduate teachers (two males and six females). The interviews were conducted between 2009 and 2010 with teachers of varying ages and years of service and whose schools were situated across Scotland. The names of the participant teachers have been changed to retain their anonymity.

Sport Education and the PgCert in 3–14 physical education

The PgCert in 3–14 physical education has two main aims. The first is to build teachers' competence and confidence to create and deliver a primary school physical education curriculum appropriate to their individual contexts, and the second is to help teachers collaborate with colleagues to support and develop primary school physical education across their schools. As such, the programme positions Sport Education and authentic applications as the culminating feature of the programme by focusing on the development of a knowledge and experiential base that highlights:

- the interdisciplinary nature of the Scottish CfE;
- developmental, inclusive, connected and lifewide principles informing primary school physical education;
- the holistic nature of the developing child in the primary school physical education context;
- children's developing movement competence;

- early years and upper primary core primary school physical education learning;
- developmental applications in the early and upper primary years;
- the key principles of authentic applications;
- an inclusive pedagogy that acknowledges the complexity of the learning context;
- teachers as curriculum innovators within their own settings.

Consequently, Sport Education has become the logical concluding feature of the PgCert by providing an authentic context for the knowledge teachers have accumulated. As one of the PgCert students has commented:

> Sport Education was one of those light bulb moments for me where everything fell into place. It brought together everything I had learned through the 3–14 programme: Basic Moves leading to applying these movements through developmental games and then bringing all of this together in an authentic sense through Sport Education. For me, Sport Education was an integral cog in the physical education curriculum.
>
> *(Heidi, 3–14 graduate teacher)*

For many of the teachers, Sport Education was not viewed as an add-on to the primary school physical education curriculum; rather they saw the possibility of incorporating elements of Sport Education into everyday physical education and extending it across the general curriculum. Oslin (2002) has suggested that this adaptation is required if Sport Education is to create an 'educationally rich sport experience' and aid the promotion of lifelong physical activity.

Another attraction of Sport Education has been its inclusive nature, an outcome also highlighted in much of the Sport Education literature (Clarke and Quill, 2003; Hastie and Curtner-Smith, 2006). For example, in the quote below, one teacher highlighted the often problematic relationship between sport and physical education (Green, 2000) and indeed between sport and Sport Education (Oslin, 2002).

> I remember the thing that struck me about it [Sport Education] was the inclusive nature of it and the lifelong learning aspect . . . and the role that sport can play in people's lives in terms of giving them a sense of belonging even if they're not elite athletes. I saw it as having a real place in life, real life; because of that I actually just bought the book at the time and I thought, I was desperate to try it out.
>
> *(Laura, 3–14 graduate)*

PgCert teachers regularly commented that they appreciated Sport Education's inclusive attributes. They were also drawn to Sport Education for other reasons: they considered it a natural link to their primary school physical education and class-room curriculum activities; it made them reconsider and even challenge the prevailing role of sport within primary school physical education and, most importantly, they had often used parts of it before in their previous primary school physical education teaching. This latter perspective is noted in the following quote:

> It was only after finding out about Sport Education that I realised I had used elements of it before in my teaching when I had organised a mini Olympics with a class where the pupils worked in the same team, took on the role of judges and were involved in pupil-led practice and competition.
>
> *(Heidi, 3–14 graduate)*

This combination of factors provided the PgCert teachers with a sense of competence and confidence which encouraged them to explore the possibilities of Sport Education within their teaching practice.

Building on the growing number of teachers completing the PgCerts, two national Sport Education seminars were held in 2009 and 2010. The second seminar was led by colleagues from England and Ireland with an expertise in Sport Education who were able to report on contemporary international projects and research findings. Directly linked to these national seminars, the first cohort of 20 Sport Education tutors attended tutor training courses and are now in a position to commence dissemination of Sport Education within their local contexts. A third national seminar, to be led by a colleague from the United States, will be the centrepiece of the national primary school physical education Summer School in July 2011. Consequently, in a short period of time, Sport Education has become a feature of primary school physical education in many Scottish primary schools and, as will now be discussed, is having a significant impact on the nature of the primary school physical education experience for individual classes and across schools.

Sport Education in Scottish primary schools: the impact

The process of disseminating Sport Education within the Scottish primary school context is gathering momentum and could be characterised as having a 'snowball effect'. As the number of teachers completing the PgCert in 3–14 physical education increases, the DPEG has been able to evaluate the various impacts that Sport Education is having on primary school physical education across Scotland. Through discussions with teachers, it has become apparent that Sport Education has impacted on three particular aspects of their teaching: the primary school physical education curriculum; their pedagogy; and collaborative experiences with colleagues in and beyond their schools (see Table 4.2). These impacts will be discussed in the following subsections.

Sport Education and curriculum experiences

Since the introduction of Sport Education, teachers report a broadening of the primary school physical education curriculum experiences in their classes to

TABLE 4.2 The impact of Sport Education on teachers' curriculum, pedagogy and collaborative practices

Curriculum	Holistic learning experiences
	Interdisciplinary learning
Pedagogy	Emergent
	Assessment for learning
	Engaging and inclusive
Collaboration	Across schools
	Beyond schools

incorporate wider learning experiences and also to connect Sport Education experiences in the gymnasium with those in the classroom. From a holistic perspective, while teachers continue to recognise the importance of children's physical skill development, they also highlighted that it is easier to address cognitive, social and emotional issues as they emerge. For example, one PgCert teacher working with a behaviourally difficult class in an area of economic deprivation reported how Sport Education helped her focus on social learning issues that regularly impacted on physical education sessions when she said:

> The major focus was . . . getting the children to work cooperatively . . . we have a lot of boys who just want to fight each other at the weekend . . . they were very individual and for themselves . . . we wanted them to work cooperatively . . . a lot of social . . . personal and social education . . . most of the time. [Before Sport Education] we would start to do something and it wouldn't work because they couldn't cooperate together . . . they work much better now.
>
> *(Jennifer, 3–14 graduate)*

This statement highlights that working with others as an individual, in cooperation and in competitive environments is a social skill that is learned and practised over time (Johnson and Johnson, 1999). Reflecting the strong correlation between Sport Education and cooperative learning (Dyson *et al.*, 2004), Sport Education has arguably afforded teachers the time and opportunity to explore the concept of cooperation with their students.

Teachers have also commented on how Sport Education has challenged children to think for themselves, by regularly engaging them in tasks that require problem-solving. These thinking tasks contribute to enhancing children's cognitive understanding in physical education. One teacher spoke about developing a structure of playing, reflecting and planning in a season of Sport Education, where the children were encouraged to think about how they were engaging with the season and how they could develop their skills and understanding. Rather than simply transmitting the knowledge required to appreciate an activity, teachers have engaged children in investigating their own learning experiences; examples include discussion, video assessment and written assessment tasks. By experimenting with the possibilities of Sport Education, teachers have subsequently commented on how children access learning outcomes that range from improved physical performance to greater depth of understanding, increased participation, taking responsibility, elevated levels of behaviour, cooperation and higher work rate (Hastie, 2003).

Sport Education has also helped the teachers, often for the first time, link primary school physical education experiences to the children's learning experiences in the classroom setting. This perspective was noted by one teacher:

> Sport at the centre was really easy . . . close links . . . it was trying to fit it all in! The kids could see the links . . . they would say, 'Is this what we were doing yesterday in the gym hall?'
>
> *(Charlotte, 3–14 graduate)*

For the teachers, the potential to make this connection between primary school physical education and other subject areas has not only become a key process but also a vehicle to create interdisciplinary links in line with the new CfE guidelines. With these new national curriculum guidelines placing the child at the centre of the learning process, Scottish teachers are being encouraged to take a more interactive approach to teaching, and promote interdisciplinary learning (Scottish Executive, 2007). Consequently, when asked how Sport Education relates to CfE, one of the teachers simply stated: 'do I even have to answer that, I mean yeah absolutely.' Many of the primary teachers similarly commented that the Sport Education model aligns with the new curriculum developments:

> Sport Ed fits in perfectly [with CfE] because . . . it's about personalisation and choice for a starter, the children have got ownership of the season, they've got ownership of the teams, ownership of the rules and the responsibilities, so it fits in perfectly with that . . . and as I say the number of interdisciplinary learning and teaching activities ties in . . . the quality of the writing or maths when it's about their own team or character [mascot] that they have imagined . . . in terms of Health and Wellbeing[2] (HWB) too . . . we have had a lot of nice subjective feedback from teachers and children and most of it related to increased participation . . . so in terms of fitness and HWB it is definitely making a difference.
>
> *(Mark, 3–14 graduate)*

By bringing physical education into the classroom and immersing it with other subject areas, these practitioners are challenging the traditional view of physical education as a separate 'fun' subject and a break from the other academic subjects (Green, 2000).

Within an international context Siedentop (2002) reflects positively on recent research that has emerged where the original Sport Education model has been adapted and extended. While there is evidence of teachers extending the model to promote cross-curricular learning (Hastie, 2003), this is an area which has received limited attention in Sport Education literature. However, within the Scottish context, Sport Education has been linked with the experiences and outcomes of CfE, and interdisciplinary learning has emerged as a key component of the Sport Education model. As one head teacher working in a school in an area of economic deprivation has reported, Sport Education 'snowballed' to such an extent that

> we tried to keep it with maths only originally because we thought there would be loads of data, loads of analysis they could do, personal research that they could do . . . figures . . . players, searches, even the finance side . . . so there were a lot of really natural links there . . . but to be honest it did start to grow and we started to focus on personal writing . . . it was hard to pull it in because the kids were so enthusiastic . . . they really wanted to go and do more . . . they didn't actually want to go on holiday . . . it was about trying to keep a lid on it.
>
> *(Felicity, 3–14 graduate)*

It is encouraging that Scottish teachers are reporting how this interdisciplinary learning has enhanced the Sport Education experience for the children, particularly leading to increased motivation and connecting learning in physical education with other subject areas. As most of the PgCert graduates are classroom primary teachers, it has become apparent that they have access to a broader curriculum than the subject-specific physical education specialists and have been able to use sport as the mechanism to draw out a myriad of connections across many different learning experiences.

Sport Education and teachers' pedagogy

As teachers introduce Sport Education to their classes, they are responding to its unpredictable nature and are beginning to use a more emergent pedagogy. They discuss how their pedagogy is moving beyond the more controlling, behaviourist approach which has long held a strong foothold in physical education (Light, 2008) and is now more receptive to issues of inclusion and uncertainty. As such, the teachers are beginning to acknowledge the complex, self-organising and non-linear nature of the children's learning in primary school physical education contexts (Jess *et al.*, 2011). A teacher reflecting on her first experience of introducing Sport Education to her class highlighted this emergent pedagogy when she noted:

> It's quite scary as you don't really know where they are going to go with it and how they are going to take it, but when they get to a place where they know what they're doing and they know how to take things on and do it themselves you get much more time to stand back and observe and be able to facilitate their learning more . . . learning things for themselves instead of you telling them what to do . . . they [the children] have loved it.
>
> *(Kirsty, 3–14 graduate)*

Another teacher similarly highlighted how Sport Education fostered a more learner-centred approach and even suggested that he would regularly ask the children for advice:

> We had these 'friendly' sessions at the start . . . there were lots of different kinds of problems when using the model . . . but we always found creative solutions for it . . . when I became stuck I would ask the children to suggest something.
>
> *(Mark, 3–14 graduate)*

These quotes capture the emergent and exploratory nature of the Sport Education process whereby both teachers and children actively participate in the learning process. Rather than working as holders of 'expert' knowledge and teaching in linear and 'top-down' ways, teachers suggested that Sport Education provided them with opportunities 'to stand back and observe' in order to support and guide the children's learning. However, as McCaughtry *et al.* (2004) highlight, taking this 'first step' into Sport Education and incorporating student ownership into the season can prove challenging for practitioners and can even lead to rejection of the model.

Furthermore, it is important to stress that an emergent pedagogical approach is not an 'anything-goes' approach, but rather one that is bounded by many contextual factors including the key tenets of Sport Education and the parameters of the focus sport or physical activity. Teachers, as a consequence, are reacting by increasingly employing techniques from 'assessment for learning': an approach which seeks to actively engage children in the learning process (Black and Wiliam, 1998). Many now undertake a detailed baseline assessment to help them plan the Sport Education experiences best suited to the particular 'starting point' of the children. Because Sport Education is delivered over a longer period of time, it has proved to be an ideal context for teachers to find out more about children's previous experiences in the specific focus sport and also to assess the children's psychomotor, cognitive, social and emotional starting point in relation to this sport. As part of a baseline assessment, one teacher has described how a Sport Education season commenced by videoing a 'traditional' game of rounders[3] with the class split into two large teams. By observing the video, the teacher was not only able to assess the children's physical performance but also could identify many of the issues befalling this traditional game including the girls talking to each other when fielding, the boys pushing to the front of the line to bat, girls avoiding batting and various arguments between and/or within teams.

Also, rather than continually directing the children on 'what to do', Sport Education has further provided the opportunity for teachers to guide and support the children in constructing their own learning experiences. Actively involving the children in Sport Education and providing opportunities for decision making during a season has helped develop a sense of ownership among the children. As discussed above, the teacher-led 'friendly sessions' in the initial stages of a season were also used to help the children explore the concepts of team and roles as well as the rules, skills and strategies of the game. However, as the children's abilities and confidence in the game grew, the teacher was also able to initiate discussion and directly involve the children in shaping the remainder of the season. Although many of the class teachers initially found handing over more responsibility to the children quite difficult, they were to increasingly acknowledge the range of positive, although awkward but solvable, outcomes.

We have also found that Sport Education is creating contexts in which the children benefit from an ongoing reflective process that encourages them to think about their own learning and the learning happening around them. This reflective process is highlighted by the earlier rounders example, when, after the experience of playing the game, the children engaged in the task of assessing their performance. This process entailed them identifying what they liked and disliked about the game, the movement skills required to play the game, how they could break down the game to make it more exciting and also how the rules and structure of the game could be changed to make it more inclusive. Instead of the teacher telling the children what to do with the game, children were involved in a process of exploration and discovery where, guided by the teacher, they were learning about the game by participating and then reflecting on their experience. At the end of the season, the teacher again videoed the modified game of rounders developed by the children. By then watching the videos from the start and end of the Sport Education season, the children were able to comment on the difference in the way they were playing. They were able to observe how, in the first game, they were arguing and not playing as a team, whereas they were all to comment how in the second game they were cooperating and working as a team and all team members were more involved and enjoying the experience. Critically, this example highlights how the Sport Education season can engage the children in a reflective process that helps them think about their own learning and is part of the assessment process during the Sport Education season.

Collaboration across and beyond the school

Working with Sport Education is not only directly impacting on teachers' pedagogy but is also impacting on broader school cultures as well as local communities. Many PgCert graduates are reporting on-site collaboration with colleagues to consolidate and extend the principles and practices of Sport Education. Sport Education is beginning to connect primary school physical education with the more inclusive values of the national CfE guidance and placing primary school physical education in a more central position in school life. Teachers have spoken about Sport Education 'taking off' in their schools as colleagues, senior management, parents and outside agencies became involved in the implementation process. One primary school physical education graduate practitioner recalled how the first time she tried Sport Education a colleague came and asked her about it and she shared resources with her. From here the interest in Sport Education within the school escalated through informal discussions, resource sharing and most recently whole school professional learning sessions. This 'snowball effect' was described by another practitioner when she noted:

Other teachers have asked for my help in setting up Sport Education
. . . Sport Education got a lot of interest from upper-stage teachers and how
they could implement it in their class and I was able to work alongside
them . . . now the school has taken it on as a topic that will be carried out
every year.

(Kirsty, 3–14 graduate)

In another primary school, Sport Education was used as a vehicle to implement
an interdisciplinary unit of work across the whole school centred on football and
the World Cup.

There was a really positive influence on behaviour across the whole school
. . . increased participation . . . increase in the standard of pupils' work on
the Sport Education-linked subjects . . . parents were invited along to the
culminating event and mentioned that they had been hearing about the project . . . Active Schools[4] delivered some of the sessions and were positive and
provided some valuable resources.

(Felicity, 3–14 graduate)

The result of this Sport Education season was to create a very 'positive feeling'
within the whole school among staff and children. Consequently, one of the more
compelling features of Sport Education has been the emerging mix of informal
and formal networks which help build momentum for its wider implementation.
Informally Sport Education seems to be spreading through staffroom discussion,
observation of Sport Education seasons in operation, and literature and resources
being passed between some of the PgCert graduates and their colleagues. These
informal mechanisms are increasingly leading to more formal developments as primary school physical education graduate teachers work in partnership with their
colleagues in their schools and local authorities to develop locally situated Sport
Education professional learning opportunities.

While examples of Sport Education impacting beyond the school are currently
less in evidence (MacPhail *et al.*, 2003; Penney, 2003; Siedentop, 2002), teachers
are acknowledging the need to explore the potential links to the 'real' lives of the
children. For example, one teacher has commented that:

the more I'm beginning to understand about the community I work in, the
more I can see we can authenticate some of the experiences on many different levels . . . it's allowing these different levels to come into play for the individual children and the roles that they perhaps aspire to.

(Laura, 3–14 graduate)

However, as the following quote highlights, Sport Education does have the
potential to directly link with many different people beyond the school. First, the
teacher working in a rural area of north-east Scotland commented on how she

> spoke to the Scottish Rugby Union and they sent two rugby coaches in to speak to us about the sorts of things that make a good coach in rugby and the sorts of things that they had to learn to be a coach, what makes a good rugby player, a good captain . . . they also did some rugby coaching with them . . . we got a professional footballer in from the Scottish Football Association as well and he spoke about being in a professional sports team . . . what that involves . . . he did coaching with them too . . . he gave them individual tasks with the ball that they could go away and work with at home.
>
> *(Kirsty, 3–14 graduate)*

And then, as the Sport Education season moved towards its conclusion:

> We put on a Sport Education festival and invited parents in to show all the good work that we had been doing in school . . . the league tables were up on the wall . . . the mascots that we made . . . the strips that we designed. We took the parents outside and the pupils coached their parents in the things that we had been learning in sport.
>
> *(Kirsty, 3–14 graduate)*

This example highlights how, with careful planning on the part of the teacher, outside agencies can be appropriately engaged in Sport Education to make positive, and possibly long-lasting, connections between the school and local community.

Therefore, although most teachers initially focus on the introduction of Sport Education with their own class, it is becoming increasingly apparent that their colleagues and senior management are being attracted to the more authentic goals of Sport Education and are starting to explore the educational possibilities that Sport Education offers across and beyond the school context.

Sport Education in Scotland: what next?

As the DPEG continues to develop its curriculum ideas, the PgCert in 3–14 physical education will, in the short term, consolidate and support the growth of Sport Education in Scottish primary schools. However, the long-term development of primary school physical education, including Sport Education, will depend on the effectiveness of local efforts to introduce, support and sustain these new innovations. As such, any development of this nature will require a network of local primary school physical education tutors who are able to support colleagues over an extended period of time. From a Sport Education perspective, with the first cohort of 20 tutors already in position, the initial phase of this dissemination process is in its early stages. The intention is for the local Sport Education tutors to move beyond the traditional short, stand-alone and off-site CPD courses by working to develop professional learning communities built up over time and situated within the local class, school and cluster context (Armour and Yelling, 2004). To date, as local Sport Education courses are held and Sport Education resources developed

(Begg and Watson, 2010), the Sport Education network will need to consider the most effective ways to strategically cope with the many challenges ahead, particularly finding the time for collaborative planning, to support colleagues and to create a context in which staff share a common purpose and goal. In addition, and in tandem with these primary developments, Sport Education is now being included at the beginning of the undergraduate secondary physical education programme at the University of Edinburgh. Pre-service physical education teachers are now considering the place of Sport Education early in their discussions about physical education and are being encouraged to access Sport Education literature and professional learning opportunities to support their ongoing development. As a consequence, the first Sport Education professional learning course specifically for secondary physical education specialists was recently held in Scotland.

Therefore, from a teacher education perspective, and building on the initial dissemination by the PgCert teachers, the infrastructure to support the long-term development of Sport Education as a core component of physical education in Scottish schools is gradually, but strategically, being put in place.

Conclusion

This chapter has highlighted how primary school physical education in Scotland has changed in a short period of time. The emergence of lifelong learning and lifelong physical activity agendas at the national level has created a context in which curriculum and professional learning projects are receiving considerable support. Subsequently, the developmental curriculum innovation by the DPEG at the University of Edinburgh, in which Sport Education plays a central part, is now being disseminated across part of Scotland by hundreds of primary teachers and tutors. With teachers reporting a range of curriculum, pedagogy and collaborative benefits, the long-term future of Sport Education in Scotland now needs to be considered from a strategic perspective. It is critical that Sport Education is not a curriculum add-on but becomes an authentic application that connects learning experiences within physical education and across and beyond the primary school curriculum. In addition, the ongoing dissemination of Sport Education cannot simply be via the traditional short 'tips for teachers' courses but through a collaborative professional learning process which aims to create robust and supportive learning communities. If these traditional pitfalls can be avoided, and there is good evidence that this may be the case, then the story of Sport Education in Scotland may prove to be both positive and sustainable.

Notes

1 A PgCert was created at each university. Glasgow University developed the PgCert in primary physical education and the University of Edinburgh the PgCert in 3–14 physical education. Both certificates have similar aims.
2 Health and Well-Being is one of the new curriculum areas within the Curriculum for Excellence. Physical education has been moved from Expressive Arts where it was positioned in the previous national 5–14 curriculum into Health and Well-Being.

3 Rounders is a striking and fielding game with similarities to baseball and softball. It is commonly played in primary schools in the United Kingdom, often by dividing the class into two large teams.

4 The Active Schools Programme is managed by Sportscotland, the national agency for sport. Their main remit is to support children in becoming regularly physically active. This includes developing activities such as walking to school, play, dance, sports and games. Active Schools employs full-time co-ordinators, who are each responsible for a 'cluster' of primary schools.

References

Armour, K. and Yelling, M. (2004) 'Continuing professional development for experienced physical education teachers: Towards effective provision', *Sport, Education and Society*, 9(1): 95–114. doi:10.1080/1357332042000175836

Bailey, R., Armour, K., Kirk, D., Jess, M., Pickup, I. and Sandford, R. (2009) 'The educational benefits claimed for physical education and school sport: An academic review', *Research Papers in Education*, 24(1): 1–27. doi:10.1080/02671520701809817

Beames, S., Atencio, M. and Ross, H. (2009) 'Taking excellence outdoors', *Scottish Educational Review*, 41(2): 32–45.

Begg, M. and Watson, C. (2010) *Sport Education at Donibristle Primary School*, Glenrothes, Fife: Fife Regions Local Education Authority.

Black, P. and Wiliam, D. (1998) 'Assessment and classroom learning', *Assessment in Education*, 5(1): 7–71. doi:10.1080/0969595980050102

Bryce, T.G.K. and Humes, W.M. (eds) (1999) *Scottish education*, Edinburgh: Edinburgh University Press.

Clarke, G. and Quill, M. (2003) 'Researching Sport Education in action: A case study', *European Physical Education Review*, 9: 253–266. doi:10.1177/1356336X030093004

Davis, B. and Sumara, D. (2006) *Complexity and education: Inquiries into learning, teaching, and research*, London: Lawrence Erlbaum Associates Publishers.

Dyson, B., Griffin, L. and Hastie, P. (2004) 'Sport Education, tactical games, and cooperative learning: Theoretical and pedagogical considerations', *Quest*, 56: 226–240.

Gallahue, D.L. and Ozmun, J.C. (1999) *Understanding motor development*, Dubuque: Brown and Benchmark.

Green, K. (2000) 'Exploring physical education teachers' everyday "philosophies" from a sociological perspective', *Sport, Education and Society*, 5: 109–129. doi:10.1080/713 696029

Hastie, P.A. (2003) 'Sport Education', in A. Laker (ed.) *The future of physical education: Building a new pedagogy*, London: Routledge.

Hastie, P.A. and Curtner-Smith, M. (2006) 'Influence of a hybrid Sport Education–teaching games for understanding unit on one teacher and his students', *Physical Education and Sport Pedagogy*, 11: 1–27. doi:10.1080/17408980500466813

Humes, W.M. (2003) 'Policy making in Scottish education', in T.G.K. Bryce and W.M. Humes (eds) *Scottish education: Post-devolution* (2nd ed.), Edinburgh: Edinburgh University Press.

Irvine, W. (2009) *Dance education tutor programme*, presented at the SPPEP Tutor Training Seminar at the University of Edinburgh, June.

Jess, M., Dewar, K. and Fraser, G. (2004) 'Basic Moves: Developing a foundation for lifelong physical activity', *British Journal of Teaching in Physical Education*, 35(2): 23–27.

Jess, M., Pickup, I. and Haydn-Davies, D. (2007) 'Physical education in the primary school: A developmental, inclusive and connected future', *Physical Education Matters*, 2(1): 16–20.

Jess, M., Atencio, M. and Thorburn, M. (2011) 'Complexity theory: Supporting curriculum and pedagogy developments in Scottish physical education', *Sport, Education and Society*.

Johnson, D.W. and Johnson, R.T. (1999) *Learning together and alone: Cooperative, competitive, and individualistic learning* (5th ed.), Boston: Allyn & Bacon.

Kirk, D. (2004) 'New practices, new subjects and critical inquiry – possibility and progress', in J. Wright, D. MacDonald and L. Burrows (eds) *Critical inquiry and problem solving in physical education*, London: Routledge.

Kirk, D. and Kinchin, G. (2003) 'Situated learning as a theoretical framework for Sport Education', *European Physical Education Review*, 9: 221–235. doi:10.1177/1356336X0300 93002

Lave, J. and Wenger, E. (1991) *Situated learning: Legitimate peripheral participation*, London: Cambridge University Press.

Light, R. (2008) 'Complex learning theory – its epistemology and its assumptions about learning: Implications for physical education', *Journal of Teaching in Physical Education*, 27: 21–37.

McCaughtry, N., Sofo, S., Rovegno, I. and Curtner-Smith, M. (2004) 'Learning to teach Sport Education: Misunderstandings, pedagogical difficulties, and resistance', *European Physical Education Review*, 10: 135–155. doi:10.1177/1356336X04044068

MacPhail, A., Kinchin, G. and Kirk, D. (2003) 'Students' conceptions of sport and Sport Education', *European Physical Education Review*, 9: 285–299. doi:10.1177/1356336X0300 93006

Newell, K. (1986) 'Constraints on the development of coordination', in M. Wade and H.T.A. Whiting (eds) *Motor development in children: Aspects of coordination and control*, Amsterdam: Elsevier Science.

Oslin, J. (2002) 'Sport Education: Cautions, considerations, and celebrations', *Journal of Teaching in Physical Education*, 21: 419–426.

Penney, D. (2003) 'Sport Education and situated learning: Problematizing the potential', *European Physical Education Review*, 9: 301–308. doi:10.1177/1356336X030093007

Scottish Executive (2003a) 'Educating for excellence: Choice and opportunity. The Executive's response to the national debate'. Available HTTP: http://www.scotland.gov. uk/Resource/Doc/47021/0023968.pdf (accessed 4 January 2011).

Scottish Executive (2003b) *Let's make Scotland more active: A strategy for physical activity – physical activity task force*, Edinburgh: HMSO.

Scottish Executive (2004a) *A curriculum for excellence*, Edinburgh: HMSO.

Scottish Executive (2004b) *The report of the review group on physical education*, Edinburgh: HMSO.

Scottish Executive (2007) *Building the curriculum 2*, Edinburgh: HMSO.

Siedentop, D. (1994) *Sport Education: Quality physical education through positive sport experiences*, Champaign, IL: Human Kinetics.

Siedentop, D. (2002) 'Sport Education: A retrospective', *Journal of Teaching in Physical Education*, 21: 409–418.

Thelen, E. and Smith, L. (1994) *A dynamical systems approach to the development of cognition and action*, Cambridge, MA: MIT Press.

Thorburn, M. (2004) 'Providing "opportunity for all" through higher still: A continuing challenge for physical education in Scotland', *Scottish Educational Review*, 24: 66–78.

Vygotsky, L.S. (1978) *Mind and society: The development of higher mental processes*, Cambridge, MA: Harvard University Press.

5

APPLYING SPORT EDUCATION IN UNIVERSITY BASIC INSTRUCTION COURSES

Wesley Meeteer II, Lynn Housner, Sean Bulger, Andrew Hawkins, and Robert Wiegand

Introduction to the university basic instruction program—why Sport Education?

The development and evaluation of a variety of pedagogical models represent an important advancement in physical education and physical education teacher education (PETE) (Lund and Tannehill, 2005). The Sport Education model is growing in popularity and researchers have accumulated a substantial body of evidence to validate its effectiveness in school-based settings (Siedentop, 2002; Wallhead and O'Sullivan, 2005). The widespread support for Sport Education can be attributed to (a) its effectiveness in developing competence and excitement among children and adolescents in a variety of sports and activities (e.g., basketball, hockey, dance, fitness), (b) its successful application in physical education settings around the world (e.g., Australia, England, Korea, New Zealand, Russia, the United States), and (c) its demonstrated use at various grade levels with learners in elementary, middle, and secondary schools (Sinelnikov and Hastie, 2008). Research reviews on Sport Education (Curtner-Smith and Sofo, 2004; Wallhead and O'Sullivan, 2005) indicate that it is particularly effective at promoting student engagement in learning activities and facilitating more responsible, trusting, and cooperative interactions among participating students.

Based on the popularity and effectiveness of Sport Education, it is not surprising that many PETE programs have embraced it and enthusiastically endorse its use. Ayers and Housner (2008) examined PETE programs across the United States and found that 52 percent introduce Sport Education to their preservice teachers. Less is known, however, about the use of Sport Education with college-aged students in the context of the university general instruction or basic instruction program (BIP) within the United States. Despite the recent emergence of numerous fields of study and academic majors within kinesiology, the BIP has remained a highly visible component of the physical education department on most college and university campuses (Hensley, 2000). The courses that constitute the BIP can be required or elective in nature but share the common goal of promoting health-enhancing levels of physical activity among college-aged students that persist across the lifespan (Hensley, 2000). The university BIP has evolved over the years to reflect changing trends in physical activity programming (Hensley, 2000; Oxendine, 1969, 1972; Oxendine and Roberts, 1978; Trimble and Hensley, 1984, 1990, 1993), and is "generally recognized by students and faculty as the most prominent part of the physical education program on most college campuses" (Hensley, 2000, p. 30). In many instances, the BIP represents a final opportunity for the physical education profession to influence those young adults who will soon transition to postcollege life as parents, community members, classroom teachers, school administrators, school board members, and other elected public officials whose positive or negative experiences may determine future decisions regarding curricular space, resource allocation, and hiring practices in public schools.

The continued use of outdated and ineffective curricular models and instructional methods within the university BIP is problematic because college students are likely to find little personal meaning in their physical activity experience, thus decreasing the likelihood of sustained behavior change, and we ultimately risk reinforcing many of the negative public perceptions of physical education that persist (Bulger and Housner, 2009; Kretchmar, 2006). Given the important goals of promoting healthy lifestyles among college-aged students and the need for modeling best practice in physical education teaching, it is surprising that we know so little about the use of Sport Education and other evidence-based curricular models within the context of the BIP. Toward this end, Housner (1993) argued that BIPs should be employed as on-campus teaching laboratories for investigating the effectiveness of various models while also enhancing the quality of the physical education experience for college-aged students. For example, Bennett and Hastie (1997) examined the effects of Sport Education at the university level and found that it contributed to high perceived engagement and skill improvement among students. Bennett and Hastie also described that team affiliation was one of the most attractive elements of Sport Education for students and instructors as evidenced by the high rate of course attendance observed across the season.

Based on the related scientific literature, past success implementing Sport Education within the professional preparation curriculum, and limited availability of quality field placement sites in K-12 physical education settings, PETE faculty members at West Virginia University (WVU) initiated a curriculum reform that formally integrated Sport Education into the BIP across the past decade. This curricular innovation was intended to achieve the PETE programmatic objectives of providing additional quality field placements for preservice teachers within the PETE program while enhancing the quality of instruction in selected BIP courses. The primary focus of this chapter is to share the key lessons learned regarding this systematic implementation of Sport Education in a university setting for the complementary purposes of providing a more enjoyable, engaging, and authentic Sport

Education experience for the general student population while simultaneously improving teacher education. The following sections include detailed descriptions of the process used to integrate Sport Education along with related program evaluation data that provide insight into the challenges and opportunities associated with this type of curricular modification.

Sport Education use in the BIP at WVU—how is it implemented?

The BIP at WVU serves approximately 4,000 college students per year through elective course offerings in a range of team sports (e.g., basketball, flag football, softball, soccer) and individual lifetime leisure pursuits (e.g., outdoor adventure, conditioning, weight training, tennis). Despite the fact that there is no physical education requirement at WVU, these courses remain highly enrolled for a variety of reasons including the college students' interest in (a) learning a new sport or lifetime leisure pursuit, (b) fitting physical activity into a busy daily routine, (c) interacting with peers in an enjoyable social environment, (d) earning academic credit for physical activity participation, and, perhaps more problematically, (e) boosting their grade point average with what is perceived to be an easy "A" in gym class. In other words, college students enroll in BIP courses for a number of purposes, some of which maintain their own preconceived notions about physical education (both positive and negative) based on the previous school experience.

These BIP courses were traditionally delivered by graduate teaching assistants with a range of academic backgrounds (including physical education teaching, athletic coaching, sport and exercise psychology, and sport management) and teaching proficiencies. While graduate teaching assistant qualifications have always been screened during the hiring process, PETE faculty members were able to provide limited instructional supervision within the BIP due to other research, teaching, and service commitments. The observed variation among college student motivation level, graduate teaching assistant expertise, and lack of instructional supervision interacted to produce a high degree of inconsistency regarding the quality of instruction observed across BIP courses at WVU. Faced with these impediments, most graduate teaching assistants resorted to traditional teacher-directed instructional approaches that focused on abbreviated introductions to basic skills/tactics and isolated practice opportunities followed by full-sided game play for most of the designated instructional time. While potentially enjoyable for higher skilled students in the class, this instructional approach is not likely to result in the development of the knowledge, skills, and attitudes that contribute to lifetime participation in the sport of activity. Furthermore, these traditional instructional approaches also tended to resemble and reinforce the marginal physical education classes that students participated in (or avoided at all costs) during their own K-12 experiences.

While college administrators worked to address these concerns and improve the teaching effectiveness of BIP instructors, faculty members within the PETE program were confronting several of their own issues related to curricular modification for the PETE major program. The modification called for the systematic integration of Sport Education across multiple semesters and courses for preservice teachers. However, the selection of appropriate field placement sites represented a serious impediment to this process for the following reasons: (a) the physical educators in the schools at that time were unfamiliar with Sport Education and could not provide adequate supervision; (b) the limited number of quality middle- and high-school placements were already used to host student teachers across the semester; (c) the physical education curriculum at the available public schools were organized around a multiactivity approach that did not accommodate the time required for the effective implementation of a Sport Education season; and (d) the typical concerns associated with practice teaching opportunities in K-12 settings including lack of control regarding content, classroom management protocol, problem student behaviors, and cooperating teacher compliance with stated university requirements. As an end result, PETE faculty members found that they could teach preservice teachers Sport Education in their courses but opportunities to actually plan, manage, instruct, and assess using the model in school-based settings were restricted for a variety of logistical reasons.

In response to these concerns regarding both BIP and PETE programs, college administrators and faculty at WVU collaborated to implement a model that achieves the complementary goals of (a) improving the quality of the BIP by providing university students with a motivating and enjoyable physical education experience that focuses on actual learning and (b) developing well-supervised field placements during which preservice teachers can practice Sport Education and focus on instructional content without the typical administrative concerns and behavioral problems that present themselves when teaching children and young adults in K-12 settings. The following subsections briefly describe the planning and implementation of this process which has continued to evolve over the past decade.

Preparing for BIP field placement

The PETE program at WVU is organized developmentally with preservice teachers progressing through the program in an intact cohort. The initial semester after admission to the program focuses on curriculum and instruction and is composed of courses that address pedagogical models and principles of effective teaching. Sport Education is introduced in a curriculum course in which preservice teachers learn the basic tenets of the model and the related benefits of providing children and young adults with authentic sport experiences that facilitate the development of competence, literacy, and enthusiasm (Siedentop et al., 2004).

In the following three semesters, preservice teachers are provided with content knowledge, pedagogical knowledge, and pedagogical content knowledge (PCK) at the elementary, middle-school, and secondary levels. During the middle-school and secondary semesters, preservice teachers experience Sport Education directly as they participate as students, practice various Sport Education roles, and engage in peer teaching opportunities across all courses. In the middle-school semester, the preservice teachers take team sport-oriented PCK courses in volleyball, soccer, basketball, flag football, hockey, and softball. During the secondary semester, preservice teachers take PCK classes focused on individual sports or activities including archery, bowling, golf, outdoor leisure pursuits, tennis, and badminton. During the early years of adopting Sport Education, faculty members delivered 15 lesson seasons in these activities using 5-week blocks. Preservice teachers participated in Sport Education within these 5-week blocks, but actual teaching experiences were limited to a peer teaching format which was less than desirable.

The PETE faculty was not satisfied with the amount or quality of practice teaching opportunities afforded preservice teachers using the previously described approach. In 2003, they implemented a new approach in which preservice teachers learn Sport Education in PCK classes taught by PETE faculty for the first 10 weeks of the semester participating as students. During the last 5 weeks of the semester, the preservice teachers are assigned to an actual university BIP course and deliver a Sport Education season of about 15 hours (ten 1.5-hour lessons 2 days per week or fifteen 1-hour lessons 3 days per week) under the direct instructional supervision of a PETE faculty member. In the middle-school semester, the preservice teachers conduct season planning and assessment using a team-teaching format, and plan lessons and instruct individually. During the secondary semester, the students progress to conducting all phases of the BIP course, including season and lesson planning, instruction, and assessment, independently. Accordingly, the preservice teachers are provided with an authentic practice teaching experience of sufficient length in which they are held accountable for delivering Sport Education in a BIP course that the general student population enrolls in for academic credit. Following the secondary semester and BIP field placements, the preservice teachers are required to use Sport Education during their middle-school or secondary student teaching placements as a final step in this developmental process. More detailed descriptions of the PCK courses and the BIP clinical teaching experience are provided below.

PCK course description

A unique aspect of PCK development at WVU is that Sport Education has been adopted across all courses during the middle-school and secondary semesters. Faculty members share the dual responsibility of teaching content in specific sports while infusing the principles of Sport Education. Each semester, the preservice teachers are placed into teams which learn cooperatively across the first 10 weeks of the semester in all PCK courses. The preservice teachers receive the opportunity to experience the various roles in Sport Education (e.g., coach, fitness trainer, official, and statistician) and their teams compete for an overall course championship. Therefore, preservice teachers experience Sport Education from several perspectives: as a student participating in a season, as a preservice teacher observing how Sport Education seasons are delivered, and as a practicing teacher during periodic peer teaching episodes. This is significant because most of these preservice teachers have not experienced genuine Sport Education during their public school experiences. During the middle-school and secondary semester PCK courses, preservice teachers acquire a number of competencies in each sport or physical activity: (a) motor skill competence; (b) game performance concepts; (c) rules, strategies, equipment, and safety; (d) historical and cultural foundations as well as developmental, psychosocial, community-based, and health-related fitness justifications for including the activity in the school curriculum; and (e) analysis of critical elements of skills. In addition, a number of opportunities for peer teaching occur in each PCK course. These peer teaching opportunities occur naturally as part of the Sport Education model as it is applied within each course, as coaches and fitness trainers plan and implement lessons for their own teams. These PCK courses, therefore, address both content and pedagogical objectives for these preservice teachers.

It should be noted that such a balance is necessary for these students because, as typical physical education majors, there are a wide variety of skill levels across these activities in each cohort. Some are accomplished players of certain sports and novices at others. Each PCK course thus reflects heterogeneity of background and skill in each sport. It is thus necessary to provide solid instruction in the content of each of these activities, while at the same time recognizing that these preservice teachers will likely be called upon to teach any or all of these activities in public school contexts. So the courses are designed to provide strong content-oriented instruction along with plenty of opportunities to teach lessons in these activities, all delivered through Sport Education.

In order to accomplish this balance between content and pedagogy, PCK instructors develop modules of instruction in which they teach a module of sport content for 1 week, just as a teacher in a school using Sport Education would— presenting content and then working through the team coaches utilizing the instructor's practice plans. The following week, those who are assigned coaching roles develop practice plans for their own teams and during a portion of the class teach the content to their team that was taught the previous week by the instructor. Thus, preservice teachers, regardless of previous background or skill, are not asked to teach content that has not already been presented by an instructor.

BIP field placements

Bennett and Hastie (1997) suggested that university BIP activity courses represent an ideal setting to use Sport Education. They argued that BIP courses are "ideally suited" for application of Sport Education because their length allows for implementation of the model with fidelity and the inherent popularity of athletics on college campuses. The application of Sport Education in the BIP takes advantage of college student predispositions toward competitive athletics. We would add that the BIP also provides opportunities for preservice teachers to implement Sport Education without certain constraints, such as large class sizes, lack of equipment or facilities, and limited accountability, that often present during K-12 physical education field placements.

Preservice teachers are provided with an authentic teaching experience implementing Sport Education in the last 5 weeks of the middle and secondary semesters when they teach university BIP classes. Within the PETE program, each preservice teacher delivers two different BIP courses in successive semesters. At the end of the middle-school semester, preservice teachers implement Sport Education as they collaborate to teach a team sport including flag football, soccer, basketball, volleyball, and softball. As suggested by Siedentop (1994), the preservice teachers are permitted to teach a sport with which they are familiar during this initial Sport Education field placement. Preservice teachers rate the available sports according to their experience and knowledge and are assigned to the sport that they are comfortable with early in the semester. Furthermore, because this is the preservice teachers' first attempt at applying Sport Education to an entire group or class, planning for the delivery of content, class management, and assessment is both time and labor intensive. To ease the transition to "teacher" and ensure a manageable workload, the preservice teachers collaborate in groups of three or four and meet regularly with a PETE faculty member during the 5 weeks leading up to the BIP placements. During this time, the preservice teachers develop season plans, lesson plans, course syllabi, and all related instructional materials. The preservice teachers are supervised by the PETE faculty member in this planning process who also serves as the BIP course instructor of record. This approach in the middle-school semester serves to minimize preservice teachers' content planning, through the use of more familiar sports, while concentrating on model planning.

The second opportunity for the preservice teachers to instruct a BIP course is during the secondary semester in which they learn various lifetime leisure pursuits. The protocol for the second BIP teaching experience is similar to the previous semester with several important developmental differences. First, the preservice teachers do not work in groups to plan, manage, deliver, instruct, or assess the course. Each preservice teacher assumes responsibility and is held accountable for a particular class (again working under the direct supervision of a PETE faculty member). Second, the students do not choose the physical activity or sport that they will teach. Random assignment is used to challenge the preservice teachers and place them in a position to interact with content that may be outside of their comfort zone. Other aspects of the second BIP field placements remain the same. The PETE faculty supervise the preservice teachers throughout the entire process. The second BIP experience is the final opportunity for preservice teachers to use Sport Education before entering student teaching.

Most of the BIP courses that are taught by PETE preservice teachers follow a similar schedule. The courses run for 5 weeks and include about 15 hours of contact time (typically 3 days a week, an hour each day). Normally, the first day of the course involves a skills combine. BIP students are assessed in the basic skills of the activity or sport as well as in general game performance. Preservice teachers design those combines, collect data on student skill and game performance, collect additional useful information depending on the sport (height and weight are usually helpful), and then prior to the second class they rank order the students and conduct a draft. During the second day of the class, the preservice teachers conduct affiliation activities, placing students on teams, having team members learn names and other information about their teammates, having teams select team names and colors, make up cheers, and so forth. Also on that day, the Sport Education roles are explained, along with general course expectations, grading policies, assignments, and class schedule.

From that point, the course unfolds according to a preseason, regular season, and postseason format. During the preseason, usually lasting 3 or 4 days, the basic course content is introduced. Informing and extension tasks are delivered by a preservice teacher for a given lesson, and tasks are designed to be conducted by the coaches with their own teams. Some intrasquad application tasks normally take place during this phase of the season as well. The preservice teacher works through the team coaches to make sure the tasks are accomplished according to their design. In order to enhance the coaches' effectiveness in implementing these tasks with their teams, the preservice teacher holds a coaches meeting while the fitness trainer for each team is conducting the fitness training and warm up at the beginning of the class. That way, the coaches will already be somewhat familiar with the tasks before they have to implement them with their teams.

During the regular season portion, usually lasting 4 or 5 days, following fitness training, the teams' coaches conduct practices for about half of each class using tasks designed by the preservice teacher, often tasks that were introduced during the preseason. Team coaches typically have more flexibility in choosing from the previously presented tasks depending on the strengths and weaknesses of their team. The preservice teacher continues to teach and provide feedback, working primarily through the coaches of each team. The other half of each class involves competitions between teams, and regular season records and statistics are kept. The regular season records usually provide the basis for seeding in the postseason tournament.

The postseason tournament lasts 3–5 days and culminates in the course championship. Fitness training still comprises the first portion of each class, followed by a brief team practice based on a scouting report of the upcoming opponent. This portion of the season is the time when additional roles are used by teams that are not involved in the games, like officials, scorekeepers, statisticians, journalists, and so on. Each course finishes with the appropriate festivity, as champions are crowned, awards given, and the typical celebrations are enjoyed.

Evaluation of Sport Education in the BIP—how has it worked?

As previously described, this systematic use of Sport Education within the university BIP was intended to benefit the general student population through the use of an evidence-based curriculum and instruction model to promote physically active lifestyles and preservice teachers by providing additional quality field placements within the professional preparation curriculum. Given the resource intensiveness of this particular curricular initiative and resultant concerns with the associated cost-benefit, PETE faculty members have engaged in a considerable amount of informal and formal program evaluation related to Sport Education use in the BIP. While a detailed account of each program evaluation effort is beyond the scope of this chapter, the key findings are reported in the following subsections.

Impact of Sport Education use on BIP effectiveness

The PETE faculty members supervising BIP field placements have anecdotally reported positive experiences using Sport Education from an instructional standpoint. In particular, consistent with the findings of Bennett and Hastie (1997), they reported strong affiliation among students who had no prior relationship. For example, it is not unusual for teammates to travel to and from class together, practice together before and after class, and/or provide positive social support for teammates during practice and competition. Due to the high degree of teacher accountability that is in place during these BIP field placements, Sport Education is delivered with fidelity and a number of desirable student behaviors are readily apparent including high rates of moderate-to-vigorous physical activity and motor appropriate behavior. As university BIP courses, the assigned PETE faculty member is responsible for grading participants based on their achievement of the learning outcomes described on the course syllabi. Accordingly, considerable attention is paid to the assessment and documentation of student learning in these BIP courses and those data typically indicate that the students are learning.

While these informal observations are valuable and help to support the use of Sport Education in university BIP courses, PETE faculty have engaged in a series of related program evaluation studies to examine the effects of this curricular innovation in a more formal manner. Housner *et al.* (2006) conducted an experimental study to compare BIP courses taught using a traditional approach and Sport Education. A sample of BIP students ($n = 231$) were randomly assigned to bowling and Ultimate Frisbee courses taught using Sport Education or a traditional approach. The participants randomly assigned to the experimental condition were involved in team affiliation, multiple roles, culminating activity, and accountability measures typically associated with Sport Education. The participants assigned to the control condition were provided with a more traditional physical education experience. Researchers used systematic observation to verify the fidelity of both the experimental and control conditions.

Pre–post class comparisons of participant skill, knowledge, and attitudes indicated that traditional and Sport Education courses were equally effective at improving knowledge and skill in Ultimate Frisbee, but the traditional approach was more effective for developing bowling skill. The students in the experimental condition perceived a stronger sense of affiliation with their peers. They valued competition, learning, and affiliation, but some did not like testing, being on the same team across an entire season, and having their grade partially contingent on a teammate's performance. Researchers also concluded that Sport Education seemed to work in providing positive socialization experiences for college-aged students.

In a follow-up study, Choi *et al.* (2008) examined the effects of Sport Education on group affiliation in university BIP courses. Using a qualitative case study approach, participants enrolled in two bowling courses were studied: one emphasized team affiliations and the other did not. The results did not initially reveal a significant difference between groups; students from both groups reported feelings of affiliation early in the course. Sport Education students, however, showed more cohesiveness as the class progressed over time. Although the results suggested that Sport Education is associated with positive student affiliation and supported the findings of the previous study and anecdotal reports of PETE faculty, more research is needed to understand how and why affiliation develops in Sport Education seasons.

In the most recent study of Sport Education use in the BIP, surveys were administered to college students ($n = 342$) enrolled in BIP courses during the spring of 2010 semester. The survey instrument focused on student perceptions of Sport Education and was administered in all BIP courses taught by preservice teachers. The overwhelming majority of respondents enjoyed the roles they were assigned (93.8 percent) and considered themselves to be an integral part of their team (90.6 percent). Again, it appears that affiliation is a key aspect related to college students' enjoyment of Sport Education. In relation to their own learning, respondents perceived that they became more skillful (88 percent), learned about fitness (93 percent), felt they became more fit (90 percent), and increased their knowledge of rules, strategies, and tactics (91 percent).

The respondents recognized that Sport Education was different from traditional physical education (75 percent), enjoyed it more than other physical education classes they had taken (78 percent), and would have liked Sport Education in high-school physical education (79.5 percent). Somewhat surprisingly, a slightly lower percentage of respondents indicated that they liked the physical education course they just completed (63.3 percent). There are a few possible explanations for this inconsistency. First, the BIP courses under investigation required actual work (e.g., skill testing, fitness training, role performance, graded application tasks, required attendance) and this may have been a new experience for students in physical education. The subjective warrant for college-aged students is that BIP courses represent a convenient route to an easy grade. This might explain why there were many seniors (75 percent) enrolled in these BIP sections. It seems likely that many students were enrolled to improve their grade point average and/or complete the total number of academic credits required for graduation. Despite this unfortunate reality, roughly half of the respondents (52.5 percent) indicated that they would participate in the specific sport or activity in the future. Given the heavy emphasis placed on traditional team and individual sports in the BIP, one wonders if this percentage could be increased significantly by applying Sport Education to more culturally relevant alternative activities like martial arts, skateboarding, triathlons, rock climbing, ballroom dance, hip-hop dance, adventure racing, and so forth (McCaughtry, 2009).

The competitive background of the BIP students may be another factor influencing the respondents' overall satisfaction with their specific BIP course. Almost all respondents reported having competitive interscholastic sport experiences at the middle- or high-school levels in the types of traditional team and individual sports taught in the BIP. These students may have entered BIP courses with an expectation that they would engage in recreational game play immediately and perceived little need for instruction and skill practice. Finally, the BIP courses were taught by preservice teachers and only 69.8 percent were rated as competent by the survey respondents. Although the preservice teachers were required to plan extensively and received direct supervision by PETE faculty members, their lack of teaching experience may have contributed to lower ratings of student satisfaction regarding the particular course.

Impact of BIP field placements on preservice teachers

Given the collegial relationships established during BIP field placement planning, implementation, and assessment, PETE faculty gain uncommon access to the preservice teacher's underlying assumptions and beliefs about teaching. During these BIP placements, the PETE faculty member, who remains the instructor of record and is ultimately responsible for the quality of the course, plays an active role in guiding the preservice teachers through all decision-making and reflective processes. Accordingly, that faculty member is afforded a much clearer understanding of that preservice teacher's technical competence and professional dispositions when compared to a university supervisor during student teaching whose interactions may be limited to three or four occasions across a semester. While lacking scientific rigor, the informal accounts of these preservice teacher and faculty interactions have helped to shape and improve the BIP and PETE programs over time.

Anecdotally, preservice teachers have reported positive outcomes regarding their implementation of Sport Education in their respective BIP field placements. During the initial BIP placements in the middle-school semester, preservice teachers often describe that they are shocked by the amount of time and discretionary effort required to deliver an effective Sport Education season. They also value the opportunity to collaborate with peers and an experienced PETE faculty member as they plan, manage, instruct, and assess their Sport Education seasons. The preservice teachers appreciate the opportunity to teach in a content area in which they maintain a higher level of perceived competence, an important consideration for other PETE faculty considering similar approaches. During the subsequent BIP placement in the secondary semester, preservice teachers comment on how fast class events unfold when they are solely responsible for the teaching–learning environment. Because of the pace, the preservice teachers are thankful for the amount of planning required before they teach, although most complain about the extensive planning initially.

Faculty who supervise the preservice teachers during their BIP placements find the experience extremely rewarding. It seems much like a coaching relationship than it does a supervisory relationship as in student teaching. Generally, faculty receive advance electronic copies of lesson plans, meet with the preservice teachers prior to teaching the lesson, and then provide feedback during and after each lesson. Since the faculty are instructors of record, and are ultimately responsible for the quality of instruction in their BIP course, they are required to be present at all classes, and are motivated to invest all the time necessary to assure a successful

Sport Education course. They evaluate the season plans prior to the start of the course, oversee the development of the course syllabus, evaluate and approve lesson plans prior to each lesson, evaluate the in-class interactive teaching conducted by the preservice teacher in charge of each lesson, evaluate the assessment plan used by the preservice teachers, and eventually complete a Field Placement Evaluation Instrument covering all these areas. That evaluation becomes 20 percent of the grade for those preservice teachers in the PCK courses taken during that semester. Clearly, the level of mentorship far exceeds anything a university supervisor for a student teaching placement might provide, and is even more systematic and thorough than the kind of mentorship a cooperating teacher might employ. To date, a single program evaluation study has been conducted to formally investigate the effects of the BIP field placements on preservice teacher preparation. In 2006, a group of doctoral students were charged with investigating the efficacy of Sport Education within the PETE curriculum. Using semistructured group interviews, researchers conducted a study on preservice teacher beliefs regarding Sport Education when applied during BIP field placements and student teaching (Sager *et al.*, 2007). Participants reported that they were able to build confidence in their own teaching and collaborate effectively with other preservice teachers during BIP field placements. These results support the previously described anecdotal accounts that indicate that the preservice teachers value the BIP field placements as an integral part of their professional development.

The preservice teachers indicated, however, that they had some difficulty convincing college students to adhere to certain team affiliation aspects (e.g., wearing a team color each day, developing team cheers or team names) in their BIP classes. The BIP students sometimes felt team colors, names, and so on were a bit childish. This finding also parallels anecdotal PETE faculty reports that the preservice teachers are often reluctant (and sometimes even apologetic) when presenting some of the fundamental characteristics of the model (e.g., festivity, affiliation, record keeping) to their BIP students. It is likely that the lack of enthusiasm in their presentation of the model directly contributes to the lack of enthusiasm they sometimes receive in return. In reference to Sport Education use during the student teaching semester, preservice teachers generally had trouble in implementing Sport Education in its entirety. This was usually due to contextual constraints at the student teaching placements such as the prevalent use of the multiactivity curricula within schools, cooperating teachers' lack of familiarity with, and reluctance to use, Sport Education, inadequate facilities and equipment, and larger class sizes. Furthermore, cooperating teachers tended to be very selective regarding the features of Sport Education that they allowed their student teachers to implement. This finding lends support for the continued use of the university BIP as a field placement for preservice teachers because they are afforded the opportunity to implement Sport Education without impediment or restriction. The unfortunate reality is that authentic opportunities to implement Sport Education in K-12 schools remain limited and complete reliance on school-based settings could leave preservice teachers with an incomplete understanding of the model's true potential.

Summary

The findings of the research conducted at WVU on the use of Sport Education and on the BIP as an application laboratory generally support the effectiveness of the approach in both instances. While there remain significant opportunities to investigate Sport Education within a BIP context, data indicate that Sport Education can be advantageously employed to enhance skill acquisition in a wide variety of team and individual physical activities. At least as interesting are the data suggesting that quality Sport Education implementation in the BIP promotes an atmosphere of enjoyable competition for the BIP students which has the potential to increase the market desirability of the BIP, and perhaps increase physical activity participation in recreational settings. Additionally, this growing data set provides evidence that the BIP is a viable environment for developing Sport Education competence in PETE preservice teachers. The BIP is a reduced management environment which permits preservice teachers to focus on practicing instructional skills under close supervision from PETE faculty with Sport Education expertise. In general, these parallel purposes interact well with the mutual benefit of both, in essence forming a curriculum developer's dream.

Over time, faculty have refined both Sport Education as applied in the BIP as well as the PETE laboratory connections. Sport Education has been modified for effective use with college-age students engaged in a fairly time-limited Sport Education season. Fidelity to the course objectives requires a strong content orientation which must be integrated into Sport Education experiences. As a result, some roles have been deemphasized, others emphasized, and objectives in all domains evaluated for grading purposes. Such adaptations may not need to be employed, or employed to that degree, in secondary or middle-school contexts.

In addition, faculty have refined the training process and materials that are used by PETE preservice teachers in implementing Sport Education in the BIP. Faculty supervising those experiences, some of whom are graduate assistants, have also experienced enhancements in their training, so the entire experience is more uniform and effective across the spectrum of team and individual sport and physical activity courses. All preservice teachers now use the same planning protocols, and all faculty use the same evaluation processes and materials, making the relative satisfaction of both faculty and preservice teachers much higher.

Finally, faculty are considering using Sport Education, not just for the portion of the BIP which serves the PETE laboratory, but for the entire BIP program as well. That would involve training all BIP instructors in Sport Education, but would also have far-ranging benefits as those advocating for more highly motivating ways of engaging in physical activity. Those who take these BIP courses are, of course, the future parents, legislators, and even school board members.

References

Ayers, S.F. and Housner, L.D. (2008) "A descriptive analysis of undergraduate PETE programs," *Journal of Teaching in Physical Education*, 27: 51–67.

Bennett, G. and Hastie, P. (1997) "A Sport Education curriculum model for a collegiate physical activity course," *Journal of Physical Education, Recreation, and Dance,* 68(1): 39–44.

Bulger, S.M. and Housner, L.D. (2009) "Relocating from easy street: Strategies for moving physical education forward," *Quest,* 61: 442–469.

Choi, Y., Wiegand, R., Housner, L.D., and Metcalf, A. (2008) "Affiliation effect of bowling skill acquisition within a Sport Education season," paper presented at AAHPERD National Conference, April 8–12,. Dallas/Fort Worth, Texas.

Curtner-Smith, M.D. and Sofo, S. (2004) "Preservice teachers' conceptions of teaching within Sport Education and multi-activity units," *Sport, Education and Society,* 9: 347–377. doi:10.1080/13573320412331302430

Hensley, L.D. (2000) "Current status of basic instruction programs in physical education at American colleges and universities," *Journal of Physical Education, Recreation, and Dance,* 71(9): 30–36.

Housner, L.D. (1993) "Research in basic instruction programs," *Journal of Physical Education, Recreation, and Dance,* 64(6): 53–58.

Housner, L.D., Hawkins, A., and Wiegand, R.L. (2006) "Application of the Sport Education curriculum model in a university basic instruction program," paper presented at the AIESEP Conference, Jyvaskyla, Finland.

Kretchmar, R.C. (2006) "Life on easy street: The persistent need for embodied hopes and down-to-earth games," *Quest,* 58: 345–354.

Lund, J. and Tannehill, D. (2005) *Standards-based curriculum development in physical education,* Sudbury, MA: Jones and Bartlett Publishers.

McCaughtry, N. (2009) "The child and the curriculum: Implications of Deweyan Philosophy in the pursuit of 'cool' physical education for children," in D.L. Housner, M.W. Metzler, P.G. Schempp, and T.J. Templin (eds.), *Historic traditions and future directions of research on teaching and teacher education in physical education* (pp. 221–226), Morgantown, WV: Fitness Information Technology.

Oxendine, J.B. (1969) "Status of required physical education programs in colleges and universities," *Journal of Health, Physical Education, and Recreation,* 40(1): 32–35.

Oxendine, J.B. (1972) "Status of general instruction programs of physical education in four-year colleges and universities: 1971–72," *Journal of Health, Physical Education, and Recreation,* 43(3): 26–28.

Oxendine, J.B. and Roberts, J.E. (1978) "The general instruction program in physical education at four-year colleges and universities: 1977," *Journal of Physical Education and Recreation,* 49(1): 21–23.

Sager, J., Sidwell, A., Jahn, J., Choi, Y., Langley, L., Metcalf, A., and Towner, B. (2007) "Student teachers' experiences, attitudes, and beliefs in utilizing the Sport Education curricular model," paper presented at the Historic Traditions and Future Directions for Research on Teaching and Teacher Education in Physical Education, October 11–13, Pittsburgh, PA.

Siedentop, D. (1994) *Sport Education: Quality PE through positive sport experiences,* Champaign, IL: Human Kinetics.

Siedentop, D. (2002) "Sport Education: A retrospective," *Journal of Teaching in Physical Education,* 21: 409–418.

Siedentop, D., Hastie, P.A., and van der Mars, H. (2004) *Complete guide to Sport Education,* Champaign, IL: Human Kinetics.

Sinelnikov, O.A. and Hastie, P.A. (2008) "Teaching Sport Education to Russian students: An ecological analysis," *European Physical Education Review,* 14: 203–222. doi:10.1177/1356336X08090706

Trimble, R.T. and Hensley, L.D. (1984) "The general instruction program in physical education at four-year colleges and universities: 1982," *Journal of Physical Education, Recreation, and Dance,* 55(5): 82–89.

Trimble, R.T. and Hensley, L.D. (1990) "Basic instruction programs at four-year colleges and universities," *Journal of Physical Education, Recreation, and Dance,* 61(6): 64–73.

Trimble, R.T. and Hensley, L.D. (1993) "Survey of basic instruction programs in physical education: 1993 [summary]," in *Proceedings of the National Conference on Basic Instruction in Physical Education* (pp. 18–21), Reston, VA: National Association for Sport and Physical Education.

Wallhead, T. and O'Sullivan, M. (2005) "Sport Education: Physical education for the new millennium?" *Physical Education and Sport Pedagogy*, 10: 181–210. doi:10.1080/17408980500105098

PART II

Students' and teachers' responses to Sport Education

6

SPORT EDUCATION IN THE ELEMENTARY SCHOOL

A report from Cyprus

Niki Tsangaridou

During the past few decades sport pedagogy has moved from a narrow focus on the processes of teaching to an examination of the operational curricula that include both content and process (Lund and Tannehill, 2010; Metzler, 2005; Silverman and Ennis, 2003). Rather than limiting research to an examination of teacher behaviors, scholars have begun to study programs and instructional models that may influence student learning and positive experiences (McCaughtry *et al.*, 2004). According to Metzler (2005), "Instructional models are essentially planning and decision-making tools that teachers can use to provide students with the most effective instruction possible in a given context" (p. 50).

Research that focuses on elementary physical education programs, however, "has not been substantial, rigorous, prolific and systematic" (Hunter, 2006, p. 581). Several scholars call for more attention for studies that describe the implementation and impact of physical education programs and models in elementary settings (Kirk, 2006; Siedentop, 2002). Despite an increase in the uptake and investigation of Sport Education, most of the literature examining its effectiveness is within middle or secondary schools (Mowling *et al.*, 2006; Penney *et al.*, 2005; Wallhead and O'Sullivan, 2005). As Mowling *et al.* (2006) indicated, "Despite this abundance of positive responses to Sport Education by older students, there is little or no data on the perceptions or representations of the model by students in elementary settings" (p. 11).

Today there is some evidence indicated that Sport Education can be achieved successfully by third-grade (see Chapter 8 in this text), fourth-grade (Mowling *et al.*, 2006), and fifth-grade students (MacPhail *et al.*, 2003, 2004, 2005). For example, MacPhail *et al.*'s (2004) findings indicated that the opportunity to become affiliated with a team was an attractive feature of the students' physical education experiences. In addition, Mowling *et al.* (2006) reported fourth-grade students' thoughts and feelings toward Sport Education. The results of the study suggested that Sport Education could be successfully implemented in the elementary settings. The authors concluded that "the flexibility of the Sport Education model allows for age-appropriate developmental modifications" (p. 33). Metzler (2005) also proposed that Sport Education can work in any setting where the students are able to assume developmentally appropriate responsibilities. He suggested that "adaptations must be based on students' abilities as players (performers and team members) and their ability to assume the duty job roles that are critical to the functioning of the Sport Education season" (Metzler, 2005, p. 323).

In his chapter "Sport Education: A View of the Research," Kinchin (2006) proposed that the model should be implemented by teachers in the early years of primary education. According to him, the model can be modified in such a way that it can be used with younger students. Kinchin reported Lewis's (2001) study as an example of how Sport Education may be implemented with young students. Lewis (cited in Kinchin, 2006) described the views of twenty-two 5- and 6-year-olds following an 8-day unit of a modified throwing and catching invasion game. Data were collected through observation and focus group interviews with teams. Affiliation, competition, records, and festivity were the major features in the unit. Roles, responsibilities, and team names were also included. The findings of the study indicated that the young children had very positive and memorable experiences during a Sport Education unit. They talked positively about the roles they performed and were able to accomplish their duties.

Although the literature includes few examples of Sport Education developed with children of primary age, to date there has been no insights into how young students experience Sport Education from non-English-speaking countries and with a non-western sport culture. As Hastie and Sinelnikov (2006) noted, "We have little knowledge of how the model might be interpreted and responded to by students in countries with a non-western sport culture" (p. 132). Kim *et al.* (2006) also pointed out that

> it is notable that to a great extent SE literature has to date reflected physical education literature more broadly in being dominated by western voices and research within English-speaking countries. Language has invariably proved a barrier and limitation to potentially very informative cross-cultural pedagogical debate.
>
> *(p. 362)*

This study was undertaken to deepen our knowledge based on Sport Education by providing descriptions of Year 4 Greek-Cypriot students' experiences of Sport Education. More specifically, the purpose of this study was to describe the experiences of a class of Year 4 (ages 7–8 years) Cypriot students within a developmentally appropriate Sport Education season. A qualitative methodology was used to explore the implementation of a modified version of a basketball game based on the Sport Education model. This study represents an effort to provide an account of young Cypriot students' experiences in Sport Education. The findings from this study may serve to extend our knowledge of Sport Education and further to facilitate efforts to develop cross-cultural pedagogical perspectives.

Method

Participants and setting

Participants in the study were 25 Year 4 students (7- to 8-year-olds), 12 boys and 13 girls, from a public elementary school in Cyprus; Natasa, an elementary classroom student teacher; and Diamando, the regular class teacher who was assigned by the university as Natasa's mentor. Natasa and Diamando participated in the study voluntarily. Consent was obtained from all the students' parents. Natasa and Diamando were informed that confidentiality and anonymity procedures would be established in the study and that all the data and reports would be given to them to check, known as "member checks." They were also informed that pseudonyms would be used in the study to protect the identity of the children.

Natasa was assigned by her university to the specific school and class and she was responsible for teaching all subjects on the elementary core curriculum during the student teaching experience. The student teaching experience was structured in the form of a 13-week period, during the fourth year of teacher education. Student teachers are assigned to teach 82 lessons in subject areas contained in the national curriculum, to particular classes in state primary schools. During the first 3 weeks of the semester, student teachers attend relevant orientation seminars at the university. The fourth week is spent in the assigned school and classroom observing their students and discussing the content of future teaching with their mentors. Between weeks 4 and 13, student teachers progressively teach all the subject areas in the elementary school curriculum.

Natasa decided with her mentor to teach a developmentally appropriate Sport Education basketball season during her physical education lessons because it was one of the sports Natasa knew well and felt that the children would enjoy it. The class met twice per week for 40 minutes for their physical education class. None of the students had any prior experience with the Sport Education model. The season was designed and taught by Natasa. The physical education facilities and equipment in the school were poor and only outdoor spaces were available for classes, as is the case with most elementary schools in the country of study. The season's duration was nine 40-minute lessons. Diamando, Natasa's mentor, assumed the role of an observant during the whole period that lessons were taught.

Data collection

Data were collected through observations (field notes and video analysis), interviews (formal and informal), journals, and document analyses (unit and lesson plans). All physical education lessons taught by Natasa were observed by the researcher using nonparticipant observation. Field notes were kept that related to instructional tasks and practices and these were expanded on and typed after the lesson. In addition, all lessons were tape-recorded and used in the analysis.

Qualitative interview techniques were also used in the study for a better understanding of the meaning of the participants' experiences as seen "through their eyes." All interviews were based on a qualitative theoretical framework. The major principle of qualitative interviewing according to Patton (2001) is to provide a framework within which respondents can describe their own understandings in their own words.

Formal interviews at the end of the Sport Education season were given by the participants: (a) Natasa, (b) Diamando, and (c) representative students. Open-ended questions were developed by the investigator and provided a frame of reference for the interviews. With respect to Natasa's interview protocol, the questions focused on her pedagogical goals and actions during the season. More specifically, Natasa was asked about the planning and the preparation she made for the season, the difficulties presented during lessons, the way she divided the groupings and the allocation of responsibilities between students, the reward system she used, and the bulletin board they used during the season. She was also asked about her feelings and overall impression of the implementation of the model and, finally, on what was obtained from the implementation of the model. The interview with Natasa took place in the author's office and lasted 60 minutes.

The regular classroom teacher Diamando, who was Natasa's mentor and observed all the lessons, was also interviewed. This interview aimed to elicit Diamando's overall impression, feelings, and personal comments regarding the implementation of the model. This interview took place at the school and lasted approximately 40 minutes. The last interview was conducted with representative students from the five groups. Students were asked to comment on the roles they undertook, the groupings, and the reward system, and in general what they liked or did not like about the new teaching approach. This interview also took place at the school and lasted approximately 15 minutes with each student.

Natasa held a personal journal for all her lessons in which she put down her comments, the students' performance, and any difficulties that arose during lessons. The purpose of the journal was to explore the meanings Natasa gave her experience, as well as to elicit information regarding the implementation of the model. No specific prompts were given in the journal and the researcher did not interact with Natasa's writings during the student teaching experience. Finally, documents such as the unit plan and lesson plans were collected for a later analysis. Because the study was conducted in a non-English-speaking country, the researcher translated the data into English after the data analysis. A professional translator assisted in the translation process of each quote appearing in the results section.

Data analysis and trustworthiness

Data from all sources—interview transcripts, observational field notes, tape-recorded field notes, and documents—were analyzed inductively (Patton, 2001).

Through multiple and careful examination of the data, the key links, properties, themes, and patterns in the data were identified in order to locate common categories. Based on this process, the data were organized and sorted into major thematic clusters. To ensure the soundness of the data collection and analysis, four strategies were employed (Patton, 2001). First, triangulation was used to ensure that the findings were accurate. Data were triangulated across sources by comparing data from interviews, observations, and documents. Second, data were scrutinized for negative cases that would dispute or undermine the interpretations. Third, a peer-debriefer was used to share developing interpretations and to challenge the researcher to support interpretations with data. Finally, member checks were conducted. The interview transcription packages were provided to Natasa and Diamando and they were invited to clarify, elaborate, or suggest changes to the original responses. Both participants agreed that the transcriptions were accurate and did not suggest any changes other than minor editing corrections.

The Sport Education season

Lesson nature

The specific Sport Education basketball season was designed in a way that would be developmentally appropriate for the age of the children based on some of Metzler's (2005) adaptations. The lessons were planned in such a way that students would have the opportunity to practice several locomotor, nonlocomotor, and manipulative skills relative to basketball and to apply them in modified game situations. During the particular season, dribbling, passing, receiving, and shooting were the primary areas of skill development. Also, basic basketball rules and simple strategies were introduced and practiced as the unit progressed. A description of the content taught during the course of the unit follows.

In the first lesson, the students were introduced to the concept and organization of the Sport Education model. In better understanding the new way of working, the pupils watched short videos of the model and segments of a basketball game. After that, a discussion took place about the model and comments were exchanged regarding what the children would be doing during the unit. Consistent with the model, the students were divided into teams, picked a color and a team name, and undertook roles and responsibilities.

In the second lesson, the pupils practiced moving at various speeds, in various directions and at various levels, and in making sudden stops. They also practiced tackling, defense positions, and faking. In the next lesson, they exercised passing and receiving (i.e., chest pass, smacking pass) and how to fake before the pass. In the fourth lesson, pupils practiced ball control and dribbling and basic regulations. Regarding the learning of basic regulations of the game, it should be noted that the pupils were informed of how fouls and steps are done and what to do in each case. It should be stressed that these basic regulations were not taught through formal presentation by the teacher; however, mention was made each time that there was a violation of the basic rules within each lesson.

In the fifth lesson, the children applied the passes in a modified game, the dribbling, the tackling, the defensive position, and faking, while in the sixth lesson they practiced shooting and, in the seventh, the zone as a form of defense. It should be also noted that refereeing on the part of the pupils started from the fourth lesson, when children went on to more complex forms of sports meets. Thereby, from the fourth lesson and thereafter, the pupils had the opportunity to realize what violations were made and to try to avoid them. In the eighth lesson, everything they learned was combined in a developmentally appropriate game, and in the last lesson an interdepartmental tournament was organized.

Grouping of children

The grouping of children was carried out by Natasa because time was short and she did not have enough time to cooperate with the children for the sort of grouping she would have preferred. The grouping was made according to her own criteria and after Diamando's suggestions regarding which pupils were particularly capable and responsible, who had leadership qualities, and so on. The criteria of the grouping were (a) the equivalence of the teams regarding the pupils' capabilities, (b) an equal number of boys and girls in each group, (c) the division of responsible pupils in all groups, (d) the diffusion of problematic pupils in all groups, (e) the creation of an even number of groups, and finally (f) the creation of an even number of teams so that subgroups would be able to be formed whose duties were to report, at the beginning of the lesson, the absent members of the team and report the members of the team who were not suitably dressed for the lesson of physical education and, finally, to divide the team into subgroups and report anything else which was preoccupying the team. The end result of this grouping was the creation of five teams: Clouds, Skies, Moons, Violets, and Marines. The first four groups consisted of four members and the last team of five. To ensure the cohesion of team members, in the case of absence of a pupil, it was decided that a member of the larger group was to replace the absentee pupil. Each team had some specific characteristics such as: color, name, photograph on the bulletin board, and its own area for practice in the field.

Student roles

During the season, all students undertook permanent duty roles. The allocation of tasks took into account the age of the children and their contact with completely unknown concepts. Some students were responsible for the decoration and updating of the bulletin board; others were responsible for the transportation of equipment from the storeroom to the playing field; others were responsible for returning equipment from the playing field to the storeroom; and others still were responsible for collecting and transporting graphic material (pencils, files, forms of recording of data, etc.). All students, apart from players, undertook the role of referee and scorekeeper during the season. In addition, some students assumed team roles (i.e., captain of the team, assistant captain, coach, etc.).

For the individual reward of the participants, a system of "grading cards" was developed. Here, cards were issued for industriousness, for best performance in skills, and for fair play. Each card equaled one point. The industriousness cards were given to the pupils responsible for various tasks and to those who helped voluntarily. The cards for best performance were given to those pupils performing the skills taught, while the cards for fair play were given to pupils who had made the smaller number of fouls during lessons. These cards were given to those who fulfilled the criteria at the end of every lesson.

For the group reward, a system of competition was used with stickers between the teams. At the end of each lesson, the team or teams that fulfilled the criteria received a sticker next to their name. Also at the end of the season, the pupils with most cards in each category were awarded a prize, according to the number of stickers accumulated. The prizes were mainly the diploma for the fairest player, the diploma for best performance, the diploma for industriousness, and the diploma for the champion team.

The tournament

The tournament took place in three phases. In phase A, the Moons played against the Clouds, and the Skies against the Violets. The refereeing and the recording of fouls in the games were undertaken by the Marines. The winning teams played among themselves in phase B. In this phase, the role of referees and recorders of fouls was undertaken by the Moons. In phase C, the role of refereeing was undertaken by George and Constantinos and the role of recorders of fouls was undertaken by Markella and Michalis. Each game lasted for 5 minutes. The members of the winning team were awarded a diploma for the champion team and a jumping rope. The team with the most stickers was declared the winning team of the competition and was applauded by the other teams. Additionally, the pupils with most cards for industriousness and best performance were also awarded prizes.

Results

The findings of the study are presented and discussed as a set of five themes: (a) program goals and student outcomes, (b) persisting teams, (c) having responsibility and roles, (d) rewarding student efforts, and (e) better than the traditional model. More specifically, in the first theme, mention is made of the goals and student outcomes placed by Natasa, which were defined according to the philosophy of the model and the needs of the pupils. The second theme examines the way in which the grouping of the pupils was made, while the third theme refers to the undertaking of roles and the defining of duties undertaken by pupils during the process of implementation of the model. In the fourth theme, mention is made of the reward system used, and finally, in the fifth theme, better than the traditional model, the participants' perceptions about the model are presented.

Program goals and student outcomes

One of the primary aims of Sport Education is turning the pupil into a critical participant and into an enthusiastic sports fan (Siedentop, 1994). In other words, into a person appreciating fair play, regardless of the results, who will act toward the protection of this virtue. So that the pupils embrace the value of fair competition, the teacher works toward this aim, by placing both short-term and long-term targets.

The short-term targets placed by Natasa, which come up from lesson planning, were defined according to the philosophy of the model and the needs of the pupils. These aims were the development of several fundamental skills (e.g., various passes, dribbling) and their application in the modified games situation, the undertaking of responsibilities and roles, and, finally, developing capabilities for reasoning regarding basic basketball issues. Regarding the long-term targets, the expected outcomes were the cultivation of a healthy, correct, and humanitarian sport culture maximized by the children's participation. Regarding this issue, Siedentop (1994) states that the model of Sport Education aims at reforming sports, since all participants are given the opportunity to participate and undertake responsibilities. With wide participation, the pupils, on the one hand, form in their mind a more integrated idea of sports and, on the other, they get acquainted with, and work on, sports.

The findings of the study, made evident from observing the videotaped lessons, suggested that the pupils progressed due to their participation in the Sport Education model. Specifically, the students, when comparing the first to the last lesson, showed an undeniable progress regarding the use of the skills they were taught in the modified basketball games. While at the beginning the pupils had no knowledge whatsoever about performing skills relevant to basketball such as passes, dribbling, faking, and so on, during the course of the lessons it was made clear that they were able to, not only perform all of the above, but also point out to their teammates the mistakes they made, regarding the particular skills. The following comments of the pupils are characteristic:

> We learned to strike the ball and shoot, we learned the pass, the goes down and hits the ground and then goes up, and the chest pass. (Andreas)

> We are able to perform the moves we learned, like turn to the right and throw the ball over to our teammate. (Eleni)

> Our opponent has to have his hands up in the air and his knees bent, so that when the ball goes to him, he will run and catch it. (Konstantina)

The progress made by the pupils during the process of implementation of the model is also recorded by Natasa, in her journal:

> I corrected some working sheets I distributed the day before the games regarding the skills I taught, and the mistakes made by the pupils were very few. They had an 11/14 success and this shows that the pupils know what they are allowed and what they are not allowed to do.

Progress, however, was shown by the pupils in learning and applying the regulations as well. The three basic violations were taught (steps, foul, out of court), were understood by all the children by mid-season, and constituted an integral part of the game through refereeing. Natasa in her interview says:

> During the last 3–4 lessons I noticed that the pupils had made a lot of progress because they could play, by now, a defensive game, dribble, pass, and judge whether someone had made steps or was out of court. I believe that, compared to the first lesson, they have made a lot of progress.

The pupils, on the other hand, report:

> When a player gets the ball and another player from the other team tries to tackle him and puts his hands on the ball, this is a foul. (Michalis)

> In basketball, when we have the ball in our hands, we can't hold it and run. We must dribble and throw it to a teammate. The ball is thrown in a special way, it is not just throwing it up in the air. (Georgia)

The success of the pupils of this particular class in relation to the pupils of the other classes of the school in the painting competition organized by the Ministry of Education themed "Basketball" proves that Natasa's targets were realized. She characteristically says:

> The school had to send four drawings under the subject of basketball, according to a circular sent to the headmistress by the Ministry of Education . . . On that particular day, the art teacher used the sketches we had on our bulletin board and, therefore, the rest of the school's pupils had some stimuli. Later on, my cooperative teacher told me that three out of the four drawings belonged to our class because the pupils in our class had more stimuli and therefore they displayed their experiences in a better way even though they were very young children.

Diamando also pointed out that the pupils improved since the aim was to acquaint themselves with basketball and learn to cooperate. She noted that "the aims put forward by Natasa were achieved, since all students cooperated and learned the fundamentals of basketball to a satisfactory level." Furthermore, by the end of the season, it was made clear that the children had particularly enjoyed Sport Education because it gave them the opportunity to socialize and have fun with their friends. Two of the children say:

> I was a referee and I really liked my role. I also like ringing the bell because it's fun to enjoy yourself and learn at the same time. (Andreas)

> I liked to point out to others the mistakes they made so as to improve their game. We really liked the lessons because we cooperated with the others. (Eleni)

Following the realization of the program targets, it seems that the model of Sport Education can offer positive experiences in teaching school physical education, even for very young pupils.

Persisting teams

The model provides that all pupils are divided into teams at the beginning of the season and remain in the same teams until the end of the season. It was suggested that, during the season, the pupils formed friendships and gradually ended up practicing and playing as a team. Socializing resulting from the participation of children in groups, combined with their gradual maturing, makes a decisive contribution to achieving positive experiences from participating in sports (Kinchin, 2006; Siedentop, 1994, 2002; Wallhead and O'Sullivan, 2005).

The grouping of children in this study was made by Natasa because she was not afforded the opportunity to cooperate with the pupils for grouping, due to lack of time. Natasa noted: "Grouping was made according to criteria decided by me and after the suggestions of my mentor regarding which pupils were particularly skilled, particularly responsible, who were leading personalities, etc." On the other hand, Siedentop (1994) also writes that it would be preferable if the teacher would be, initially, the one who would do the grouping, so as to achieve parity between members.

The five groups created functioned during the season with the same pupils in each team. Diamando is in agreement regarding the unity of the team during the season. She pointed out that, "when the pupils are continuously changed, you cannot achieve the acceptability you can achieve within the group, because the groups consist of children of mixed abilities. Cohesion is not maintained if students are constantly removed or changed." It was clearly shown from the observations that the groups functioned very well without any particular problems because an atmosphere of cooperation was created both between the members of a team and between teams. The very few reactions of some individual pupils regarding the members of the teams disappeared after the first lessons. Specifically, when addressing the members comprised in each team, there were two pupils who initially reacted, claiming that they did not want to participate in the specific groups either because they did not like being with the rest of the children or because their friends were in the other groups. The following field notes are characteristic:

Stefanos protests to Natasa because he doesn't want Alexandros in his team.

Marios objects because his best friend was in another team.

During the course of the lessons, however, these particular pupils bonded with the rest of their teammates and ended up playing as a team and facing their opponents collectively. Natasa mentions regarding this issue:

There were two pupils who reacted to the division of the teams. One is reactive due to psychological problems he faces. The other one is reactive due to the fact that the issue of unity is not within his preferences. After the first lessons, however, they both started to cooperate with the rest of their teammates.

It was evident that the students had the opportunity to experience the benefits of being in the same team. They appreciated the opportunity of having more time to interact, work, and play with the same teammates. Characteristically, one student, following a question he was asked on whether he liked the division into groups and the cohesion of his group until the end of the lessons, answered:

I like being in the same team. Everything was so good. We worked together and became good friends and good players. We learned a lot of things. (George)

The socializing of the participants as a result of grouping contributed to their obtaining positive experiences from the unit, something that does not happen in traditional physical education lessons since pupils are part of a broader whole in the classroom, they never make up the same teams, and, consequently, the feeling of cohesion is lost.

Having responsibility and roles

Research showed that Sport Education helps pupils undertake responsible roles (Kinchin, 2006; Wallhead and O'Sullivan, 2005). After the pupils were divided into groups by Natasa, it was deemed expedient to designate roles that could be easily applied since this was their first experience with the model. It was clearly shown from the observations and videotaped lessons that the participants undertook their roles enthusiastically, responsibly, and industriously. This disposition of the children had the most positive effect on all aspects of the season. The pupils showed particular interest in even fulfilling duties undertaken by their teammates. Indeed, in many cases, they disagreed among themselves because they wanted to perform duties that were not incumbent upon them. The following field note excerpt is characteristic:

One pupil from each team, following Natasa's instructions, undertook the duty to take the envelope and write down the mistakes of his/her teammates. The envelope was placed in a cardboard box outside the basketball court. Some groups initially disagreed on who would hold the envelope because all members wanted to jot down the mistakes of their teammates in the envelope. After Natasa's intervention, they agreed that the envelope would be held by the pupil who had first taken it out of the box.

The findings from the study indicated that the duties accompanying each role were completely realized and understood by the pupils. The students noted:

The referees rang the bells for the other team to take the ball when a foul was made or when the ball was out. (Konstantina)

When I rang the bell he had to ring his, too, and put them in their place, to see where the ball had hit and gone out and make sure that the other team's player went there and retrieved the ball. (Georgia)

Natasa in her diary also writes that she is quite pleased with the pupils who undertook responsibilities because they showed that they could undertake responsibilities and fully respond to them and at the same time understand and learn the rules more easily. She wrote:

These were new concepts altogether, therefore I had some difficulty at first, until they got the hang of it. Soon, however, they got the hang of it—what the referee does, what the marker does. This helped them a lot to understand and learn the rules more easily.

Based on the data analysis, evidence suggested that the pupils enjoyed the roles which gave the games prestige and the capability to exert control in the development of the game. Diamando, for example, reports:

When you allocate responsibilities to children, they become more responsible and at the same time they realize and feel the value of what they are doing because they feel that they are participants that they are taking part in what they are doing.

What made a particular impression was the interest shown by the majority of the students during the process of implementation of the model which previously had not been observed in traditional physical education. Diamando notes that it was the first time that the majority of students wanted to assume more responsibilities in lessons of physical education.

Undoubtedly, the undertaking of responsibilities and roles gave the pupils additional knowledge and a well-rounded and integrated picture of basketball, making them in this way critics who are participating in this sport. Natasa points out:

I found out that there was one pupil who came up with a defense plan for his team. The same plan would be used in offense, as well. He discussed the plan with his team and it was decided that they put it into action.

An undisputed value of Sport Education is the undertaking of roles on the part of the participants, since the model allocates more roles than the simple, typical role of "player" during more traditional lessons of physical education. In Sport Education, pupils learn to be captains, referees, and data collectors at the same time. In this way, on the one hand, they have a more integrated idea in mind regarding sports and, on the other hand, they acquaint themselves with, and dabble with, roles and responsibilities related to sports.

Rewarding student efforts

For the support of pupils, a reward system was developed by Natasa. The basic elements characterizing the reward system was that it was easy to use and practical for use in every lesson, and was aimed both at individuals (for diligence, better performance in skills, and fair play) and groups (i.e., for cooperation between the members of the team as well as between the members of other teams, appropriate dress for all members, full utilization of teaching time, will for fair play, show consideration to the teacher's instructions). The following field note excerpt refers to an incident that occurred in one lesson:

> Some pupils are rewarded with bonus cards for good effort and mention is made for the reason why they receive a bonus card . . . Natasa indicates that, in spite of the fact that some pupils made progress in skills, they will not get a bonus card because they were not properly dressed for the lesson.

As noted previously, "grading cards" were used for individuals, and stickers were awarded to teams. The grading cards system surpassed the expectations even of Natasa. In her interview, she says:

> I was very impressed by the motives we gave with the grading cards because I did not expect them to be so successful. The pupils were really excited. I was impressed by a particular child; it was obvious that he liked the grading cards very much because every day in the lesson he used to tell me that he had played very well and he wanted a grading card. He was excited and made a lot of effort.

The pupils, at the end of the lessons, were excitedly asking to be rewarded for their behavior. Natasa wrote in her diary that the pupils waited impatiently for the grading cards to be handed out:

> Because in the previous lesson there was no time left to hand out grading cards, the children were asking me anxiously when they would be handed out. Also, today, after getting their grading cards, they held onto them all day and asked one another how many they had got so far.

Observational data suggested that the reward system created enthusiasm and promoted cooperation between the teams. Undoubtedly, the reward system, combined with group interaction, allowed the pupils to pay attention to what they were learning. They knew that they would later have to use these lessons to defeat their opponents, knowing that victory leads to reward and moral contentment, something of paramount importance for children of this age (Kinchin, 2006; Kirk, 2005).

Better than traditional physical education

It was evident that Sport Education was a more attractive and meaningful approach than the traditional method of physical education for the participants in the study. This is in agreement with the findings of Kinchin and Kinchin (2005) and MacPhail *et al.* (2005) that Sport Education's pedagogical features have positive influences even in young children. Reflecting back to the season, Natasa was pleased with the students' learning, enthusiasm, and enjoyment, but she also noted that "Sport Education had a positive impact on me as well. It is an attractive model and makes teaching and learning meaningful." Due to the model's authentic nature, Natasa's teaching was affected since she had to teach based on situated experiences. She pointed out that

> during the lessons I always had in mind that I had to find the appropriate opportunities to stress regulations and support forms of behavior through games and not a simple presentation or an isolated and unsupported observation that would have absolutely no significance to the children.

Students also emphasized that Sport Education was beneficial and a valuable learning experience for them. They indicated that they liked it better than the traditional model of physical education. The following interview vignette illustrates the students' views:

Researcher: Before basketball, what did you do in physical education lessons?
Paul: We used to play on the steps and jumped over the hoops.
Researcher: How do you like the physical education lessons now?
Paul: I like these lessons better because, instead of playing on the steps and jumping over hurdles, we learned better things with Mrs. Natasa. I learned what the referee does and when other people make mistakes. I learned to make turns. The only thing I didn't do very well was the turn. After I tried it, though, I managed to do it well. The first time I didn't do it well but I tried and tried and finally learned to do it!
Researcher: Do you like this type of lesson?
Paul: Yes, I liked it much better. It was better than what we used to do with the other teacher. We must tell her what we did, so that she will learn to do similar things.

Conclusions

The purpose of this study was to describe the experiences of a class of Year 4 (ages 7–8 years) Cypriot students within a developmentally appropriate Sport Education unit. Overall, the results of the study suggested that Sport Education was implemented successfully and the general reaction of the participants regarding the value of the model was very positive. The reasons for this preference seemed to stem from the structural arrangements of Sport Education (Siedentop, 1994). It appears that a key factor in this study was that the students enjoyed the format of the unit. Data suggested that the students learned enough about basketball in order to play and enjoy modified games. In other words, the nature and features of the Sport Education model seem to contribute to the enjoyment and participation of the students during this unit.

While this Sport Education experience lasted only nine lessons, this was still a significant time increase for them. The regular lesson allocation for these students was usually only two, or at most three, lessons. Many students commented on how they spent more time practicing and playing games. The idea of an authentic sports experience is important here. In this Sport Education season, fair play was promoted and openly rewarded, thus diminishing arguments with referees and the open abuse of teammates. Teams were small and players were seen as important to the team, particularly as the teams remained the same throughout the entire season. The key however was that the students played more modified games than in a regular physical education unit because the unit allowed for age-appropriate developmental modifications to include both skill practices and game situations. As has been previously found in other studies, students practiced to improve and be able to play well and win in games. These experiences provide students with a means of fun because they work together and unified their energies during practice in order to have success in game situations (Kinchin, 2006; MacPhail *et al.*, 2003; Mowling *et al.*, 2006; Wallhead and O'Sullivan, 2005).

This study is one of the few that examines the possibilities of this model with young students. The findings of this study support Mowling *et al.*'s (2006) findings that Sport Education could be successfully implemented in elementary settings and that the Sport Education model was most appealing to the participants than the traditional model (MacPhail *et al.*, 2004). These findings support previous findings that Sport Education is a valuable and significant pedagogical model (Kinchin, 2006; MacPhail *et al.*, 2003, 2004; Mowling *et al.*, 2006; Wallhead and O'Sullivan, 2005).

Given the exploratory nature of this study and the fact that its findings are based on data provided by one participant and her students, further studies should be conducted in enriching the Sport Education literature in the elementary level. Although the model was "originally designed for high school physical education classes, the flexibility of Sport Education allows for age-appropriate developmental modifications" (Mowling *et al.*, 2006, p. 33). Sport Education, if applied correctly, can offer positive experiences in teaching physical education in schools, something needed by both pupils and teachers. At the first stages of its application, various challenges might arise, but while the children and the teachers are getting familiarized with the model, this becomes a long-term investment. In later stages, when everyone will know their roles and how to work, physical education will no longer be a boring and monotonous lesson, but an educational amusement (Siedentop, 1994).

Scholars have suggested that we must pay more attention to what kind of learning experiences we are providing in physical education, especially to young students. As Kirk (2005, p. 242) notes, "The early years are critical years for the development of the kind of physical competences that place individuals in position to access and engage actively in the physical culture of society." Kirk (2006) also argued that school physical education can provide students with learning experiences that are inherently pleasurable and intrinsically satisfying. According to him, the Sport Education model is an example "of how sport can be represented in physical education in an educationally valuable form" (p. 263). Based on the findings of this study, I suggest that Sport Education has a great value in primary physical education and I must agree with Kinchin and Kinchin (2005) who pointed out that "a window of opportunity now exists for other early years teachers to develop this flexible and broad foundation in order to promote a more holistic emphasis to their instruction across the curriculum at this stage of the education process" (p. 120).

References

Hastie, P.A. and Sinelnikov, O.A. (2006) "Russian students' participation in and perceptions of a season of Sport Education," *European Physical Education Review,* 12: 131–150. doi:10.1177/1356336X06065166

Hunter, L. (2006) "Research into elementary physical education programs," in D. Kirk, D. Macdonald, and M. O'Sullivan (eds.) *Handbook of physical education* (pp. 580–595), London: Sage.

Kim, J., Penney, D., Cho, M., and Choi, H. (2006) "Not business as usual: Sport Education pedagogy in practice," *European Physical Education Review,* 12: 361–379. doi:10.1177/1356336X06071469

Kinchin, G. (2006) "Sport Education: A view of the research," in D. Kirk, D. Macdonald, and M. O'Sullivan (eds.) *Handbook of physical education* (pp. 596–609), London: Sage.

Kinchin, G. and Kinchin, V. (2005) "Laying the foundation for Sport Education," in D. Penney, G. Clarke, M. Quill, and G. Kinchin (eds.) *Sport Education in physical education: Research based practice* (pp. 111–121), London: Routledge.

Kirk, D. (2005) "Physical education, youth sport and lifelong participation: The importance of early learning experiences," *European Physical Education Review,* 11: 239–255. doi:10.1177/1356336X05056649

Kirk, D. (2006) "Sport Education, critical pedagogy, and learning theory: Toward an intrinsic justification for physical education and youth sport," *Quest,* 58: 255–264.

Lewis, J. (2001) "Is it possible that Siedentop's Sport Education model can be used with key stage 1 physical education to aid pupil development?" Unpublished undergraduate dissertation, De Montfort University, Bedford.

Lund, J. and Tannehill, D. (2010) *Standards-based physical education curriculum development,* Sudbury, MA: Jones and Bartlett.

McCaughtry, N., Sofo, S., Rovegno, I., and Curter-Smith, M. (2004) "Learning to teach Sport Education: Misunderstandings, pedagogical difficulties, and resistance," *European Physical Education Review,* 10: 135–155. doi:10.1177/1356336X04044068.

MacPhail, A., Kinchin, G., and Kirk, D. (2003) "Students' conceptions of sport and Sport Education," *European Physical Education Review,* 9: 285–299. doi:10.1177/1356336X030093006

MacPhail, A., Kirk, D., and Kinchin, G. (2004) "Sport Education: Promoting team affiliation through physical education," *Journal of Teaching in Physical Education,* 23: 106–122.

MacPhail, A., Kirk, D., and Kinchin, G. (2005) "Sport Education in key stage 2 games," in D. Penney, G. Clarke, M. Quill, and G. Kinchin (eds.) *Sport Education in physical education: Research based practice* (pp. 122–138), London: Routledge.

Metzler, M. (2005) *Instructional models for physical education* (2nd ed.), Boston: Allyn and Bacon.

Mowling, C., Brock, S.J., and Hastie, P.A. (2006) "Fourth grade students' drawing interpretations of a Sport Education soccer unit," *Journal of Teaching in Physical Education*, 25: 9–35.

Patton, M.Q. (2001) *Qualitative research and evaluation and methods* (3rd ed.), Beverly Hills: Sage.

Penney, D., Clarke, G., Quill, M., and Kinchin, G. (2005) *Sport Education in physical education: Research based practice*, London: Routledge.

Siedentop, D. (1994) *Sport Education: Quality PE through positive sport experiences*, Champaign, IL: Human Kinetics.

Siedentop, D. (2002) "Sport Education: A retrospective," *Journal of Teaching in Physical Education*, 21: 409–418.

Silverman, S. and Ennis, C. (2003) "Enhancing learning: An introduction," in S. Silverman and C. Ennis (eds.) *Student learning in physical education: Applying research to enhance instruction* (2nd ed., pp. 3–7), Champaign, IL: Human Kinetics.

Wallhead, T. and O'Sullivan, M. (2005) "Sport Education: Physical education for the new millennium?" *Physical Education and Sport Pedagogy*, 10: 181–210. doi:10.1080/17408980500105098

7

SPORT EDUCATION THROUGH THE EYES OF A TEACHER-RESEARCHER AND HIS STUDENTS

Ashley Casey

This chapter has emerged out of my two careers: the first as a secondary school teacher of physical education in England and the second as an action researcher involved in a 7-year longitudinal study of my evolving pedagogy and the curricular that I designed. It is the fact that, for the majority of this time, these two careers were undertaken simultaneously that gives credibility to my writing as a 'teacher-researcher'. Over 30 years ago Lawrence Stenhouse was at the forefront of advocacy for the notion of teacher-as-researcher (Stenhouse, 1977), which positioned the teacher as an 'extended professional' (in a phrase borrowed from Hoyle, 1974), living in an evolving classroom and striving for continuing growth through thoughtful experimentation. While it has been argued that this notion of teacher-researcher has not reached the dizzy heights to which Stenhouse aspired (see Greenwood, 2002, for a fuller discussion), it has been integral in the pedagogical change of thousands of educators, with a consequent effect on their students. Indeed the educational benefits afforded to my students through the use of both teacher research and Sport Education are the key catalysts to the writing of this chapter.

With the importance placed on enhanced student experiences by both approaches, it should be unsurprising to note that there will be a second voice (or collection of voices) in this exploration of Sport Education: that of my students. Their narrative around Sport Education formed a key lens for my study, alongside my own examination of practice, the help I received from colleagues and the theoretical literature (Brookfield, 1995). This chapter will explore Sport Education through my eyes and the eyes of a number of groups of students who, over 7 years, experienced the approach through a number of different units of work and a number of activities.

Drawing upon Siedentop's (1994) original intent that Sport Education would help students become literate, competent and enthusiastic sportspeople, I will present my use of the model through the same, albeit somewhat doctored, themes of competent, literate and enthusiastic (p. 7). I believe that, while Siedentop envisioned pupils working in roles other than that of player, there are other roles to be played by the Sport Educator other than that of teacher. With this in mind I will explore how I sought to become a *competent*, *literate* and *enthusiastic* proponent of this model of learning.

1   Becoming a *competent* sport educator: in this section, I examine how I developed the skills and strategies inherent in Sport Education so that I could construct, develop and teach a unit of work. To this end, I will explore my first use of Sport Education and will try to show how I learnt to use the model with my students and in my school.
2   Becoming a *literate* sport educator: in this segment, I examine how I developed my basic competency and began to understand and be more knowledgeable about the rules, traditions and values associated with Sport Education. Furthermore, I will try to demonstrate how I came to distinguish between good and bad Sport Education practices. I will investigate my use of Sport Education with a group of challenging students and show how my desire to use appropriate approaches to teaching needed to be 'backed up' with a knowledgeable approach to the use of Sport Education.
3   Becoming an *enthusiastic* sport educator: in the final section, I will explore how I aspired to be someone who taught and behaved in ways that preserved, protected and enhanced student learning through Sport Education. I examine my use of the model in my last year of secondary school teaching with groups of students who were now literate, competent and above all enthusiastic themselves about this approach to learning in physical education.

Competent

As Plato suggested, 'The beginning is the most important part of the work.' Significantly, my first encounter with Sport Education was neither an absolute success nor an unmitigated failure. Instead it went OK. Yet it was this level of 'success', and my move towards 'Sport Education literacy' as a teacher, that prompted me to continue to engage with the model and find new ways of using it. Such learning allowed me to find ways of using Sport Education so that it fitted into my school with all its baggage of tradition, achievement and competition.

Teaching through Sport Education emerged from a personal desire that my pupils learn about leadership, cooperation and responsibility. The literature around the Sport Education approach has extensively explored and extolled its virtues as a means through which social skills can be taught alongside the fundamental skills inherent in actual game play (Siedentop, 1994). Yet it was more than that. My idea for using it emerged out of a desire to do something that physical education, despite its high aspirations, had almost singularly failed to do – explicitly teach leadership, cooperation and responsibility as part of a designed curriculum (Hellison, 2003). I was inspired to try this by the words of Don Hellison when he suggested that physical education claims much more than it should:

Past and present sport, exercise, and physical education leaders have often claimed that a number of personal and social benefits result from participation in physical activities. Sport builds character. Running makes you feel better. Fair play in class and you will fair play in life. The list goes on.

(2003, p. 7)

However, in aspiring to do something new and start again, I should have understood that, despite my 7 years of teaching to that date, I would be returning to being a beginning or neophyte teacher. I have subsequently concluded that the very act of 'trying something new' deprives a teacher of his or her previous expertise and requires them to learn again from the ground up (Casey and Dyson, 2009; Casey *et al.*, 2009). Fortunately, when I was looking for an opportunity to learn about and use the Sport Education model, I found Kinchin's article 'A Closer Look at Sport Education' (2002) in which he used cricket as an example of how Sport Education might work within the traditional British summer curriculum. The choice of cricket was further supported by Bell (1998) who recommended that first-time Sport Educators should position the model within a familiar and comfortable sport. Given my lifelong involvement with cricket and the school's cricket traditions, this choice allowed for a greater focus to be placed upon the instigation of the model rather than the development of a new sport. Armed with the scheme of work Kinchin exemplified in his article, and my additional background reading, I was able to convince my Head of Department (HoD) that it would be worthwhile to undertake a season of Sport Education, focusing on cricket with the Year 9 boys.

Therefore, through the medium of World Cup Cricket, six teams played out what I intended to be 11 weeks of competition (but which was terminated after five by my HoD – more on that later). Within this structure, I helped students to organise and lead their own warm ups, practices and matches while simultaneously supporting them as the players, coaches, managers and officials of the Sport Education season.

Nonetheless, as I recalled at the time, despite my efforts it did not turn out to be plain sailing:

The re-establishment of the summer curriculum away from athletics and formal cricket coaching was a hurdle, and one that the department would eventually fail to clear, thus prematurely ending the whole programme. The school is traditionally a strong performer in the county in cricket, which is reflected in the county quarter and semi final appearances of three school teams at key stages 3 and 4. The prevalence of 'practitioners in both the world of sport and education . . . to view physical education, primarily, as a training ground for young sporting talent' (Armour and Jones, 1998, p. 15) is mirrored in the traditional practices of the department and the Head of Boys physical education, who expressed his discomfort with the adoption of sport education on numerous occasions.

(Master's degree assignment, 2003)

Fortunately, the students' enthusiasm generally remained high and they expressed overall satisfaction in and enjoyment of the project. For example, it was noted, by the student himself and by his peers, that Tom (the captain of team 'India' and an U14 county cricketer) could have taken a dominant role in every match. Yet he chose instead to mix up his involvement and in the process established himself as a competent leader:

> I thought everyone got a chance at the team. I didn't open the batting or bowling every week, I sort of gave everyone else a chance.
>
> *(Tom, Team India interview)*

> I think that [Tom] was like watching other people and seeing how they were doing before he went in, so he was sort of seeing how well other people did and see whereabouts they should bat. I thought he was a good captain.
>
> *(Team India, interview)*

Other groups found that the Sport Education approach helped them to learn about leadership responsibilities through cooperative behaviours:

> A lot of cooperation with your team members, you shouldn't be always fighting like cat and dog with the other team members, you shouldn't feel like you're on your own against everybody else, you should feel like you're part of the team.
>
> *(Team Pakistan, interview)*

> You got to know people's strengths and weaknesses so the stronger players could encourage the weaker players, like in my group Nick could help me, or someone like that who wasn't as strong as he was or as capable a player.
>
> *(Team New Zealand, interview)*

However, despite my efforts and enthusiasm and a personal desire to be innovative and student centred, my HoD was finding it harder and harder to be involved in a change that was not (a) instigated by him nor, in his opinion, (b) required in either the summer timetable or the specific approach to teaching cricket. On some occasions, he faced his concerns by detaching himself from the process and simply observing. At other times he got directly involved and in doing so foregrounded himself as the expert. For example, in my field notes I observed him filling the role of umpire. Umpire was supposed to be a student role and therefore the HoD was wrong to start umpiring himself. His teaching of aspects of the game including taking a guard and leg before wicket (LBW) fitted into the model and players seem to be appreciative (field notes). Yet I believed that he was in error to lend his support as an umpire as this could be seen as a return to the skills-based curriculum that the

Sport Education model was replacing. This lapse highlighted the lack of a shared ideal between HoD and myself, and created a major (and eventually insurmountable) stumbling block to the successful completion of the unit.

In the penultimate lesson of the unit we talked privately, and at length, about the intervention. Afterwards I noted HoD's concerns with regard to the longevity and tenability of the programme.

> HoD still expressing grave concerns about application for top end players . . . the elite few . . . he is not very impressed with the model . . . doesn't seem to see the kids running around enough . . . having involvement . . . or the higher end kids being stretched in their technical batting or bowling skills . . . is happy to continue the model but I am unsure how long this will last.
>
> *(Field notes, p. 6)*

This conversation served as a warning that the unit would soon end (in reality this was the next week: 6 weeks shy of the 11 weeks planned) and now serves as a cautionary tale for those looking to bring Sport Education into a traditional department. However, it is worth noting that Sport Education was not for everyone first time around and it was not only HoD who struggled with this new iteration of physical education. A couple of the more able students – both of whom had a lot of cricket experience and expertise – also resisted the changes, as listed in the following field note extracts:

> Possible, potential problem with Sri Lanka who are, once again, not on task . . . Ricky isolated from the group . . . needs to be brought onto task.
>
> James is off task . . . using spare tennis balls from the practices with a cricket stump to smack them [the balls] around . . . very little involvement . . . rest of the players all on task and all involved in the game . . . spectators avidly watching the game and supporting . . . James continues to wander around hitting tennis balls into the middle of the game, disruption . . . messing around with the stump . . . so . . . vast majority [counts to 14] players on task . . . one deliberately disruptive, obstructive.

This reaction to Sport Education was not dissimilar to the reported response of a high-skilled pupil during his first experience of the approach. Kinchin (2001) reported that 'Don' needed to make a number of alterations to his perceptions of sport before he could take responsibility for working with less-ability peers, helping them and playing on the same team as them. However, the relatively brief 5-week programme was not sufficient for 'Ricky' and 'James' to place their needs below those of their teams.

In many respects, Sport Education was a success. The pupils enjoyed the match play, the team ethos and the opportunity to assume a higher profile within their own learning. Support for the model was evident from the majority of the students, although some of the higher-ability students (as shown) felt that their development as cricketers would have been better served working exclusively on their skills in the nets. Despite this resistance, Sport Education was able to provide a means through which I, as a teacher, could make leadership, cooperation and responsibility as the focus of my teaching rather than a by-product.

The sentiments expressed by Hellison (2003) when he wrote 'My ideas, just emerging and not yet fully formed at that time, were about building character and helping kids' (p. 5) are mirrored within this section. After one curtailed use of Sport Education, I felt that I was developing the skill and strategies needed to use the model in a rudimentary fashion. In the next section, I will explore my attempts to adopt an inclusive 'Sport Education for All' approach to my teaching and become increasingly literate in the 'ways' of Sport Education.

Literate

Following the completion of my master's degree, I undertook a PhD (Casey, 2010). This longitudinal study explored my expanded use of models-based practices, including Sport Education, and benefited from the support of a handful of colleagues: two of whom are mentioned in this section.

My original aim for my PhD was to use my new pedagogies with classes that I trusted and who trusted me, and examine the impact of some new approaches to teaching. However, thanks to my conversations with a critical friend, 'Wayne' (a colleague who taught English at another school), I changed my mind. I decided that, in an effort to move my teaching forwards and keep becoming a more child-centred teacher, I needed to include more classes in my budding pedagogy. Wayne had read my daily reflective diaries and challenged me to think about my teaching, and the difficulties inherent within it, in different ways.

The main catalyst for the unit of Sport Education I will examine now – a term-long football season – was one critical conversation with Wayne. In one of our meetings, he questioned me about class 10Z and the 'constant clashes' that I had with them; and in particular with David, a troublesome student for most of the teachers in the school. I explained how all my attempts to control the class through a didactic approach had continually failed and my frustrations with the whole process. I confessed to him that I was considering trying a models-based approach but was worried that it would fall flat on its face and things would be even worse. Wayne challenged me to try my new pedagogies with this class; after all, why should only the best students be rewarded? Besides, it might just work. Eventually, and following much deliberation, soul-searching and planning, I devised a unit of Sport Education. Furthermore, rather than simply reward 10Z for their bad behaviour, I offered the other two classes I taught in their year group the option to be taught in my usual manner or through a Sport Education approach (one accepted Sport Education and the other declined). Finally, and in an effort to placate David, I offered the students concerned a choice of activity and was unsurprised to see them choose football (soccer).

I resolved that I wanted to involve everyone in my new way of teaching and not simply 'cherry-pick' the 'brilliant classes' that Wayne talked about and thereby guarantee my successes. I wanted to test out this models-based practice and see if it could really 'cut the mustard'. However, despite my resolution to try, I was still nervous about the outcome, as this reflection shows:

> I am still unsure how some will take to this. 10X don't concern me or even 10Y, but 10Z – this could go very well or could blow up. Still, nothing ventured and all that. It is exciting and a little nerve-racking at the same time.

Through these anxieties and my decision-making processes around the Sport Education unit I concluded that by telling them what to do through my didactic approach I could teach in my comfort zone. In this way, if anything went awry, I could blame my failures on the class, not my tried-and-tested approach. However, would I be able to protect myself in the same way if the celebrated new approaches failed to deliver the goods?

I was fortunate to work with a second colleague, 'Burt', on this Sport Education unit. Burt, who was employed by the school as a teaching assistant, witnessed first-hand each of the Sport Education lessons. While Burt worked as an unqualified teacher, he was on hand to offer a different perspective on my developing competence as a Sport Educationalist. What follows are extracts from Burt's observations of my teaching. The diary importantly records his reflecting on 10Z and the ways in which I sought to use my nascent pedagogy with my classes. As you read his reflections on the difficulties that he saw over a 4-week period of changing the learning landscape for this group of boys, note how his own social construction of physical education, and his personal belief about teaching, influences his observations:

> What is this class on about? They get what they want, football, and they still muck around. From my understanding they do football and are given almost total control over their lesson and they fart around, then complain about the lesson and the lack of time they have in it. Ash doesn't want to admit defeat and make them do a more structured 'get in and sit down' lesson but I think these guys need to be told and guided a bit more. All in all I don't think this lesson structure has worked because all they do is walk all over Mr Casey.
>
> *(Burt's Teaching Log, 2 March 2006)*

> An enormous change from last week with this class. They were given a last chance effort by Mr Casey this morning so maybe that's why. But like the 1st years they were given complete control of their lesson. Total independence except for the setting up. So, whatever it was, either the independence or the telling off, it was a big change and a very nice one. But the independence has worked with all classes.
>
> *(9 March 2006)*

> These guys have finally worked it out. There was absolutely no input from Mr Casey today and the lesson worked. They were all on time and doing the

right thing and the whole lesson went without a hitch. It's taken these guys a while. They thought they were too good for school when they were under instruction and then were given control of themselves, a potentially devastating move. Now they've realised that they have to answer and take responsibility for their own actions which has brought them into line.

(16 March 2006)

Last lesson for football outside for these guys and it wasn't hard to tell. Everything just went out the window. Nobody performed any of the roles: nobody even played the game. The non-playing team were probably the worst. They hardly had to do anything and they couldn't even manage that. I think these guys actually need to be taught, not given the lesson. They did it well under pressure but they were given an inch and they took a mile.

(23 March 2006)

As Wayne and I discussed, this class was a problem before, during and after the study. It was always going to be a risk to try something new with them: a class that thrived on the willingness to try and take a mile even when the inch was not offered. Burt often argued (and on many occasions I found myself agreeing with him) that they needed to be didactically teacher led, but I wanted to give everyone a chance at being taught in this new way. The potential ability of pupils to be unofficial change agents in the development, modification or abandonment of curriculum change (Metzler and McCullick, 2008) was clearly demonstrated here. However, I did not want the new pedagogical approach to be limited only to the 'good' classes and I wanted to take risks. In this way I continued, as a veteran teacher, to resist the pupils' attempts to scupper the innovation (Metzler *et al.*, 2008).

I do not know if it was the freedom to sink or swim based on their own efforts, or the old-style dressing down that I gave them on 9 March 2006, but it seemed to shake them up enough to show the real potential for this class of Sport Education. The effect was surprising, particularly to Burt who had been sceptical from the start. However, it simply did not last. This was not a pedagogical choice that could overcome the resistance to change that these experienced pupils were demonstrating. Eventually the wheels fell off and the boys remembered their established role within the school as the troublemakers. Despite the end of unit collapse, I learnt a lot about changing my teaching from replication to interaction through the intransigence and truculence of this class. I was like a newly qualified teacher who was timetabled against the form that no-one wanted to teach. I forced myself to battle and it was not a battle I always – or Burt would say frequently – won. It was not, however, as if I went into this change blindly hoping to transform the infamous 10Z into a dream teaching group. I went into the challenge because I believed that Wayne had been right and that if I was to really change what I did in the classroom it has had to be unilateral not selective change.

The reactions of the pupils in 10Z, as noted by Burt, sit in stark contrast to the positive responses noted by Curtner-Smith *et al.* (2008) about British students in their recent study. While the demographic of the pupils seems to be very similar, the responses were quite different. That is not to say that their difficulties with innovative practice were unique. Indeed in the same study by Curtner-Smith *et al.*, the authors reported the negative influences the American pupils had on their teachers. These pupils showed considerable resistance to Sport Education in which they fought the change in approach that their teacher was trying to engender. However, after the initial battles had been fought, the teachers reported that the students' attitude to the approach improved (Curtner-Smith *et al.*, 2008).

While I have painted a 'lukewarm' picture of Sport Education, the pupils in 10Z and their companion class 10X did report some great gains through the use of this alternative pedagogical model. Some pupils reported in the group interviews that they enjoyed the added competition that came with the Sport Education unit:

> I think the competitive edge really helped because, um, when we were prac-tising water polo just as a whole class there's no competitive edge really, because you get different teams every week, it's an ongoing thing, so we wanted to work together because we wanted to practise these tactics so we could play the game and win, and even if you're not that competitive people still want to do well.
>
> *(10Z, group interview)*

However, more students were enthused by the cooperative elements inherent in Sport Education. They felt that having roles other than that of player helped them to impact more on their new team mates and not just on their own learning:

> I think it's had an impact on our learning of how to teach other people. Take guys like Stu, he doesn't like football, but we helped him in the coaching ses-sions how to, you know . . .
>
> Yes, because I think that by making us work as our own coaches and manag-ers that it's made us work with people that we don't usually get on with as well. We may not automatically fall into the groups with friends that we were in for the sports session, so it made us have to work together, so it's quite use-ful for that.
>
> The good thing about having coaching performance, we could work out what the people's strengths were before so we knew where to put them when we played the full game, so we had about ten minutes before of the training and then put it into practice in the match.
>
> *(10Z and 10X, group interviews)*

These comments show the marked contrast between the behaviours displayed on the pitch and the feelings expressed in the interviews. Yet the school itself – its traditions, the prior experiences of the pupils and the ingrained normality of didac-tic teaching – had an impact on the pupils' willingness to be taught in a new and unfamiliar way. Pupils do not just 'step into' Sport Education but have to learn to learn in a new way (Casey and Dyson, 2009; Casey *et al.*, 2009) and that takes time. Additionally, as Curtner-Smith *et al.* (2008) noted, some new teachers and new Sport Educators find it hard to negotiate the micropolitics of their schools and/or departments which favoured the more traditional approach to teaching in physical education: an approach that Kirk (2010) termed physical-education-as-sport-techniques. As I have shown earlier, I worked in a school content to develop its sports teams and yet my position as a teacher-researcher allowed me to find new ways of teaching through Sport Education. The building picture that I had of pupil responses through social and academic learning gave me enough evidence and confidence to navigate the staid traditions of the school. In the next section, I will explore my developing expertise in Sport Education which increasingly allowed me and the pupils to become *enthusiastic* proponents of the approach.

Enthusiastic

This section explores my final secondary school-based use of Sport Education. This unit was a long way away from the tentative 5-week programme that I taught in the summer of 2003 and helped me gain a degree of *competence* in the model. It was a goodly distance from the intermittent successes and failures that I experienced in the winter and spring of 2005/2006 which developed my *literacy* with the approach. My developed and sustained *enthusiasm* for the Sport Education model, and my eagerness to teach through and around it, led me to use it nearly the whole of key stage 4 (years 10 and 11 [aged 14–16 years]) and for the first time include the girls. Some of the successes of this unit have been reported elsewhere (see Casey and Hastie, in press; Casey *et al.*, in press). Yet the emphases in these papers were the participants (i.e. mine and the boys in the study) and their experiences of and learning through student-designed games rather than the Sport Education season which followed. In contrast, this section will foreground the model and bring together the experiences of the girls and boys who took part together, for the first time, in a Sport Education unit.

The arrival of a new colleague as my HoD served as a catalyst for the adoption of a term-long Sport Education unit (running from the start of September through to the end of December – longer in the boys-only groups). The key to the wholesale adoption of this approach – in key stage 4 during a single lesson every week – was the HoD's prior experiences with using Sport Education. However, and by her own admission, these experiences turned out to have been limited by the aspects of the model that she had employed in her previous school. Curtner-Smith *et al.* (2008) described three approaches to the use of Sport Education: the full version (as Siedentop, 1994, intended); the watered-down version (focused on formal competition as a management structure but failing to include many of the other aspects of Sport Education); and the cafeteria approach (where the traditional team games-centred curriculum is re-branded – but not reconstructed – as Sport Education). My new HoD had previously used a watered-down version of the model but was happy to adopt the full version with leadership and guidance from me. This relationship in itself signalled my new position as a competent and literate Sport Educator capable of mentoring others in the use of the model.

What followed was a huge divergence from the traditional model of physical education that had subjugated the learning experienced by the girls in the school from *time immemorial*. Instructor-led, didactic, 'do-as-I-do', physical-education-as-sport-techniques (Kirk, 2010) had been the only way in which the girls had 'enjoyed' physical education. Suddenly they were being asked to take on roles other than that of performer, in a physical education class that suddenly contained boys, and in non-traditional games (in fact games they had designed themselves) that were not taught through sober technical excellence. The stand-out messages that emerged from the focus group interviews with the girls were that they were 'so sick of doing netball . . . netball . . . netball . . . netball . . . and netball . . . the same way and the same topic for *five* years' (their emphasis).

It would be fair to say that almost anything different would have been seen as positive; however, the key factors for the success of the Sport Education unit were, first, 'we could actually have some choice' in what they did, second, they enjoyed the social aspects of doing physical education for the very first time with the boys in their class, and third, they perceived Sport Education to be more serious and less frivolous than the pseudo-games they had played in netball.

The boys in the same classes – who respectively had 3 and 4 years of experience of my models-based practice as a teacher – were more exhaustive in their responses.

> We learnt about the necessary sides of a game, the attacking, defensive and passive sides of games which all contribute to an enjoyable and intriguing game. How attackers can use a variety of techniques to get round defensive formations with the aim of scoring. Whilst involving views on how refereeing should occur and who should have the final say with multiple refs. We then learnt to analyse the separate sections of the game, scoring, shooting, defending, losing possession, to adapt the basic structure of the game to create a perhaps easier, or more testing and challenging, game.
>
> *(Richard, individual student interview)*

> It was good to learn about games in this way as it meant that you had to analyse every part of the game, meaning you gained a greater understanding of games. I wouldn't say it was easy but I wouldn't say it was hard.
>
> *(Oliver, individual student interview)*

The relative competence and literacy shown by the boys and girls may have differed markedly but their enthusiasm was nearly uniformed and cannot be overlooked. Moreover, the correlation between my enthusiasm as their teacher, the arrival of a new HoD with the courage to move beyond her immediate comfort zone and the emancipation of these students as learners were all contributing factors to the success of this Sport Education unit. Yet the model had to have a significant robustness in itself to stand the rigours and obstacles that a teacher might encounter when using it in his or her classroom.

Conclusion

My encounters with Sport Education, as shown in the vignettes above, came first as a result of a desire to change the way I taught: the catalyst for which was the availability of literature around Sport Education and the positive and celebratory things that people were saying about the model. My second encounter developed from a realisation that everyone deserved the chance to be taught to the best of my ability. My third and final vignette shows how I used the model to engender deeper learning about and around games.

As I have tried to show, becoming a *competent*, *literate* and *enthusiastic* Sport Educator is not a straightforward process. Having read this chapter you might wish to re-categorise my first encounter with the model as an unmitigated disaster. That might be in part due to my initial underperformance with the model, or the actions and reactions of my first HoD. However, as I have argued, this lacklustre beginning was to some extent due to my naivety as an early-career Sport Educator. On the contrary, though, I think that it was more than that – a lot more than that – in fact had I been given the opportunity to finish the unit of work that I had planned then I think I would have been able to build on the success shown in the first section.

Many, Burt included, might equally argue that the second section highlights a 'what not to do' model of Sport Education. Nonetheless, and despite these reservations, I felt that the approach showed a lot of promise. The boys did find ways of becoming independent learners and they did revel in roles other than that of player. In many ways it was their expectations of schooling and the school's expectations of them that played the greatest role in the undoing of some of the good that was done over the course of the unit.

Conversely, by the time I concluded my teaching at the school, some 7 years and numerous seasons of Sport Education later, I was using the model with whole year groups and I was doing it with the support of the new HoD and teaching it with her and another new colleague. Yes, it took me a lot of time to negotiate the spaces in which I could undertake this approach, in the times that I could do them, and in the curricular content areas that I was allowed. But I think that, when faced with tradition, teachers can either 'put up' or 'shut up'. The latter requires the maintenance of the status quo while the first means finding ways of circumventing the restrictions that can often be in place in a school. Some of these restrictions are created by teachers' naivety with the Sport Education model and others from the practice traditions inherent in physical education. However, if we are going to end the dominance of the physical-education-as-sport-techniques approach, we need to find new ways of conceptualising teaching in our gymnasium.

My experiences of Sport Education have been good and the work I did towards the end of my time in school was the best I had undertaken in a 15-year career. The steps that we take towards new and evolving practices in physical education are slow and uncertain. In fact, we may well take nearly as many backward steps as we do forwards. Sport Education for me was part of a philosophical change and move away from behaviourist pedagogy to a constructivist approach to teaching. Finally – and as my pupils said and showed – it is not just the teacher who has to learn to teach in a new way; it is also the pupils who have to learn to learn in a new way (Casey and Dyson, 2009; Casey et al., 2009). That notion of learning to learn is one that is yet to be covered in the literature but one for which Sport Education is well suited.

References

Armour, K.M. and Jones, R.L. (1998) *Physical education teachers' lives and careers: PE, sport and educational status*, London: Falmer Press.

Bell, C. (1998) 'Sport Education in the elementary school', *Journal of Physical Education, Recreation, and Dance*, 69(5): 36–39, 48.

Brookfield, S. (1995) *Becoming a critically reflective teacher*, San Francisco: Jossey Bass.

Casey, A. (2010) 'Practitioner research in physical education: Teacher transformation through pedagogical and curricular change' (unpublished PhD), Leeds Metropolitan University.

Casey, A. and Dyson, B. (2009) 'The implementation of models-based practice in physical education through action research', *European Physical Education Review*, 15: 175–199. doi:10.1177/1356336X09345222

Casey, A. and Hastie, P.A. (2011) 'Students and teacher responses to a unit of student-designed games', *Physical Education and Sport Pedagogy*, 16: 295–312. doi:10.1080/17408989.2010.535253

Casey, A., Dyson, B. and Campbell, A. (2009) 'Action research in physical education: Focusing beyond myself through cooperative learning', *Educational Action Research*, 17: 407–423. doi:10.1080/09650790903093508

Casey, A., Hastie, P.A. and Rovegno, I. (in press) 'Student learning during a unit of student-designed games', *Physical Education and Sport Pedagogy*.

Curtner-Smith, M., Hastie, P.A. and Kinchin, G.D. (2008) 'Influence of occupational socialization on beginning teachers' interpretation and delivery of Sport Education', *Sport, Education and Society*, 13: 97–117. doi:10.1080/13573320701780779

Greenwood, D.J. (2002) 'Action research: Unfulfilled promises and unmet challenges', *Concepts and Transformation*, 7: 117–139. doi: 10.1075/cat.7.2.02gre

Hellison, D. (2003) *Teaching responsibility through physical activity*, Champaign, IL: Human Kinetics.

Hoyle, E. (1974) 'Professionality, professionalism and control in teaching', *London Educational Review*, 3(2): 13–19.

Kinchin, G.D. (2001) 'A high skilled pupil's experiences of Sport Education', *ACHPER Healthy Lifestyles Journal*, 48(3–4): 5–9.

Kinchin, G.D. (2002) 'A closer look at Sport Education', *PE and Sport Today*, 10: 27–30.

Kirk, D. (2010) *Physical education futures*, Milton Park, Abingdon, Oxon: Routledge.

Metzler, M.W., Lund, J.L. and Gurvitch, R. (2008) 'Chapter 8: The diffusion of model-based instruction by establishing communities of practice', *Journal of Teaching in Physical Education*, 27: 571–579.

Metzler, M.W. and McCullick, B.A. (2008) 'Chapter 5: Introducing innovation to those who matter most – The P-12 pupils' perceptions of model-based instruction', *Journal of Teaching in Physical Education*, 27: 512–528.

Siedentop, D. (1994) *Sport Education: Quality PE through positive sport experiences*, Champaign, IL: Human Kinetics.

Stenhouse, L. (1977) *An introduction to curriculum research and development*, London: Heinemann.

8

A SPANISH TEACHER'S EXPERIENCE WITH SPORT EDUCATION

A narrative account

Diego Martínez de Ojeda, Antonio Calderón Luquin, and Peter Hastie

In this chapter, we read the story of Diego, a Spanish physical education teacher who made an attempt to introduce his third-grade students to Sport Education. Our hope was that a narrative approach, otherwise known as reauthoring conversations (White, 1995), could contribute to the skills and knowledge that inform teaching Sport Education as a novice user. We wanted to know the key factors that led to a successful (or problematic) introduction of the model for a teacher and his students. We also wanted to better understand the key components necessary for Spanish teachers wishing to undertake a similar adventure. In addition, we sought to discover and understand the meaning the teacher took from the experience and the extent to which he thought it might affect his future practice.

But first, let us better understand the context of narrative research, and the methodology of this chapter. Narrative research is the study of how human beings experience the world, and narrative researchers collect these stories and write narratives of experience (Gudmundsdottir, 2001). According to Creswell (2007), narrative research is best for capturing the detailed stories or life experiences of a single life or the lives of a small number of individuals, and such was the case in our situation. As these stories are not always presented in chronological order, the researcher uses a process known as "restorying," to gather stories, analyze them for key elements (e.g., time, place, plot, and scene; see Miller and Salkind, 2002), and then rewrite the stories to place them within a chronological sequence (Ollerenshaw and Creswell, 2002). Importantly, narratives include a chronology of events that can include past and future experiences, as well as the present. Cortazzi (1993) suggests that it is the chronology of narrative research that sets it apart from other genres.

Moen (2006) provides a particularly helpful commentary on narrative and storytelling. She notes that:

storytelling is a natural way of recounting experience, a practical solution to a fundamental problem in life, creating reasonable order out of experience. Not only are we continually producing narratives to order and structure our life experiences, we are also constantly being bombarded with narratives from the social world we live in. We create narrative descriptions about our experiences for ourselves and others, and we also develop narratives to make sense of the behavior of others.

(p. 2)

In this study, the data for this narrative were in the form of interview transcripts, documents such as lesson plans, our observations of the teacher in action, and his autobiographical writing and storytelling (Connelly and Clandinin, 1990). A story in narrative research retells events as one would find in a novel, and includes time, place, plot, and scene. However, within these stories, participants may identify epiphanies or turning points in which the story line changes direction dramatically.

The context. Time and place of our story

It is early in the year 2010, and we find ourselves in the grounds of Santa Florentina School in a small village near the city of Cartagena, Spain. The town itself is quite unremarkable, and while being well connected with the principal cities of the famous Costa Blanca, it is still largely ignored by the tourist guides of the region. While the township lacks a certain cultural richness, it does have a richness of population, with inhabitants from Morocco and South America (Ecuador, Bolivia, and Colombia). It is on the playground that we meet Diego, the central character in our story. Diego is the physical education teacher at Santa Florentina, an elementary school that enrolls children from the first through sixth grades (ages from 6 to 12 years). Physical education is scheduled two times a week for 60 minutes, and Diego has been working here since 2008 (he has 10 years of teaching in other schools) when he graduated from the University of Murcia. Throughout his time at the school, Diego has established himself as a central player in the vivacity of the school, being involved in theater productions and school sports.

The playground consists of one small multifunctional cement court with two baskets and also an area with swings and other play facilities. While there is no gymnasium, Diego suggests that his major agenda for physical education is less limited by facilities than it is by access to equipment such as hoops, cones, and ropes. Concurrent to his teaching position, Diego is studying for his master's degree at a local university. His motivation for seeking an advanced degree is to pursue a doctorate, with the intent to eventually teach in higher education.

With respect to his outlook on physical education for young children, Diego suggests he follows an instructional style which could be described as traditional, with lessons progressing through the five stages of introduction, warm-up, main part, cool down, and conclusion. Nevertheless, Diego was also concerned with "trying to connect the activities with the interests of the students, and so adapt games so that there is a relationship between what I have planned and what they like to play." Furthermore, he often chose to replace the lesson closure in cases where "the students suggest activities that can fit into the scheduled work content as long as they do not involve loss of time due to use of material not readily available or other issues."

This concern for student motivation was also apparent when Diego suggested that "it is essential to change one's teaching methods to preserve the motivation of both students and teachers." He even goes as far as suggesting that it should be compulsory for every teacher to make adjustments in their pedagogies in order to motivate students toward physical education and sport. As he notes, "In physical education you must always be innovating and presenting the subject as attractive as possible."

The plot, part 1. Factors leading to the introduction of Sport Education

It so happens that, during his master's study, Diego is introduced to Sport Education as an alternate pedagogical model. While the exposure to the model was limited to a 5-hour session in which theory and practical application were introduced, it seemed enough to entice his interest. After discussions with the presenter (Peter Hastie), Diego pursued further reading on the topic. He noted that, "to learn more about the model, I read the material of Siedentop (1994) and Dyson et al. (2004). I also consulted the reviews of Wallhead and O'Sullivan (2005) and Siedentop (2002)." Diego listed a series of other papers that followed his reading of the major reviews. These included articles on the enthusiastic participation of students (Carlson, 1995; Hastie, 1996, 1998, 2000; Pope and Grant, 1996) and teachers (Alexander and Luckman, 2001; Alexander et al., 1996); on research related to the acquired knowledge (literacy) (Hastie, 1996; Hastie and Sinelnikov, 2006); and on the level of competition (competition) (Carlson and Hastie, 1997; Grant, 1992).

Of particular importance in Diego's decision to "try" Sport Education was that he was intrigued by what he called "the proliferation of Sport Education studies that justify the application of the model as positive in many different areas." Indeed, he was particularly interested by the reported positive responses by students in terms of improving skills, autonomy, and knowledge of the game and motivation. He considered these attractive outcomes warranting an application with his third-grade students. He did note, however, that "I think that teachers unconsciously have carried out some similar methodologies, but not so structured and with the main features of Sport Education." What was additionally attractive, however, was his interpretation that "students are one important point in their learning process, because of the being on a team during the season [affiliation], and helping each other to improve the team and the individual performance." As he commented:

> This third course is probably the most well committed and responsible of all I teach; I would like to try Sport Education to develop in them the autonomy

behaviour and to see if they are competent enough to solve the problems and to decide what to do during the season.

Finally, the fact that Sport Education provided some authentic characteristics of how his students perceive sport, but coupled with the foregrounding of fair play, also contributed toward Diego's interest in trialing a season. In particular, Diego noted that

> until now I had never prepared a teaching unit in which the components of the methodology were: 1) season planning, 2) grouping into teams, 3) regular competition, 4) final competition, 5) score keeping, and 6) culminating event. For this, my initial interest was very high.

This interest was accompanied by a level of optimism, and Diego believed his students would have a favorable response to the season. He commented that, by selecting a game the students had played before (and enjoyed), it would be easier to focus on fundamental aspects of the model. He was also confident that the students would be motivated by the fact they would be taking so much of the responsibility for the season.

The plot, part 2. Resolving further questions and issues of concern

After his initial exposure to Sport Education within the master's coursework, and after his reading of the literature, Diego identified a number of issues that he still found problematic should he choose to deliver a season to his students. His primary concern was whether his students could persist with the same content over an extended period of time. He was apprehensive about the extent to which students could persist without becoming bored or getting tired. Historically, games were not afforded extensive curriculum time as distinct units, but more as a part of the unit focusing on sending and receiving skills. That is, students would first practice isolated skills of throwing, hitting, and receiving light balls of different sizes, as well as throwing for accuracy. This would be followed by one or two lessons playing games using these skills.

Consistent with the extended curricular time, Diego wondered how students would respond to being on the same team from the beginning until the end of the unit. In principle, he did not believe that there would be problems, but he also recognized that some students might struggle with the idea of consistently being members of a team in which they had no choice of membership.

Other questions which arose during this period of extended reflection related mostly to the change in pedagogy. As he commented, "At first I didn't have a very clear understanding of the role of the student-captain and his responsibility in giving feedback. I think with the third grade, it might be a little complicated, because they don't have enough autonomy." Coupled with this was Diego's concern about the lines of communication between the teacher and captain, and then between the captain and the team. In particular, concerns related to "Which information to give them, how to do this, and when to do this?" In terms of the curriculum, issues related to the appropriate modification of the game, the kind of competition, and the calendar of that competition. In addition, Diego was aware of the need to design score sheets that would be appropriate for the grade level.

The plot, part 3. Planning and preparing to teach

When planning for the season, Diego began with the primary goal of increasing students' knowledge of different aspects of play (such as officiating and keeping score) that would then allow them to play later with more autonomy. He noted:

> Especially that the students recognize, apply, and respect the rules of the game and respect the referee decisions, and also to create a good feeling about the practice of PE and sports. Thus they will be able to play this and other games in their free time. According to the main features of Sport Education I tried [to get] the students [to] respect the rules of the game, and know more about games like this in the region in which we live.

Other objectives for the unit included the students' throwing and catching skills, and through increased opportunities to play, the game was going to be more fluid.

Nonetheless it was still the social responsibility aspects of the model that seemed most attractive. Diego later commented that he wanted to see how Sport Education had an influence on students in terms of students

> assuming responsibilities in the game and also in their real life . . . As far as responsibility, if students could show commitment to their roles and accept and respect those of the teammates, this would be an indicator of autonomy and a consolidation of the proper values of physical education.

In terms of the specifics of season planning, Diego was concerned that he himself respect the three fundamental objectives of Sport Education, and it was through his analysis of competency, literacy, and enthusiasm that he planned the season. In terms of literacy, he chose a game the students found particularly exciting. He did note, however, that any modifications to the game, in this case "balón prisionero,"[1] had to respect the norms by which it was played by children in the area. Diego was conscious of maintaining not only those aspects of the game that led to its enjoyment, but also the traditions of play and social norms that resulted in its being played with high degrees of friendliness among participants. He was also concerned about threats to enthusiasm presented by an extended unit length. While Diego was expressively confident that "it was going to be a great experience," he still spent time thinking of a variety of different tasks he could present during lessons. In terms of competency, Diego began with the fundamental skills of throwing and catching, and recognized that certain aspects of throwing precision were necessary. Consequently, in order to achieve competence among the students, he spent significant time planning for the composition and size of the ball, as well as the dimensions of the playing area. Another aspect of planning was selecting student roles. Diego's challenge was to include roles that students would commit to "freely and by consensus." Eventually the roles of captain, scorekeepers, game officials, and fitness leader were selected. In the early matches, officials and scorekeepers were placed in pairs in order to help each other, while the role of fitness leader changed each lesson so that all students could practice this role.

First of all, Diego analyzed the number of sessions dedicated to each one of the parts of the model (regular competition, finals, culminating, and festivity) and the facilities and necessary material (to identify the equipment, collection of data, etc.). In this first step, he also spent considerable time thinking how to modify balón prisionero, initially in terms of establishing for it games reduced to 4 × 4 and 8 × 8, and then in terms of variations in ball type and size.

The second task was to identify details concerning teams. Diego developed a form for students to place their names, the team name and mascot, and the team responsibilities of each player. He also left two lines blank in which each team was able to propose two fair play rules that they thought could be important. His reasoning here is that "I think if the pupils participate in the creation of the norms it is easier for them to identify with them." Each team was also given strips of material in team colors that students could wear during team practice and in games.

For officiating and score keeping, Diego tried to keep the tasks simple and easy to apply, and that they picked up aspects of fair play. To achieve this, he often added the players' names on the score sheets before class. This prevented unnecessary time being wasted in class, as the students often were slow to do this. Moreover, by having score sheets with students' names already added, Diego believed the scorekeepers could concentrate better on this main role with was to gather data from the game. Finally, the challenge was to determine the format of the competition and the culminating event.

The scene. The season in action

For Diego, it was important to help the students to learn to play independently, and as such he felt he had to provide opportunities for autonomy. Nonetheless, he also appreciated that, in the earliest lessons, his intervention was often necessary. In the early lessons, score keeping was problematic, as students struggled with the process of obtaining the final scores (composed by the sum of the eliminated students plus the fair play scores). In order to rectify these difficulties, he met with the scorekeepers between games "to explain to them at great length how they had to do it," following which the scores improved.

With respect to officiating, students would frequently disagree and, instead of resolving game problems between each other, they would go to Diego and ask for him to arbitrate. In response, Diego took opportunities at the end of matches to reinforce to all students about the importance of respecting the decisions of the officials. He also encouraged the referees to collaborate more in order to quickly come to consensus. Finally, it was decided that, at the end of each match, the referees and scorekeepers would meet to agree upon the fair play of each team. Diego commented that, after these interventions, "everything worked very well, and there was significant improvement in respecting officials' decisions."

Eventually, though, the autonomy envisioned by Diego was being realized. Indeed, in one lesson, he commented that "the referees were so comfortable that they decided to act alone when they thought a student was not involved enough in the play." In these cases, the referees actually directed players to pass to a student who had not had many chances to throw. Other notes he made included the following:

> The speed of the game was still growing, with few interruptions. The scorers were showing good collaboration and accuracy, and the referees and scorers after each party met to discuss the points for sportsmanship. It is also curious that, as the unit progressed, students did not ask about other games. At the end of the unit, the groups were very structured in their work and the information given through the student-captains came pretty well.

Diego did however take numerous opportunities to promote reflection among his students. At the beginning of each lesson, he spoke to team captains about the format of the day's games and equipment, and also of the need to provide positive feedback. At the end of lessons he met with the class as a whole to discuss any issues that students brought to his attention, as well as positively reinforcing aspects of student behavior he found appropriate.

For Diego, the turning point in the season was the point at which students realized that their success in competition also depended upon their behavior with respect to refereeing decisions. This point was clearly evident with the onset of the formal competition phase. While short meetings with different students in previous lessons gave hints about this upcoming consequence, the formality of the competition phase meant specific noncompliant behaviors had real consequences.

The biggest surprises

When asked which features of the season matched his expectations, Diego suggested that, in general, all of them did. However, what was particularly surprising was the level to which students "were able to make decisions for themselves and even plan complex strategies before the game." He suggested that this development of autonomy extended beyond the season.

> In the unit teaching after the season (past 4 weeks), in the unit of alternative modified games, the students played with different teams in each session and new games for them, and the fact of having participated in the Sport Education season, I think that caused a positive transfer of activities at the

level of acceptance, respect for both themselves and the rules. The pre-sport games unit was developed in a very smooth and without a conflictive climate, and the students also demanded at times to be officials in the development of this content.

The critical learning

From his experiences throughout the season, Diego acquired a sense of liberation in his teaching. His discovery of a pedagogical model that "promotes the improvement of skills and student participation in physical education" as well as the "ability to make decisions as a team and assume responsibility in physical activity" reinforced to him the importance of physical education in the sense of a child's total education. He also noted he appreciated the role of Sport Education in "bringing all the factors of a sport as it exists in society into a relevant curriculum."

However, it was the development of student autonomy that captured Diego's attention and which provided his most significant learning as a teacher. This had the subsequent effect that he found himself becoming more and more motivated. As noted, he was surprised by the extent that, with practice and experience, students were able to make decisions for themselves and even plan complex strategies. This was something he had hoped for, but was hesitant to predict its possibility.

The future

When Diego was asked to look toward any future experiences with Sport Education, he was able to list a number of changes we would consider. Some of these were practical, in terms of issues he felt he would need to address that were neglected this time, while others were extensions he saw as possible after the students' first experience. With regard to the first of these, he suggested he would work more intensively with the student-coaches in the earlier phases of the season. Of perhaps more interest, though, was his intent to produce a longer season. While initially concerned as to whether students would become bored within an extended experience, Diego suggested that, as students become more familiar with the model and its pedagogy, he would introduce more roles, and add posters outlining the general rules of the game as well as specific role responsibilities. He also intended to give more publicity to the final party "right from the start of the season." Coupled with extended roles, a longer season would allow Diego to spend more time "introducing the principal skills and allocating more sessions where there are more complicated technical elements to learn."

As he became more confident with the expansive nature of Sport Education, Diego also felt more comfortable adopting more of the festive dimensions of the model. He suggested it was

> important to consider the advertising of events for motivation, through the
> school newspaper, charts in the school announcing the unit, or posters with

the names of teams and a record during the development of it, or posters announcing the final conclusion.

He also thought he might consider taking an interdisciplinary perspective, collaborating with other teachers within the school. Indeed, such was Diego's positive response to this season that he has planned a series of seminars for other physical education teachers who are curious about his experiences.

In terms of advice he would give to other novice users of the model, Diego suggested that they must first know well the model, because if not, it will be very difficult. He also suggested that they should pay particular attention to planning the structure of the unit and each session, and in particular, the information given to students through students–captains. The critical nature of team selection was also mentioned, with specific attention being placed on creating teams that are heterogeneous, and thereby promoting respect, tolerance, and acceptance.

What did we learn from this story? Our metanarrative

The stories in the past two chapters of this book tell of two teachers who implemented Sport Education in response to desires to help students develop leadership, cooperation, and responsibility. For other teachers, the agendas include greater levels of participation and motivation (see Chapters 6 and 12). Moreover, in all of these cases, the model was implemented in different ways, with students in different grade levels, and with different activities. In reflecting on this, it is critical to remember Siedentop's assertion that there is no one best way to enact a season. He writes:

> When one develops a curriculum and instruction model, it is futile to worry too much about possible misapplications or, even worse, to get involved in demanding that the model has to be done in some perfect form. That is not how dissemination works in schools. If one gets involved in ownership issues, one is bound to lose. I do believe it is important that teachers have very good, practical materials with which to start Sport Education, and those kinds of materials are now available worldwide from a number of sources.
>
> *(Siedentop, 2002, p. 416)*

It makes sense, then, that we pay increasing attention to the voices of teachers as they plan and implement seasons of Sport Education. While there are certain immutable features of the model (i.e., persisting teams with students taking roles other than player, periods of informality and competition, and elements of festivity), we need to recognize teachers' localized expertise and listen more to their stories of implementation. Only by acknowledging and supporting these "stories of implementation" can we meaningfully help more teachers successfully implement Sport Education seasons, while also uncovering alternative pedagogies and allowing hybrids of the model that serve students in specific educational contexts to develop.

Note

1 Balón prisionero is a Spanish form of dodgeball, a game where the main objective of each team is to remove all members of the opposing team by hitting them with thrown balls, catching a ball thrown by a member of the opposing team, or forcing them to move outside the court boundaries when a ball is thrown at them. In this form, when a student is eliminated, they go into an area behind the attacking team (cemetery) from where they can return to the field when a player on their team catches a ball thrown by the opposing team.

References

Alexander, K. and Luckman, J. (2001) "Australian teachers' perceptions and uses of the Sport Education curriculum model," *European Physical Education Review,* 7: 243–267. doi:10.1177/1356336X01007300

Alexander, K., Taggart, A., and Thorpe, S.T. (1996) "A spring in their steps? Possibilities for professional renewal through Sport Education in Australian schools," *Sport, Education and Society,* 1: 23–46. doi:10.1080/1357332960010102

Carlson, T.B. (1995) "Now I think I can: The reaction of eight low-skilled students to Sport Education," *ACHPER Healthy Lifestyles Journal,* 42: 6–8.

Carlson, T.B. and Hastie, P.A. (1997) "The student social system within Sport Education," *Journal of Teaching in Physical Education,* 17: 176–195.

Connelly, M.F. and Clandinin, J.D. (1990) "Stories of experience and narrative inquiry," *Educational Researcher,* 19(5): 2–14.

Cortazzi, M. (1993) *Narrative analysis,* Washington, DC: The Falmer Press.

Creswell, J.W. (2007) *Qualitative inquiry and research design: Choosing among five approaches,* Thousand Oaks, CA: Sage.

Dyson, B., Griffin, L., and Hastie, P. (2004) "Sport Education, tactical games, and cooperative learning: Theoretical and pedagogical considerations," *Quest,* 56: 226–240.

Grant, B.C. (1992) "Integrating sport into the physical education curriculum in New Zealand secondary schools," *Quest,* 44: 304–316.

Gudmundsdottir, S. (2001) "Narrative research on school practice," in V. Richardson (ed.) *Fourth handbook for research on teaching* (pp. 226–240), New York: Macmillan.

Hastie, P.A. (1996) "Student role involvement during a unit of Sport Education," *Journal of Teaching in Physical Education,* 16: 88–103.

Hastie, P.A. (1998) "Skill and tactical development during a Sport Education season," *Research Quarterly for Exercise and Sport,* 69: 368–379.

Hastie, P.A. (2000) "An ecological analysis of a Sport Education season," *Journal of Teaching in Physical Education,* 19: 355–373.

Hastie, P.A. and Sinelnikov, O.A. (2006) "Russian students' participation in and perceptions of a season of Sport Education," *European Physical Education Review,* 12: 131–150. doi:10.1177/1356336X06065166

Miller, D.C. and Salkind, N.J. (2002) *Handbook of research design and social measurement,* Thousand Oaks, CA: Sage.

Moen, T. (2006) "Reflections on the narrative research approach," *International Journal of Qualitative Methodology,* 5(4): Article 5. Available HTTP: http://www.ualberta.ca/~iiqm/backissues/5_4/html/moen.htm (accessed January 5, 2011).

Ollerenshaw, J. and Creswell, J.W. (2002) "Narrative research: A comparison of two "restorying" data analysis approaches," *Qualitative Inquiry,* 8: 329–347. doi:10.1177/10778004008003008

Pope, C. and Grant, B.C. (1996) "Student experiences in Sport Education," *Waikato Journal of Education*, 2: 103–118.

Siedentop, D. (1994) *Sport Education: Quality PE through positive sport experiences*, Champaign, IL: Human Kinetics.

Siedentop, D. (2002) "Sport Education: A retrospective," *Journal of Teaching in Physical Education*, 21: 409–418.

Wallhead, T. and O'Sullivan, M. (2005) "Sport Education: Physical education for the new millennium?" *Physical Education and Sport Pedagogy*, 10: 181–210. doi:10.1080/17408980500105098

White, M. (1995) *Re-authoring lives: Interviews and essays*, Adelaide: Dulwich Centre Publications.

9

PURSUING SOCIAL AND EMOTIONAL LEARNING OUTCOMES THROUGH SPORT EDUCATION

An Australian case study

Swee Chong Ang, Dawn Penney, and Karen Swabey

As this book and previous literature reflects, since its initial development by Siedentop (1994) Sport Education has been adopted in many and varied physical education teaching and teacher education contexts internationally. Some of the research arising has directed attention to the potential for Sport Education to specifically support learning associated with cooperation skills (Pope and Grant, 1996), personal and social responsibility (Hastie and Buchanan, 2000; Hastie and Sharpe, 1999) and/or the development of an inclusive learning environment (Carlson, 1995; Carlson and Hastie, 1997; Ennis, 1999). Meanwhile, research in England explored the suitability of Sport Education as a pedagogical model for teachers faced with the challenge of fulfilling national curriculum aims and requirements (Penney *et al.*, 2005).

The project reported here specifically sought to extend research addressing the capacity of Sport Education to facilitate the achievement of particular learning outcomes, and therefore its prospective alignment with national and/or state curriculum frameworks. The project thus directed attention to the *adaptation* of Sport Education from curriculum and instructional perspectives to reflect context-specific learning priorities. As we explain further below, those priorities related specifically to the social emotional learning outcomes identified in the new Health and wellbeing (HWB) curriculum in Tasmania (Tasmanian Department of Education, 2008). Following Kim *et al.* (2006), the message here is that developing and implementing Sport Education with a specific agenda certainly does not equate to 'business as usual' in physical education lessons for either teachers or students. The teacher and students involved in this research were introduced to and adopted approaches to teaching and learning that were clearly new to them.

Social emotional learning as a curriculum priority

The Collaborative for Academic, Social, and Emotional Learning (CASEL) define social emotional learning as the process of developing fundamental social and emotional competencies in children (CASEL, 2008). With mental health problems identified as adversely affecting behaviour, academic performance and social functioning (Hunter Institute of Mental Health, 2000), social emotional learning has become acknowledged as an increasingly significant aspect of education and as fundamental to children's mental health (Australian Government Department of Health and Aging, 2006). Across the states and territories of Australia (each of which have their own respective curriculum frameworks and requirements), social emotional learning is thus embedded within the health and physical education learning area.[1]

In 2008, in Tasmania, the learning area was renamed HWB, with the new curriculum focusing on developing health and well-being skills, knowledge and understanding across three strands:

> Strand 1: understanding health and wellbeing
> Strand 2: skills and concepts for movement and physical activity
> Strand 3: skills for personal and social development
> *(Tasmanian Department of Education, 2008, p. 9)*

The social and emotional wellbeing of children is a particular focus in strand 3, which encompasses identity, relationship and self-management skills as key foci for learning and teaching. These foci are in turn reflected in the learning outcomes identified. For example, the HWB curriculum is intended to extend students' understanding of the concepts of identity and relationships, and it is expected that students will be able to 'demonstrate self-management skills that promote personal identity and relationships' (Tasmanian Department of Education, 2008, p. 11). As we have discussed elsewhere (Ang *et al.*, 2009), the content of the HWB curriculum clearly connects with the five social emotional learning 'core competencies' as defined by CASEL (2008): self-awareness; social awareness; self-management; responsible decision-making; and relationship skills.

Exploring the potential of Sport Education to facilitate social emotional learning

This project recognised and sought to pursue the potential alignment of Sport Education with a focus on social emotional learning outcomes. While much of the existing research pointed towards the key features of Sport Education lending themselves to the development of skills, knowledge and understandings associated with social emotional learning, our emphasis was that achieving such outcomes is by no means guaranteed as a consequence of employing Sport Education as a pedagogical model. Following other research highlighting interpretation and adaptation as critical aspects of teacher engagement with Sport Education (Kim *et al.*, 2006;

Penney *et al.*, 2005), we saw a need for the specific focus on social emotional learning to be explicit at all stages of planning to implement Sport Education in physical education in order for the intended learning outcomes to be achieved. A crucial phase of the research was, therefore, the mapping of prospective connections between Sport Education and social emotional learning in relation to curriculum planning at a unit and lesson level, and in relation to pedagogy. This involved us thinking critically and creatively about the ways in which the features of Sport Education, and particularly the team-based learning structure, the various roles for students, and competition, could be adapted to achieve an explicit focus on social emotional learning from teaching and learning perspectives.

A unit of Sport Education was thus designed and developed by Swee Chong Ang using Sport Education literature and resources (Hellison *et al.*, 2000; Penney *et al.*, 2005; Siedentop *et al.*, 2004) in conjunction with the new Tasmanian HWB curriculum document (Tasmanian Department of Education, 2008) and taking into account the specific school context for this project. The unit sought to directly connect with the prior learning experiences and learning needs of the students involved: a class of 26 grade 5/6 students from a low socio-economic status (SES) school in Tasmania. A low SES school was selected in recognition that social emotional learning may be particularly pertinent to these students. It is suggested that the potential incidence of mental health or propensity to mental illness may be greater in low socio-economic contexts (McGrath, 2000).

The unit comprised eight lessons of modified volleyball (Newcombeball), with two lessons per week, each lasting 45 minutes. The unit was conceptualised and organised in three phases that related specifically to progressive development of social emotional learning and, in parallel, an increasing emphasis on independent learning within a Sport Education framework. As indicated above, the unit sought to employ the key features of Sport Education in a manner that would facilitate the focus on social emotional learning. Specifically:

- Sport Education's *season structure* was acknowledged as supporting continuity in learning. While the time constraints of this project meant that the season was notably short, it was nevertheless regarded as a beneficial characteristic, potentially enhancing the ability of the unit to support growth in students' self-confidence and contributing to feelings of affiliation or belonging.
- *Affiliation* was recognised as particularly important for social emotional learning. Small group situations can promote social emotional learning by facilitating cooperative learning and giving all children a sense of membership and belonging. Persisting groups provide enhanced opportunities for this and, potentially, position students to come to appreciate individual and group similarities and differences. They may also present a context in which students develop a greater awareness of how individual interests relate to those of others (and the team as a whole) and in which they can learn to become active citizens of their team. Team meetings were acknowledged as situations that could provide opportunities for focused self and group reflection relating to social emotional learning.

- *Roles* in Sport Education are intended to support the development of interpersonal and social skills and encourage critical awareness of social issues and responsibilities. In this unit, this was reaffirmed and specific links to social emotional learning were made explicit in roles. For example, the roles of captain and coach were identified as particularly important in learning relationship building skills such as conflict management, persuasion and fostering collaboration. Responsible decision-making was also identified with these roles. The roles of sports board members, referee and scorekeeper were all recognised as involving students in making ethical decisions. In choosing roles, students were encouraged to reflect on and apply learning relating to issues of identity and relationships, by assessing their own and others' interests, values and strengths and potentially negotiating roles.

- In Sport Education, *competitions* are designed to facilitate and celebrate learning relating to all of the roles that students have been challenged to take on. Competitions presented a context to specifically promote social emotional learning by providing opportunities for learning relating to values such as resilience, respect and fairness, and presenting situations whereby students could learn about responsible decision-making and the expression and control of emotions under stressful situations.

- *Records* provide feedback for individuals and teams in Sport Education and can be used as a reference point to set goals for future learning and performance. Tailoring the 'measures of performance' and thus record keeping to the unit learning objectives enabled the focus on social emotional learning to be further reaffirmed. Thus, record keeping was used as a basis to teach self-management skills such as evaluating, planning and goal setting. Points were awarded to teams for fair play and for fulfilling team duty responsibilities, with students made aware of the link between this 'accountability system' and positive social behaviour. Fair play and refereeing award schemes were designed to explicitly encourage responsible decision-making.

- The *culminating event* provides a platform for celebrating the achievements of all students throughout the Sport Education season. In this project, it was seen as a further opportunity to promote social emotional learning through the celebration of individual and team strengths with the intention of enhancing self-esteem and self-confidence among all students.

Table 9.1 provides an overview of the structure and content of the Sport Education–social emotional learning unit. Content to be addressed in the lessons and across the unit as a whole was aligned with the learning expectations appropriate for the grade level as defined by the new HWB curriculum document. 'Standard 4 stage 10' performance criteria[2] for learning relating to Strand 3 (skills for personal and social development) (Tasmanian Department of Education, 2008, p. 79) were therefore used in conjunction with the core social emotional learning competencies described above to evaluate students' social emotional learning associated with participation in the Sport Education–social emotional learning unit.

TABLE 9.1 Overview of the Sport Education–social emotional learning unit: modified volleyball (Newcombeball)

Lessons	Learning activities
PHASE 1 (teacher-directed)	
1	Introduction to Sport Education and group formation
	Teacher observes and assesses ability of students' individual motor skills in a 1 vs. 1 cooperative game (focus on the dig and the set)
	Election of team captains and Sports Board members
2	Awareness (social skills) talk (Hellison *et al.*, 2000)
	Level 1 responsibility: effort
	Announce groups and practise non-playing roles
	Intra-team cooperative game, 1 vs. 1
	Inter-team scrimmage, 1 vs. 1 (game sense: long and skinny court)
3	Awareness (social skills) talk (Hellison *et al.*, 2000)
	Level 2 responsibility: self-direction
	Team game skill practice. Practice focuses on the serve, set technique, dig and set rally
	Preparation for pre-season games: inter-team scrimmage, 2 vs. 2 (game sense: two square bounce)
PHASE 2 (students taking increasing responsibility)	
4	Awareness (social skills) talk (Hellison *et al.*, 2000)
	Level 3 responsibility: self-direction
	Preparation for formal competition: round-robin pre-season games 2 vs. 2, Part 1
	Practice session (game sense: two square bounce)
5	Awareness (social skills) talk (Hellison *et al.*, 2000)
	Level 4 responsibility: helping others
	Round-robin pre-season games 2 vs. 2, Part 2
	Practice session
PHASE 3 (student-directed)	
6	Awareness (social skills) talk (Hellison *et al.*, 2000)
	Level 5 responsibility: helping others
	Round-robin formal competition 3 vs. 3, Part 1
	Practice session (game sense: space ball)
7	Social skills awareness talk (Hellison *et al.*, 2000) – reinforcement
	Round-robin formal competition 3 vs. 3, Part 2
	Practice session (game sense: space ball)

Source: Adapted from Ang *et al.* (2009).

Progression in content also related to a tactical games or 'game sense' approach being embedded in the unit (see, e.g., Australian Sports Commission, 1997; Mitchell *et al.*, 2006) and use of the Hellison *et al.* (2000) Teaching Personal and Social Responsibility (TPSR) model as a key point of reference.

Unit design necessarily took account of both the teacher and students' 'pedagogical readiness' for Sport Education and for a focus on social emotional learning. Notably, the teacher did not have any prior experience of using Sport Education and had limited knowledge of social emotional learning. Ang therefore adopted the role of co-teacher in conjunction with the role of researcher for implementation of the unit. The early phase of the unit (lessons 1–3) was designed for a more teacher-directed approach to enable foundational skills and knowledge relating to the Sport Education model, the specific application of the model in this unit (in terms of roles, record keeping, etc.) and the context of volleyball to be effectively established. During this phase, cooperative play focusing on team cohesion, rather than competition, was emphasised. Inter-team competitions during this phase were therefore mainly scrimmages (games that do not count towards the championship) designed to support a focus on students learning organisational and duty team responsibilities and becoming familiar with the competition format.

The second phase was designed so that students would take more responsibility in lessons, with the teacher acting to support this transition. Competitions were pre-season games to increase the challenge for the students and allow more complex techniques and tactics to be introduced. Practice sessions involving peer coaching and team planning were also incorporated and pre-season games counted towards the championship points.

The final phase was designed as an entirely student-led and competition-oriented phase. It involved three rounds of three versus three format games with the final round culminating in a festive event, with championship games, award ceremonies for best referee, 'Most Valuable Person' and Champion Teams for both divisions in the competition, student speeches and a slide presentation of photographs taken during the season.

Social emotional learning in Sport Education: experiences and outcomes

Quantifiable data relating to students' social emotional learning were gathered before and at the end of the Sport Education–social emotional learning unit. On each occasion, two surveys were administered to participants: the Australian Council for Educational Research (ACER) social and emotional well-being survey instrument (ACER, 2008) and the Physical Activity and Sport Profile (PASP) (University of Tasmania, 2008). Basic descriptive statistics are presented for data arising from both surveys. The small sample size ($n = 24$) precluded further quantitative analysis and means that all data are treated with caution. In addition to the survey data, structured lesson observations generated qualitative data relating to both learning and teaching.

ACER social and emotional well-being survey

The ACER social and emotional well-being survey identifies four distinct social-emotional-motivational foundations that support the social and emotional well-being and achievement of students:

a   *Positive mindset for achievement* (academic confidence, work persistence and work organisation)
b   *Getting along* (social confidence, friendship, conflict resolution, rule following and collaboration)
c   *Emotional resilience* (emotional awareness, empathy, emotion regulation and behaviour control) and
d   *Social responsibility* (trustworthy, respectful, fair, caring and good citizen).

The pre- and post-unit surveys generated data relating to: (i) levels of self-reported overall social and emotional well-being as determined by survey scores; (ii) mean scores for pre- and post-unit self-reported overall social and emotional well-being; and (iii) self-reported pre- and post-unit social-emotional-motivational competency levels relating to each of the four foundations above.

In relation to overall social and emotional well-being, the maximum score for this section of the survey was 20. Students were assigned to one of four levels in accordance with their survey responses. These were 0–5 (very low), 6–10 (low), 11–15 (good) and 16–20 (very good) overall social and emotional well-being. Here and subsequently, student absences account for the variation in sample size (n) from the class size (26 students). Table 9.2 presents pre- and post-unit results for this section of the survey.

As shown in Table 9.2, pre- and post-unit, many students indicated high or very high overall social and emotional well-being. Nevertheless, there was a reduction in the number of students with very low and low self-reported overall social and emotional well-being. There was also an increase in the number of students with a very high level of self-reported overall social and emotional well-being. Further analysis of these data confirmed that these trends were apparent among both girls and boys within the class. Mean scores reaffirmed slight improvements occurring for both subgroups, as illustrated in Table 9.3.

TABLE 9.2 Levels of self-report overall social and emotional well-being

	Survey level				
	Very low	Low	High	Very high	Total
Pre–unit	2 (8%)	2 (8%)	3 (13%)	17 (71%)	24
Post–unit	0 (0%)	1 (4%)	1 (4%)	21 (92%)	24
Per cent change	− 8%	− 4%	− 9%	+ 22%	

TABLE 9.3 Pre- and post-unit mean scores of students' self-perceived overall social and emotional well-being

	Boys (n = 12)	Girls (n = 12)	All students
Pre-unit	16.41	15.33	15.88
Post-unit	18.42	17.41	17.92
Score change	+2.01	+2.08	+2.04

TABLE 9.4 Pre- and post-survey mean scores of students' social and emotional competencies under the four distinct social-emotional-motivational foundations

	Maximum	Pre-unit	Post-unit
Positive mindset	7	5.57	6.17
Getting along	7	5.57	6.17
Emotional resilience	12	8.88	10.16
Social responsibility	8	6.50	7.46

Encouragingly, students showed a consistent improvement across the four distinct social and emotional competencies measured by the survey instrument. Table 9.4 presents pre- and post-unit scores for each foundation.

Physical Activity and Sport Profile

The PASP survey was the second well-being measure used in this project, and focuses on *Sports Physical Self-Concept*. As with the ACER social and emotional survey results, the PASP results were used to allocate students to four levels of physical self-concept, with a maximum score being 200 points. In this case, the cut-offs were 0–50 (very low), 51–100 (low), 101–150 (good) and 151–200 (very good) physical self-concept.

Table 9.5 shows improvements in students' self-reported sports physical self-concept level and, once again, further analysis examined results by gender. Notably, this showed that *all* of the changes in self-reported physical self-concept were associated with responses from girls. *All* of the boys (*n* = 12) associated themselves with 'very high' sports physical self-concept in both the pre- and post-unit surveys. Table 9.6 presents the mean scores for pre- and post-unit PASP survey data.

Qualitative insights into learning in the Sport Education–social emotional learning unit

Observation data relating to learning and teaching within the context of the Sport Education–social emotional learning unit were gathered via weekly lesson

TABLE 9.5 Levels of self-report sports physical self-concept

	Survey level				
	Very low	Low	High	Very high	Total
Pre–unit	0 (0%)	1 (4%)	5 (21%)	18 (75%)	24
Post–unit	0 (0%)	0 (0%)	4 (17%)	20 (83%)	24
Per cent change	0	− 4%	− 4%	+ 8%	

TABLE 9.6 Mean scores of students' self-report sports physical self-concept

	Boys (n = 12)	Girls (n = 12)	All students
Pre–unit	176.75	149.67	163.21
Post–unit	177.17	154.75	165.96
Score change	+ 0.42	+ 5.08	+ 2.75

observations. From a learning perspective, observation specifically focused on the five core social and emotional competencies identified by CASEL (2008).

Self-awareness

During the unit, students demonstrated a propensity for self-reflection and thoughtfulness. This was observed during reflection time with students sharing how they applied the social skills learned during the season in settings such as the home, playground and street. For example, one student said, 'I practised controlling my mouth and my temper more at the playground and my friends now like to play with me more.' In another lesson, the students demonstrated high levels of personal awareness when they were asked to discuss the assigning of non-playing roles. One student made the following comment when he was asked to be a scorekeeper:

> I am not so good with numbers and so, can I give it [scorekeeper role] a go the next time? Now, I just like to be a coach 'cos I'm good at explaining the skills and I'm a patient person.

Social awareness

During the course of the unit, there were many instances where students demonstrated the capacity to sense their classmates' emotions, understand others' perspectives and take an active interest in their teammates' concerns. In completing the captain nomination forms, students were able to articulate why their nominees would be capable of undertaking the role. One student wrote, 'He makes things fun, would cheer on his team and is good at making decisions.' During the first phase of the unit, there were several occasions when players argued with the refer-ee's decision. However, there were fewer such incidents as the unit progressed. One student explained, 'Performing the role of referee myself helps me understand why it is not so easy to be a good referee. Now I argue less with the referee.'

Self-management

On occasions, competition situations generated negative emotions such as frustra-tion, anxiety and aggressiveness in some of the students. However, when this occurred, teammates were quick to try to calm students down. One student said to a teammate, 'Cool down Wally and stop arguing with the linesman, you are mak-ing us lose fair play points.' During team goal-setting sessions, students also showed that they were able to cooperatively set goals and develop strategies to improve team performance. Having agreed upon their goal as 'to improve our passing skills' one team then went to plan practice sessions during their recess.

Responsible decision-making

There were many occasions where students were observed making responsible decisions and showing respect to each other. Students shook hands with each other before and at the end of each game without prompting from the teacher. They also used the 'game sense' ideas introduced to them and, by applying tactical decision-making, started to play a much better game towards the end of the season. One team captain demonstrated a sense of personal responsibility by asking the teacher for permission to practise during their recess time. Duty teams also demonstrated responsible decision-making and associated behaviours in reporting punctually for their duty and showing commitment in carrying out their team tasks.

Relationship skills

This competency was the most visible during the season and particularly evident among the team captains. Interestingly, the teams that were doing well in the games were also the ones with captains who demonstrated strong relationship skills. For example, one captain proved herself to be a great motivator to her team. She would get her team to do a 'high-five' whenever the team scored a point and would clap and cheer her team-mates on encouragingly even if they lost a point. Another captain was particularly good at resolving conflicts among the players. In one instance, a conflict broke out between the line judge and a player over the official's decisions. The captain was able to calm his angry teammate down quickly and persuaded him to accept the decisions.

Quantitative and qualitative data thus pointed to students extending their social emotional learning in and through the Sport Education–social emotional learning unit and to the unit presenting many positive learning experiences for students. From an observer perspective, visible improvements in students' approach to learning and to their peers were apparent. These results were particularly encouraging given the short duration of the unit.

While social emotional learning was the identified learning priority, it is important to acknowledge that, as in all physical education settings, teachers are necessarily concerned to address a number of aspects of learning. In our view, the focus on social emotional learning in this unit did not come at the expense of skill development. Observation data pointed to students also improving setting and digging skills. As the unit progressed, the rallies in the volleyball game became longer and more fluid. Similarly, the setting and passing skills among team members became more accurate as fewer mistakes were made. In considering factors contributing to these improvements, it is notable that students felt supported and encouraged by both peers and the teacher. They also voluntarily spent time practising during recess and lunch break.

There was also some evidence from the observation data to suggest that tactical awareness of the students improved during the unit. As the weeks progressed, the students became much better at placing their shots into open spaces. Use of the 'game sense' (Australian Sports Commission, 1997) approach and small-sided modified games helped students to understand tactical concepts and transfer learning to their volleyball games. Other studies have similarly demonstrated the capacity for tactical skills and understanding to be developed in Sport Education contexts (see, e.g., Hastie *et al.*, 2009; Pritchard *et al.*, 2008).

Focusing on pedagogy

This section (that again draws on observation data) focuses attention on implementation of the unit from the teacher's perspective. In so doing, it seeks to foreground the importance of pedagogy in achieving positive learning outcomes in the context of Sport Education.

Here we endeavour to explain how the physical education teacher effectively leveraged characteristics of Sport Education to bring about positive changes in students' social emotional learning. As indicated in our opening comments, we advocate for more research focusing on the pedagogy of Sport Education. As a small-scale case study, this project sought to offer a modest contribution to the Sport Education literature in this regard. We identify a number of strategies that observation revealed as contributing to social emotional learning being foregrounded in learning experiences and ensuring that opportunities for students to develop and demonstrate social emotional learning were created.

Creating problem-solving situations

Using small-sided games and the assignment of roles, teacher-embedded problem-solving situations arose throughout the unit and provided opportunities for students to variously develop self-management skills, decision-making skills and interpersonal skills. Using the 'Games Sense' approach (Australian Sports Commission, 1997), the teacher presented tactical problems within the small-sided games, thereby allowing students multiple opportunities to problem solve. Problem-solving opportunities, some of which related to relationship skills, were also embedded in duty team tasks and in tasks and in expectations associated with roles such as team captain, referee and coach.

Notably, the teacher acted as a motivator and facilitator in the problem-solving process, particularly through the use of questions to help students seek solutions to their problems individually and in groups. In their research findings, Dyson *et al.* (2004) have similarly emphasised the facilitator role of teachers as a key pedagogical consideration in the implementation of the Sport Education model. With the teacher's guidance, the students responded well to the problem-solving situations and, as a result, became more confident and competent in problem-solving. Sports Board members also met with the physical education teacher and the teacher-researcher once a week during recess to resolve issues and problems arising during the season.

Fostering an inclusive learning environment

The teacher successfully used the mixed ability teams, fair play points system and 'Most Valuable Person' awards to encourage students to include all members of the class in the games, avoid an undue emphasis on winning and embrace the importance of playing fairly in a sporting manner. At the beginning of the unit, the teacher explained to the students that he would use the fair play point system to recognise their efforts to be inclusive of each other. During the unit the teacher made use of 'teachable moments' arising to award the fair play points and reinforce inclusive behaviours among students.[3] The following incident is an example of the physical education teacher reinforcing inclusion students:

> PE teacher: Randel, your teammate made a mistake in sending the ball off the court. You did not criticise her and, yet, gave her a pat on the back. I would like to award your team another fair point play for the kindness you show towards your teammate.

Incidents such as this indicated that the award system contributed to the students' ability to empathise (social awareness) with each other. The teacher also used inclusion games (Hellison, 1995) to promote empathy and inclusion. For example, he instigated the 'all-touch' rule in the volleyball game in which the ball must be passed to everyone in the team before it can be hit over to the opposition's court. The mixed gender teams and the strategies for promoting inclusion among players possibly contributed to the improvements seen in the social emotional learning measures of the girls particularly. The potential for Sport Education to be directed towards enhancing the learning experiences of girls has previously been highlighted, for example in Ennis' (1999) work. In Ennis' study and in this project, boys also valued the experience as contributing members of teams.

As the teams were formed with students of differing skill levels, the teacher also modified the competition rules to enhance involvement of all students. This was consistent with the view expressed by Dyson *et al.* (2004) that modification of the game complexity level can help teachers match game complexity with student game play development. For instance, in order to increase the chance of a player with weaker setting and digging skills successfully returning an incoming shot, players were allowed to choose their method of returning the shot. Weaker players could choose to catch and toss, the ball over the net instead of using dig or set. Better players could also choose catch and toss, but most chose to challenge themselves by using the dig and set instead. Hence, the modification of the game rules achieved its aim to increase the opportunity for players of differing skills to achieve personal success and, at the same time, contribute positively to the team.

Fostering teamwork and cooperation among students

The teacher made very effective use of the persisting team structure in Sport Education to actively promote teamwork, cooperation and affiliation and, thus, engage students with learning linked to relationship skills. This was manifested in students providing support for each other and showing respect for one another. The non-playing roles, the structure of games and competition were also oriented so as to contribute to an emphasis on mutual respect, particularly in relation to varied playing ability. The students understood that they needed to rely on and have confidence in each other in order for competitions to run smoothly. The duty team ensured that the equipment was set up properly while the refereeing team ensured that the games began on time and players abided by the competition rules. The teacher also instigated a rule whereby students were to shake hands with their opponents before and after each game. After a while, this became an integral part of team behaviour and accepted conduct in the lessons.

The choice of the Newcombeball also contributed to the smooth implementation of the unit as a whole and, specifically, to fostering teamwork and cooperation. While contact and/or territorial sports games may give rise to many conflict situations, these may be less frequent and/or 'intense' in net games. Without undue distractions from having to manage conflict, the teacher was able to focus on promoting the desired learning.

Being supported and being committed!

At this point, it is worthwhile highlighting further factors contributing to the successful implementation of the Sport Education–social emotional learning unit. First, the support of the principal was important in empowering the teacher and enabling some timetable changes to accommodate the unit. Second, the willingness of the teacher to devote additional time to aspects of Sport Education such as meetings with the Sport Board and arrangements for the culminating event was important. As others have also highlighted, Sport Education is arguably a demanding pedagogy (e.g. Kim *et al.*, 2006). The teacher also had the benefit of the fact that the class selected comprised a group of students who were generally better behaved than other classes that the teacher taught. Given that the teacher was using Sport Education for the first time, this was regarded as a desirable situation. While other classes may have presented more challenging teaching and learning situations and, possibly, also presented greater diversity in relation to students' pre-existing levels of social emotional learning, it was regarded as important for the teacher to be able to try a new pedagogy and new teaching focus in a supportive rather than overly challenging context.

Issues, problems and challenges

Despite the above emphasis that implementation constituted a positive teaching and learning experience, the unit was not without its problems and challenges. Three major issues were identified in this regard.

The first issue was the limited amount of time available for instruction in each 45-minute lesson. During the initial phase of the season particularly, trying to encompass instructional and managerial tasks associated with Sport Education, teaching through the 'Games Sense' approach and simultaneously teaching responsibility using TPSR, all in the context of 45-minute lessons, presented a demanding pedagogical challenge.

Hastie (2000) stressed the importance of establishing a rigorous managerial task system if students are to have a successful season. The early phase of the season appeared to be the most challenging for the teacher in terms of balancing instructional and managerial tasks. During this phase, the teacher devoted a lot of time to teaching class protocols such as game format and rules, instruction on scoring, keeping statistics, refereeing and learning about the various duty team functions. This meant that the time then available to explicitly focus on teaching personal and social skills while also introducing tactical game concepts was limited. However, subsequently (and particularly once students were familiar with the core features of Sport Education) the teacher found the 45-minute lessons less restrictive.

The pedagogical skills to effectively manage Sport Education learning contexts are arguably understated in much literature. This study reaffirmed that, particularly in the initial weeks of Sport Education, trying to maximise learning opportunities for all students can be a challenging task. The teacher in this study had to deal with confusion over competition rules and protocols while also trying to help a group to work out differences among themselves. With the students yet to learn conflict resolution processes, the teacher was working out the problems on the first court, just as the teams on the second court were presenting another set of problems. Amidst handling the managerial issues, the teacher struggled to teach social skills and games concepts. Hastie and Curtner-Smith (2006) alluded to this challenge in highlighting that teaching using both Sport Education and teaching games for understanding pedagogical models simultaneously could be labour intensive. The fact that this was the first time the students were exposed to more self-directed learning approaches contributed to these teething problems experienced in our study. Fortunately, the researcher acting as a co-teacher was able to provide much needed managerial support in the early part of the unit.

The third issue that we became very aware of was work intensification for the teacher as a result of adopting the Sport Education model. Although the unit ultimately provided the students with a very enriching learning experience, the time and workload contributed by the teacher and co-teacher were significant. Kim *et al.* (2006) asserted that it would be a gross mistake to interpret the promotion of greater responsibility for students as in any way reducing the work of the teacher. This study supported this emphasis and their accompanying call for research that can generate more insights into 'what it takes' for teachers to effectively implement Sport Education.

Conclusion

In conclusion, this study shed some light on the potential pedagogical connections that can be made between Sport Education and social emotional learning. This was demonstrated by the successful design and implementation of a Sport Education unit with a specific focus on social emotional learning and by positive learning outcomes being achieved. Given the small sample size and the short length of this study, we necessarily advise caution in interpretation of the findings. Most of all, this study has presented a strong case for more research which explores the prospective adaptation of Sport Education to specifically support the development of social emotional learning and which tracks the impact of such learning experiences on students' social and emotional well-being over a sustained period of time. Such research clearly needs to be undertaken in a range of school contexts and with a longitudinal design. This would prompt advances in curriculum planning within a Sport Education framework to address how learning experiences can systematically seek to extend students' social emotional learning. In our view, the Sport Education–social emotional learning partnership has much to offer physical education internationally. We hope that this study will inspire others to further explore its potential.

Notes

1 The nomenclature of the learning area varies across Australia. The term Health and Physical Education is used here to include variations.
2 The assessment framework in the new Tasmanian curriculum comprised five standards encompassing 15 stages of learning.
3 See Penney *et al.* (2005) for further discussion and illustration of 'teachable moments' being utilised in Sport Education.

References

ACER. (2008) *Social-emotional well-being survey.* Available HTTP: http://www.acer.edu.au/sewbs/survey.html (accessed 17 November 2010).

Ang, S.C., Penney, D. and Swabey, K. (2009) 'The role of Sport Education in achieving social and emotional learning outcomes in the context of the new Tasmania Health and Wellbeing curriculum', *Physical Education Matters*, 4(2): 29–33.

Australian Government Department of Health and Aging (2006) *KidsMatter implementation manual*, Barton, ACT: Commonwealth of Australia.

Australian Sports Commission (1997) *Game sense: Developing thinking players*, Belconnen: ASC.

Carlson, T.B. (1995) '"Now I think I can": The reaction of year eight low-skilled students to Sport Education', *The ACHPER Healthy Lifestyles Journal*, 42(4): 6–8.

Carlson, T.B. and Hastie, P.A. (1997) 'The student social system within Sport Education', *Journal of Teaching in Physical Education*, 16: 176–183.

CASEL (2008) *Social emotional learning skills and competencies*. Available HTTP: http://www.casel.org/basics/skills.php (accessed 17 November 2010).

Dyson, B., Griffin, L. and Hastie, P.A. (2004) 'Sport Education, tactical games, and cooperative learning: Theoretical and pedagogical considerations', *Quest*, 56: 226–240.

Ennis, C.D. (1999) 'Creating a culturally relevant curriculum for disengaged girls', *Sport, Education and Society*, 4: 31–49. doi:10.1080/1357332990040103

Hastie, P.A. (2000) 'An ecological analysis of a Sport Education season', *Journal of Teaching in Physical Education*, 19: 355–373.

Hastie, P.A. and Buchanan, A.M. (2000) 'Teaching responsibility through Sport Education: Prospects of a coalition', *Research Quarterly for Exercise and Sport*, 71: 25–35.

Hastie, P.A. and Curtner-Smith, M.D. (2006) 'Influence of a hybrid Sport Education-teaching games for understanding unit on one teacher and his students', *Physical Education and Sport Pedagogy*, 11: 1–27. doi:10.1080/17408980500466813

Hastie, P.A. and Sharpe, T. (1999) 'Effects of a Sport Education curriculum on the positive social behaviour of at-risk rural adolescent boys', *Journal of Education for Students Placed at Risk*, 4: 417–430.

Hastie, P.A., Sinelnikov, O.A. and Guarino, A.J. (2009) 'The development of skill and tactical competencies during a season of badminton', *European Journal of Sport Science*, 9: 133–140. doi:10.1080/17461390802542564

Hellison, D. (1995) *Teaching responsibility through physical activity*, Champaign, IL: Human Kinetics.

Hellison, D., Cutforth, N., Kallusky, J., Martinek, T., Parker, M. and Stiel, J. (2000) *Youth development and physical activity*, Champaign, IL: Human Kinetics.

Hunter Institute of Mental Health (2000) *Social and emotional wellbeing*. Retrieved from http://www.responseabilty.org

Kim, J., Penney, D., Cho, M. and Choi, H. (2006) '"Not business as usual": Sport Education pedagogy in practice', *European Physical Education Review*, 12: 361–379. doi:10.1177/1356336X06071469

McGrath, H. (2000) *THE BOUNCE BACK! Resiliency program: A pilot study*. Available HTTP: http://www.kidsmatter.edu.au/programs-guide/bounce-back (accessed 17 November 2010).

Mitchell, S.A., Oslin, J.L. and Griffin, L.L. (2006) *Teaching sport concepts and skills: A tactical games approach* (2nd ed.), Champaign, IL: Human Kinetics.

Penney, D., Clarke, G., Quill, M. and Kinchin, G. (2005) *Sport Education in physical education: Research based practice*, London: Routledge.

Pope, C. and Grant, B.C. (1996) 'Student experiences in Sport Education', *Waikato Journal of Education*, 2: 103–118.

Pritchard, T., Hawkins, A., Wiegand, R. and Metzler, J.N. (2008) 'Effects of two instructional approaches on skill development, knowledge, and game performance', *Measurement in Physical Education and Exercise Science*, 12: 219–236. doi:10.1080/10913670802349774

Siedentop, D. (1994) *Sport Education: Quality PE through positive sport experiences*, Champaign, IL: Human Kinetics.

Siedentop, D., Hastie, P.A. and van der Mars, H. (2004) *Complete guide to Sport Education*, Champaign, IL: Human Kinetics.

Tasmanian Department of Education (2008) *The Tasmanian Health and Wellbeing curriculum*. Available HTTP: http://www.education.tas.gov.au/curriculum (accessed 17 November 2010).

University of Tasmania (2008) *Physical Activity and Sport Profile Survey instrument*, unpublished work.

10

EXPLAINING THE ATTRACTION

Understanding the motivational responses of students to Sport Education

Tristan Wallhead

As Mr. Orr stood with his class roster in the corner of the gymnasium he noticed Jake, the equipment manager for the Eagles team, was the first to come out of the locker room. Jake headed straight for the equipment room and grabbed four cones, two rugby balls, and five sets of blue tags for his team. He quickly set up his four cones in a 15 by 15 yard square and progressed to put on his tag belt. "Morning Jake," Mr. Orr stated. "Remember today's warm-up is yesterday's 2v1 practice." Before Mr. Orr had finished his sentence several of Jake's teammates had joined him and were busy putting on their tag belts. Jake instructed his teammates to quickly split into pairs and get between two of the cones. "When I say go you can make a pass to your teammate and then you have to try and get past me to score a try between these other two cones," Jake stated. Within this short time Mr. Orr noticed that many of the other teams had also set out their cones and had started the 2v1 practice in their home base areas. "Three points to the Eagles for being the first full team getting started today," Mr. Orr shouted across the gym. "Team referees please come to me." The referees of each team quickly ran over to Mr. Orr. "Remember in the first 4v4 game you are particularly looking for forward pass violations and also fair play. A team starts with three fair play points. Every time there is a negative comment to a teammate, the opposition or the referee will take a point away. Eagles you are playing the Condors, Ravens you are playing the Hummingbirds. Let's get started." The referees ran back to their teams and within 30 seconds had organized their four starting players to their relative try line. Mr. Orr moved to the midline of the gymnasium to where the referees were situated and overheard Sarah, the coach of the Hummingbirds, say to her team, "Remember when you receive the ball run forward and don't pass until you are about to be tagged . . . oh and also remember don't argue with the referee." Mr. Orr watched carefully as his teams played a 10-minute tag rugby game. The referees were doing a good job making calls and keeping the game flowing so he decided to do some formative assessment of the Condors' performance on maintaining width in attack . . .

This scenario provides a brief illustration of typical teacher and student behavior within a lesson of Sport Education. Within the instructional structure of Sport Education, students gradually assume greater responsibility for learning as teachers relinquish traditional "up-front" direct teaching roles. The teacher assumes the role of facilitator to student skill and social development through a range of peer teaching strategies which differ from the traditional teacher-directed model of instruction. These structural features were designed to provide positive motivational sport experiences for all students in physical education through simulating key contextual features of authentic sport (Siedentop et al., 2004).

Motivation has been defined as the direction and intensity of behavior (Gill, 2000). Direction refers to the activities in which students choose to participate, and intensity is the magnitude of effort applied within those activities. From the narrative vignette, it is obvious that the students in Mr. Orr's class were exhibiting positive motivational behavior in physical education. Students attended to their specific role responsibility assignments within the structure of the group learning tasks. They were also quick to respond to instructions and maintained a high level of participation within assigned tasks. Motivated or enthusiastic student participation is a primary goal of Sport Education (Siedentop, 1994). Throughout the Sport Education literature, a common theme of student engagement in tasks and participating within the defined roles has emerged. Teacher (Alexander et al., 1996) and student (Bennett and Hastie, 1997) anecdotal accounts have provided evidence of a high level of participation within all phases of a Sport Education season. Authors who have utilized quantitative observations of student behavior have provided empirical evidence to validate these claims (Hastie, 1996; Hastie and Sinelnikov, 2006). This high level of behavioral engagement within Sport Education has also manifested in positive affective consequences including increased students' perceptions of fun (MacPhail et al., 2008), interest (Hastie and Sinelnikov, 2006), and enjoyment (Wallhead and Ntoumanis, 2004). These affective consequences of motivated behavior in physical education have increasing value within contemporary health-related discourse related to the role of physical education in promoting youth physical activity. A major motive young people give for participating in sport and physical activity is fun and enjoyment (Crocker et al., 2004). Several researchers have also shown that enjoyment of physical education is positively associated with levels of extracurricular physical activity (Sallis et al., 1999; Trost et al., 1997). Therefore, it seems plausible that providing fun and enjoyable physical education experiences may enhance students' motives for physical activity participation (Garn and Cothran, 2006).

Empirical evidence would suggest that Sport Education is an attractive and motivating experience for many students in physical education. The purpose of this chapter is to summarize what we currently understand about the psychosocial mechanisms that may undergird these motivated responses. The two psychosocial frameworks of achievement goal orientation and self-determination theory will be utilized to interpret students' motivational response to Sport Education. In addition to an overview of these frameworks, this chapter will provide a synopsis of research that has utilized these frameworks to examine students' motivational responses to Sport Education. Finally, future avenues of research will be proposed that may serve to further enhance our understanding of the widespread motivational attraction of Sport Education to students.

Achievement goal orientation

During the last two decades, achievement goal perspectives have been employed to explain and understand students' affective and behavioral responses within an achievement setting (Dweck, 1990; Nicholls, 1989). Sport-based physical education satisfies the criteria as an achievement context as the physical competence of a student is always on display and can easily and regularly be evaluated by the self and others against a normative standard (Warburton and Spray, 2009). Early iterations of goal orientation theory suggested that two primary achievement goals existed to explain students' perceptions of their competence. The first goal is to demonstrate superior ability relative to peers and is called performance (ego) goal orientation. The second goal is to develop self-referenced competence or gain mastery of a task and is labeled mastery (task) goal orientation (Dweck, 1990). These dispositional goal orientations are viewed as independent constructs (Nicholls, 1989). That is, a student could be high in both orientations, or low in both, or low in one and high in another (Walling and Duda, 1995). Research in physical education has shown that the two goal orientations relate to different behavioral and affective students' motivational responses, such as choice of task difficulty, persistence, and enjoyment. Students with a high mastery orientation tend to choose challenging tasks and report higher levels of persistence and enjoyment (Ntoumanis and Biddle, 1999). In contrast, students with a high performance orientation, particularly if low in mastery orientation, tend to avoid more challenging tasks as they may jeopardize their normative perception of competence.

Achievement goal orientations are purported to explain students' motivation at the individual level. At the situational level, achievement goal theorists (e.g., Ames, 1992) have suggested that different instructional structures influence students' adoption of the different achievement goals. Epstein (1989) coined the acronym TARGET to represent six structures of the achievement context, or motivational climate, which influence student motivation. These structures are task, authority, reward, grouping, evaluation, and time. The task structure refers to what students are asked to learn. The authority structure refers to the type and degree of participation and decision-making students are permitted in the instructional process. The reward structure addresses how students are recognized for their progress and achievement, and the grouping structure deals with the distribution of student diversity within working groups. Evaluation refers to the standards established for student learning, whether self- or normative-referenced, clear or ambiguous, and whether publicly or privately announced. The time structure is the pace of instruction, including the amount and flexibility of time allocated for student practice, task completion, and student learning.

Ames (1992) contended that the way teachers operationalize these structures determines, to a great extent, children's motivational responses. For example, an instructional structure which offers task variety, involves students in the decision-making, promotes work in heterogeneous groups, and emphasizes self-referenced criteria for evaluation and recognition would promote a higher mastery-involving motivational climate. In contrast, in a more performance-involving climate, the teacher would dictate the organization and timing of tasks, and evaluation criteria would be more public and referenced based upon the demonstration of superior normative ability. Consistent with research in the classroom settings (Ames and Archer, 1988), research in physical education has shown that a mastery climate is viewed as more beneficial for student development (Ntoumanis and Biddle, 1999). Xiang and Lee (2002) found that, as students progress into the upper grade levels, they tend to be more inclined toward a performance goal orientation. For these older students, providing a dual climate which supports both mastery and performance may be important for allowing students of both styles to perceive and demonstrate competence (Biddle, 2001).

Though not specifically designed to address the TARGET structures, it has been proposed that Sport Education has many similarities with the contextual features of a mastery-involved climate (Wallhead and Ntoumanis, 2004). Within Sport Education, students work within persistent heterogeneous groups for the duration of an extended season. The instructional structure of Sport Education also facilitates students' decision-making and responsibility within the learning process as teachers relinquish traditional "up-front" direct teaching roles. The teacher often acts as facilitator as students are given various role responsibilities for teaching each other skills and knowledge within a cooperative group learning structure. Students are also often involved in developing and utilizing evaluation systems that provide individual accountability within a group structure. These evaluation systems are clearly tied to rewards that emphasize social and team development.

Research examining the influence of Sport Education on changes in students' motivation using an achievement goal perspective has provided evidence of the efficacy of the model in eliciting positive student affective outcomes that are linked to a mastery-involved climate (Spittle and Byrne, 2009; Wallhead and Ntoumanis, 2004). Wallhead and Ntoumanis (2004) found that a season of Sport Education increased a group of male high-school students' perceived effort and enjoyment of basketball. These affective responses were predicted by changes in perceptions of a mastery-involving climate and perceived autonomy. Spittle and Byrne (2009), in a similarly designed comparative study, revealed that middle-school-aged students perceived elements of the Sport Education model to maintain their competence and perception of a mastery-involved climate better than a traditional teacher-directed unit of soccer. The relatively small effect of Sport Education on students' perception of a mastery climate across both studies suggests further research is required to clarify the cognitive mechanisms that are facilitating the positive affective responses. Although the use of persistent team membership and peer teaching responsibilities may foster a more mastery-involving climate, the inherent formal competition within the latter stages of a Sport Education season may also create a more performance-oriented environment (Wallhead and Ntoumanis, 2004). Sinelnikov and Hastie (2010) provided support for this proposition with their objective analysis of the motivational climate operant within a Sport Education season. These authors found that the Sport Education motivational climate was a combination of mastery-oriented and performance-oriented approaches, with a mastery climate predominating within the practice phase of the season and performance-based criteria operant within the latter formal competition phase of the unit. This dual climate may have positive implications for allowing students of both orientations to perceive and demonstrate competence (Biddle, 2001). For some lesser skilled low master-oriented students, this climate may be perceived more as a threat to the self and so attenuate some of the positive aspects of Sport Education. Sinelnikov and Hastie (2010) have suggested that, to promote a more mastery-oriented climate within the competition phase of Sport Education, teachers should focus on developing evaluation and recognition structures that privately reward self-referenced improvement. To provide greater insight into the cognitive mechanisms that are facilitating positive motivational responses future studies should correlate objective climate assessments with both the students' perceptions of a mastery or performance climate, and their affective and behavioral responses.

Research in which students' motivational responses to Sport Education using achievement goal perspectives have been examined is limited by its sole reliance on the dichotomous version of the achievement model. The two goals described previously focus exclusively on approach forms of motivation, that is, the need to achieve competence. More recent propositions have suggested the existence of social goals (Gable, 2006) and avoidance goals, namely mastery, performance, and social avoidance goals (Elliot, 1999; Elliot and McGregor, 2001; Elliot et al., 2006). Social goals have been added as findings in education have demonstrated that aspects of social relationships in the classroom can influence performance on achievement tasks (Shah, 2003). The addition of social goals also serves to reduce the artificial separation of social and achievement domains often seen in motivational research (Garn and Sun, 2009). The addition of the avoidance distinction was made because individuals do not always approach achievement tasks, and not doing worse than previous experiences (i.e., mastery avoidance), not being outperformed by others (i.e., performance avoidance), or being afraid of rejection (i.e., friendship avoidance) can also be motivating factors. In the physical education domain, research has shown that these qualitatively different types of motivation are associated with a differential pattern of outcomes (Guan et al., 2006; Wang et al., 2007). Social approach goals have been shown to be a powerful predictor of students' reported expenditure of persistence and effort in a physical education setting

(Guan *et al.*, 2006). Performance avoidance goals often lead to maladaptive achievement outcomes including being negative predictors of both effort and persistence. In some more contemporary studies in which goal perspectives are used, researchers have proposed that goal cluster profiles, rather than individual goals, within the 3 × 3 model may be more informative in understanding affective and behavioral motivational responses in physical education. In a sample of middle-school students, Garn and Sun (2009) reported that three main goal profiles emerged. These goal profiles were high approach, low achievement and moderate social, and low social. The high-goals group reported the most adaptive motivational responses while the low achievement, moderate social goal group reported the least adaptive responses within the PACER fitness test in physical education.

Further research is required to examine the influence of Sport Education on students' motivational outcomes using the 3 × 3 version of the achievement goal framework. A growing body of evidence suggests that Sport Education is effective in developing student social skills (Wallhead and O'Sullivan, 2005) and that team affiliation is one of the key motivating factors within the model (O'Donovan, 2003). Therefore, the inclusion of the social approach-avoidance goals would seem pertinent for better understanding the students' attraction to Sport Education. The categorization of participating students into different goal profiles may also provide a sharper lens to examine how students of different motivational orientations respond to the structural features of Sport Education. This line of inquiry would stimulate more informed discussion of student choices of specific role responsibilities and different group-based contingencies that may maximize student participation and enjoyment.

Self-determination theory

Self-determination theory (SDT) is a dialectic, organismic theory of human motivation (Deci and Ryan, 2000). Central to the theory is the distinction between autonomous and controlling forms of motivation. This distinction is often viewed on a continuum reflecting the perceived origin or cause of an individual's motivated behavior in a given context – known as the perceived locus of causality (Ryan and Connell, 1989). Autonomous motivation reflects engaging in a behavior because it satisfies personally relevant goals. The prototypical form of autonomous motivation is intrinsic motivation, which lies at one extreme of the perceived locus of causality continuum and represents behavioral engagement with no external contingency or reinforcement, either real or perceived. Individuals intrinsically motivated to perform an activity will participate in that activity spontaneously and free from any external reinforcement. Alongside intrinsic motivation lie three forms or qualities of extrinsic motivation. Extrinsically motivated behaviors are those that are instrumental to some separable outcome. Identified regulation is a motivational construct that lies adjacent to intrinsic motivation and represents motivation to engage in a behavior because the behavior services an intrinsic or personally relevant goal, for example choosing to be physically active to lose weight. Introjected regulation reflects participating in a behavior due to perceived internal pressure such as avoiding negative affective states like shame or guilt or gaining contingent self-worth or pride. Adjacent to introjected regulation lies external regulation, which reflects the prototypical form of extrinsic motivation. External regulation reflects engaging in behaviors due to external reinforcement such as rewards and praise or through the avoidance of negative reinforcements, such as punishment. Located at the opposite extreme to intrinsic motivation on the continuum, amotivation is the lack of desire to engage in, or participate within, a specific setting. While SDT does not contend to represent the different forms of autonomous motives on a linear continuum, students who operate past the threshold of autonomy between introjected and identified regulation will be more self-determined in their behavior. Higher forms of self-determined behavior in physical education have been associated with more positive cognitive, affective, and behavioral outcomes including enhanced concentration (Standage et al., 2003), student learning (Chen, 2001), and intention to participate in physical activity (Ntoumanis, 2005).

SDT posits that the form of autonomous motivation adopted within a context or activity will be dependent on the satisfaction of the three basic and universal psychological needs for autonomy, competence, and relatedness (Deci and Ryan, 2000). To the extent that the behaviors and activities fulfill the goals to satisfy those needs, individuals will experience increased levels of desirable outcomes, such as satisfaction. Autonomy refers to the basic need to experience one's behavior as self-endorsed or volitional. To provide support for autonomy within an educational setting requires providing students with a sense of control or choice over their behavior. Empirical evidence suggests that teachers who listen to students, create time for independent work, give students opportunities to talk, praise signs of improvement and effort, offer progress-enabling hints, and respond to student questions will foster an autonomy-supportive environment (Reeve and Jang, 2006). In contrast, behavioral control connotes leading and pressurizing students toward a teacher-defined way of behaving. Competence is understood as a perception of being able to demonstrate success within a given context (Harter, 1999). Several factors influence the satisfaction of the need for competence including task difficulty, reinforcement provided by others, and individual goal orientations. Experiencing success on optimally challenging tasks will enhance students' perceptions of competence and lead to more internal perceptions of control. Contingent, positive reinforcement provided for mastery attempts will also enhance perceptions of competence as it serves to foster a more mastery-involved climate, thus enhancing the students' perception of self (Harter, 1981). Relatedness is defined as having a connection with peers who are deemed significant to the student (Baumeister and Leary, 1995). Relatedness can be viewed as acceptance among peers and teachers, a high degree of social support, and/or positive friendship qualities. Social interactions that support relatedness are commonly perceived as empathetic and caring, which includes encouragement statements between peers who serve to help classmates (Baumeister and Leary, 1995). Since students may prioritize one or a combination of needs as influential for their motivation, no single need can be deemed more beneficial than another. Therefore, providing students with an educational environment which supports all three psychosocial needs has been proposed to be a critical antecedent for influencing positive student motivation (Vallerand, 2001). With its emphasis on a student-centered pedagogy, team performance competency, and affiliation strategies, contemporary sport pedagogy researchers have hypothesized that Sport Education may be an appropriate instructional model to satisfy all three needs.

One of the primary goals of Sport Education is for students to become competent performers in the focused activity. Siedentop (1994) defined competency within Sport Education as students having "sufficient skills to participate in games satisfactorily and being able to understand and execute strategies appropriate to the complexity of the game being played" (p. 4). Early large-scale trials of Sport Education in Australia provided some initial teacher evidence that Sport Education may be effective in facilitating motor skill improvement (Alexander et al., 1996). More recent quantitative assessments of changes in student game competency have suggested that the model is efficacious in developing team-play efficiency and tactical awareness (Hastie, 1998; Hastie et al., 2009). The findings on students' perceptions of increases in competency have been more equivocal. Student interview data from earlier Sport Education studies provided some initial evidence that the model was effective in facilitating individual motor skill improvement (Carlson, 1995; Pope and Grant, 1996). These findings have not been as well replicated within comparative group design studies. Participants in these studies consistently report nonsignificant increases in perceptions of competency as a result of participating in a Sport Education season (Spittle and Byrne, 2009; Wallhead and Ntoumanis, 2004). This finding may be an artifact of a relatively small sample size or short intervention duration, but more qualitative evaluative projects in which the dynamics of the teaching–learning process in Sport Education were examined suggest that there may be some didactic transposition flaws evident within peer-assisted learning tasks. A study specifically designed to analyze content development within a Sport Education season showed that the coach-led tasks were only efficacious in developing participants' knowledge and performance of lower complexity psychomotor learning goals (Wallhead and O'Sullivan, 2007). Participants failed to learn higher order content due to deficiencies in the student coach's ability to effectively elaborate content through appropriate demonstration, error diagnosis, and task modification (Wallhead and O'Sullivan, 2007). These didactic barriers to the effective transposition of content within peer-assisted learning tasks may provide some explanation for the equivocality of findings related to students' reported increase in competency.

The findings from a recent study, which utilized SDT to qualitatively examine students' perceptions of Sport Education, provide an alternative insight into students' conceptualization of changes in competence. Perlman and Goc Karp (2010) found that students within Sport Education identified participation in game play, completion of roles, and meeting fair play guidelines as key criteria to demonstrate competence. This conceptualization of competence goes beyond reflections of changes in individual skill or tactical performance that are typically accessed through motivation surveys. This finding highlights that Sport Education may develop competence but this need satisfaction is based upon a broader view of success that extends beyond perceptions of individual change in motor skill or tactical performance (Perlman and Goc Karp, 2010). Examining the influence of Sport Education on competence in future studies should include more expansive conceptualizations of this psychosocial need that includes more process and formative outcomes that move beyond typical individual skill proficiencies.

Baumeister and Leary (1995) viewed relatedness as creating a sense of support within a social context. Deci and Ryan (1985) stated that providing a social context which supports relatedness is achieved through the development of peer connections and empathetic actions, such as inclusivity-promoting behaviors. This notion of relatedness seems to have been inherent within Siedentop's (1994) original conceptualization of the model. He argued that the use of persisting groupings is one of the most important features of Sport Education as it allows students an increased opportunity to interact and work toward common group goals and thus foster social development (Siedentop, 1998). Research on this structural feature of Sport Education has provided a strong body of evidence to support this proposition. Early trials of the model provided anecdotal evidence that teachers perceived Sport Education to be fostering students to "develop qualities such as teamwork, peer support and active pursuit of socially responsible and equitable participation beyond what was evident in previous teaching" (Alexander et al., 1996, p. 37). Student data also supported these findings, with participants reporting an increase in cooperation between peers (MacPhail et al., 2004; Pope and Grant, 1996). Several authors have suggested that the key social structure within Sport Education which drives the development of positive peer interactions is team affiliation (Bennett and Hastie, 1997; MacPhail et al., 2004; O'Donovan, 2003). Recent examinations using an SDT framework has provided further support for this notion. Perlman and Goc Karp (2010) found that providing students the opportunity to be on the same team developed social connections and understanding of the uniqueness of classmates that was beyond experiences in other classes. These social connections which manifest in positive inclusive behaviors, such as providing lesser skilled teammates with positive feedback statements within game play, resulted in increased participation (Perlman and Goc Karp, 2010). Although Sport Education seems to satisfy students' need for relatedness, further research is required to identify specific instructional strategies within Sport Education that may enhance this outcome. For example, Perlman and Goc Karp (2010) identified the collaborative development of a fair play rubric as being critical for the initial enhancement of class empathy and a reduction in negative sporting behaviors during game play. Instructional strategies such as these may not be as prevalent within differing iterations of Sport Education across the globe and require more evidence-based support.

Autonomy support is achieved when students perceive their educational setting to provide them with a sense of control or choice over their behavior. Arguably, the structural feature of Sport Education that provides the greatest opportunity for control and choice resides within the pedagogy of student role responsibility. With the infusion of different role responsibilities, including coach, referee, trainer, or scorer, Sport Education teachers are provided an opportunity to utilize autonomy-supportive behaviors that are more difficult to implement within teacher-directed styles. Student role responsibilities require the formation of cooperative learning groups, where the teacher is able to provide students with time for independent work and opportunities for content-related dialog, yet still offer progress-enabling hints when required. All of these teacher behaviors, if utilized regularly within Sport Education, give students a level of choice and control over their learning that is not normally present within a teacher-directed pedagogy. Research that has specifically examined the influence of Sport Education on perceived autonomy support is limited. Using the transcontextual model of motivation (TCM) to examine the effect of Sport Education on extracurricular physical activity, Wallhead *et al.* (2010) revealed that Sport Education had only a small effect on elementary students' perception of teacher and peer autonomy support. This relatively small increase in perceived autonomy support did, however, exert a significant influence on autonomous motives in physical education, which highlights the importance of utilizing autonomy-supportive teacher behaviors effectively within Sport Education. It also provides potential insight into the difficulty some teachers have in facilitating autonomy within the prescriptive nature of instruction, which is inherently controlling (Ryan and Grolnick, 1986). To maintain more effective content development within the coach-led tasks of Sport Education students, teachers often provide student coaches task cards that delineate the organization and feedback required to maintain an effective program of action within the task (Wallhead and O'Sullivan, 2007). This pedagogy adds a level of didactic prescription to cooperative learning group dynamics that may reduce the perception of autonomy support. Teachers utilizing Sport Education must carefully balance the need for effective content development with facilitating student choice and control. This may be achieved by gradually allowing coaches more choices on the content and timing of tasks as the season progresses, or by the infusion of collaborative fair play rubrics (Perlman and Goc Karp, 2010) or game design tasks (Hastie and Curtner-Smith, 2006).

Recent studies have provided evidence that the structural features of Sport Education have the potential to move students along the continuum of perceived locus causality to more autonomous forms of motivation. Wallhead *et al.* (2010) found that two seasons of Sport Education facilitated a moderate increase in autonomous motivation in both Native American and Caucasian elementary students. This finding was replicated by Sinelnikov *et al.* (2007) who found that in a group of Russian secondary students Sport Education maintained high levels of autonomous motivation throughout all phases of the season. More qualitative examinations of changes in students' autonomous motives suggest that this effect may be explained by students passing through the threshold of autonomy from external to more intro-jected/identified forms of motivation regulation (Perlman and Goc Karp, 2010). Within the initial phases of a Sport Education season, students were compliant with the structural features of Sport Education such as role responsibilities and fair play game rubrics due to teacher provision of external regulation through rewards and punishment contingency protocols. As the season progressed, students began to internalize their motives for participation within these structures and rationalized them through introjected and identified forms of motivation (Perlman and Goc Karp, 2010). The results of these studies provide some strong preliminary evidence that the structural features of Sport Education move students toward more autonomous forms of motivation in physical education. This finding has some potentially important health-related physical activity implications for adolescent populations.

Vallerand and Ratelle (2002) hypothesized that the forms of motivation from the perceived locus of causality could be conceptualized as operating at three levels of generality: global, contextual, and specific. Motivation at the contextual level represents autonomous motivation to engage in a variety of behaviors in a given context (Ryan and Connell, 1989), such as physical education or leisure-time physical activity (Chatzisarantis *et al.*, 2003). Vallerand and Ratelle (2002) also hypothesize that there is cross-contextual interplay between motivation at the contextual level, suggesting that motives in one context can affect motivation in others. For example, if an individual exhibits a high level of autonomous motivation in an educational context, such as physical education, this may also influence the formation of an autonomous motivational orientation in another related context outside of school, such as leisure-time physical activity. This hypothesized transfer of autonomous motivation across contexts is central to the TCM (Hagger *et al.*, 2003). Research using the TCM to examine the efficacy of Sport Education in promoting motivation from a physical education to a leisure-time physical activity context is in its preliminary stages. The findings of a recent study suggested that Sport Education had a positive effect on student autonomous motivation in physical education which transferred to motivation to participate in physical activity within a school-based lunch recess sport club context (Wallhead *et al.*, 2010). Penney *et al.* (2002) suggested that physical education programs should focus on being "connective specialisms" (p. 55); in other words, agents of change to provide life chances for students in other arenas of physical activity. Much of the research completed to date has demonstrated that Sport Education is an effective mechanism to positively transform students' motivation in physical education, but this transformation has been confined to school-allocated curricular time. If a transformative agenda is to be pursued, further research utilizing the TCM to examine the influence of Sport Education on students' motivation for extracurricular physical activity participation is required. This work should include targeting "at-risk" adolescent populations, who have limited financial opportunities, but operate within a collectivist culture that highly values sport-based participation.

Summary

It is clear from the expansive empirical evidence that has emerged from the examination of students' responses to Sport Education that the structural features of the model are inherently attractive to students in physical education. Students consistently report higher enjoyment and exerting more effort within tasks in Sport Education than within traditional teacher-directed approaches to sport-based instruction. Despite this appeal, our understanding of the psychosocial mechanisms that are facilitating these positive student responses are still in their infancy. Preliminary studies using achievement goal perspectives have provided indications that Sport Education has similarities with the contextual features of both a mastery and performance-involved climate. Although this orientation may fit with the competency goals of many secondary-aged students, a more comprehensive approach which includes examination of changes in students' social goals may provide a more thorough explanation of students' positive motivational responses to Sport Education.

From a self-determination perspective, there is emerging evidence that Sport Education moves students along the continuum of perceived locus of causality to more autonomous forms of motivation. How this outcome is achieved requires further examination. Empirical evidence from other educational and work domains highlights the importance of providing students with an environment that supports all three psychosocial needs of competence, relatedness, and autonomy to move students toward more self-determined forms of motivation. Preliminary evidence would suggest that Sport Education is most efficacious in developing students' perceptions of relatedness, and to some degree competence. Since students may prioritize one or a combination of these needs as influential for their autonomous motivation, further research is needed to examine the influence of Sport Education on the satisfaction of specific needs and the influence this satisfaction has on changes in autonomous motives for physical education. Preliminary evidence of students' perception of autonomy support within Sport Education would also suggest that this is one of the most important, yet underutilized, facets of the model. Future iterations of Sport Education should include more overt use of autonomy-supportive teaching behaviors that consistently prioritize students' levels of choice and control within tasks.

In common with the predominance of sport pedagogy research in which investigations have utilized motivational theory to explain students' responses in physical education, the Sport Education literature, to date, has been limited by its deficiencies in longevity and transformation. Much of the discussion of the attractiveness of Sport Education to students has been based upon reflections of data from students' experience of one or two seasons of Sport Education within curricular time. Although encouraging, if we are to vaunt Sport Education as a panacea for sport-based instruction, a more transformative agenda needs to be pursued. This agenda should initially include research that examines changes in students' motivation in physical education after more longitudinal participation in Sport Education. It should also examine the influence of these motivational changes on students' perspectives on sport and physical activity participation from a more global perspective. This latter proposition mimics one of Siedentop's (1994) original statements about Sport Education:

> I do not pretend that a one semester Sport Education experience in the 10th grade is going to have any far reaching implications for our collective life.

On the other hand, I would be most distressed if students who experienced Sport Education repeatedly over several years of schooling were not somehow changed in ways that eventually impact on the larger sport culture.

(p. 9)

This is truly an authentic goal for any instructional model, but one that requires more empirical examination if it is to be achieved by Sport Education.

References

Alexander, K., Taggart, A., and Thorpe, S.T. (1996) "A spring in their steps? Possibilities for professional renewal through Sport Education in Australian schools," *Sport, Education and Society*, 1: 23–46. doi:10.1080/1357332960010102

Ames, C. (1992) "Achievement goals and the classroom climate," in G.C. Roberts (ed.) *Motivation in sport and exercise* (pp. 161–176), Champaign, IL: Human Kinetics.

Ames, C. and Archer, J. (1988) "Achievement goals in the classroom: Students' learning strategies and motivational processes," *Journal of Educational Psychology*, 80: 260–267.

Baumeister, R. and Leary, M.R. (1995) "The need to belong: Desire for interpersonal attachments as a fundamental human motivation," *Psychological Bulletin*, 117: 497–529.

Bennett, G. and Hastie, P. (1997) "A Sport Education curriculum model for a collegiate physical activity course," *Journal of Physical Education, Recreation and Dance*, 68(1): 9–44.

Biddle, S.J.H. (2001) "Enhancing motivation in physical education," in G.C. Roberts (ed.) *Advances in motivation in sport and exercise* (pp. 101–127), Champaign, IL: Human Kinetics.

Carlson, T.B. (1995) "Now I think I can: The reaction of eight low-skilled students to Sport Education," *ACHPER Healthy Lifestyles Journal*, 42(4): 6–8.

Chatzisarantis, N.L.D., Hagger, M.S., Biddle, S.J.H., Smith, B., and Wang, C.K.J. (2003) "A meta-analysis of perceived locus of causality in exercise, sport, and physical education contexts," *Journal of Sport and Exercise Psychology*, 25: 284–306.

Chen, A. (2001) "A theoretical conceptualization for motivation research in physical education: An integrated perspective," *Quest*, 2: 35–58.

Crocker, P., Hoar, S., McDonough, M., Kowalski, K., and Niefer, C. (2004) "Emotional experience in youth sport," in M. Weiss (ed.) *Developmental sport and exercise psychology: A lifespan perspective* (pp. 197–222), Morgantown, WV: Fitness Information Technology.

Deci, E.L. and Ryan, R.M. (1985) *Intrinsic motivation and self-determination in human behavior*, New York: Plenum.

Deci, E.L. and Ryan, R.M. (2000) "The 'what' and 'why' of goal pursuits: Human need and the self-determination of behavior," *Psychological Inquiry*, 11: 227–268. doi:10.1207/S15327965PLI1104_01

Dweck, C.S. (1990) "Self-theories: Their role in motivation, personality, and development," in R. Dienstbier (ed.) *Nebraska symposium in motivation: Perspectives on motivation* (Vol. 38, pp. 199–235), Lincoln, NE: University of Nebraska Press.

Elliot, A.J. (1999) "Approach and avoidance motivation and achievement goals," *Educational Psychologist*, 34: 169–189.

Elliot, A.J., Gable, S.L., and Mapes, R.R. (2006) "Approach and avoidance motivation in the social domain," *Personality and Social Psychology Bulletin*, 32: 378–391. doi:10.1177/0146167205282153

Elliot, A.J. and McGregor, H.A. (2001) "A 2 × 2 achievement goal framework," *Journal of Personality and Social Psychology*, 80: 501–519. doi:10.1037//0022-3514.80.30501

Epstein, J. (1989) "Family structures and student motivation: A developmental perspective," in C. Ames and R. Ames (eds.) *Research on motivation in education: Vol. 3* (pp. 259–295), New York: Academic Press.

Gable, S.L. (2006) "Approach and avoidance social motives and goals," *Journal of Personality*, 74: 175–222. doi:10.1111/j.1467-6494.2005.00373.x

Garn, A.C. and Cothran, D.J. (2006) "The fun factor in physical education," *Journal of Teaching in Physical Education*, 25: 281–297.

Garn, A.C. and Sun, H. (2009) "Approach-avoidance motivational profiles in early adolescents to the PACER fitness test," *Journal of Teaching in Physical Education*, 28: 400–421.

Gill, D.L. (2000) *Psychological dynamics of sport and exercise* (2nd ed.), Champaign, IL: Human Kinetics.

Guan, J., Xiang, P., McBride, R., and Bruene, A. (2006) "Achievement goals, social goals, and students' reported persistence and effort in high school physical education," *Journal of Teaching in Physical Education*, 25: 58–74.

Hagger, M.S., Chatzisarantis, N.L.D., Culverhouse, T., and Biddle, S.J.H. (2003) "The processes by which perceived autonomy support in physical education promotes leisure-time physical activity intentions and behavior: A trans-contextual model," *Journal of Educational Psychology*, 95: 784–795.

Harter, S. (1981) "A model of intrinsic mastery motivation in children: Individual differences and developmental change," in W.A. Collins (ed.) *Minnesota symposium on child psychology* (Vol. 14, pp. 215–255), Hillsdale, NJ: Erlbaum.

Harter, S. (1999) *The construction of the self: A developmental perspective*, New York: Guilford Press.

Hastie, P.A. (1996) "Student role involvement during a unit of Sport Education," *Journal of Teaching in Physical Education*, 16: 88–103.

Hastie, P.A. (1998) "Skill and tactical development during a Sport Education season," *Research Quarterly for Exercise and Sport*, 69: 368–379.

Hastie, P.A. and Curtner-Smith, M. (2006) "Influence of a hybrid Sport Education–teaching games for understanding unit on one teacher and his students," *Physical Education and Sport Pedagogy*, 11: 1–27. doi:10.1080/17408980500466813

Hastie, P.A. and Sinelnikov, O.A. (2006) "Russian students' participation in and perceptions of a season of Sport Education," *European Physical Education Review*, 12: 131–150. doi:10.1177/1356336X06065166

Hastie, P.A. Sinelnikov, O.A., and Guarino, A.J. (2009) "The development of skill and tactical competencies during a season of badminton," *European Journal of Sport Science*, 9: 133–140. doi:10.1080/17461390802542564

MacPhail, A., Gorely, T., Kirk, D., and Kinchin, G. (2008) "Children's experiences of fun and enjoyment during a season of Sport Education," *Research Quarterly for Exercise and Sport*, 79: 344–355.

MacPhail, A., Kirk, D., and Kinchin, G. (2004) "Sport Education: Promoting team affiliation through physical education," *Journal of Teaching in Physical Education*, 23: 106–122.

Nicholls, J.G. (1989) *The competitive ethos and democratic education*, Cambridge, MA: Harvard University Press.

Ntoumanis, N. (2005) "A prospective study of participation in optional school physical education using a self-determination theory framework," *Journal of Educational Psychology*, 97: 444–453. doi:10.1037/0022-0663.97.3.444

Ntoumanis, N. and Biddle, S.J.H. (1999) "A review of motivational climate in physical activity," *Journal of Sports Sciences*, 17: 643–665.

O'Donovan, T.M. (2003) "A changing culture? Interrogating the dynamics of peer affiliations over the course of a Sport Education season," *European Physical Education Review*, 9: 237–251. doi:10.1177/1356336X030093003

Penney, D., Clarke, G., and Kinchin, G.D. (2002) "Developing PE as a 'connective specialism': Is Sport Education the answer?" *Sport, Education and Society*, 7: 55–64. doi:10.1080/13573320120113576

Perlman, D.J. and Goc Karp, G. (2010) "A self-determined perspective of the Sport Education model," *Physical Education and Sport Pedagogy*, 15(4): 401–418. doi: 10.1080/17408980903535800

Pope, C. and Grant, B.C. (1996) "Student experiences in Sport Education," *Waikato Journal of Education*, 2: 103–118.

Reeve, J. and Jang, H. (2006) "What teachers say and do to support students' autonomy during a learning activity," *Journal of Educational Psychology*, 98: 209–218. doi:10.1037/0022-0663.98.1.209

Ryan, R.M. and Connell, J.P. (1989) "Perceived locus of causality and internalization: Examining reasons for acting in two domains," *Journal of Personality and Social Psychology*, 57: 749–761.

Ryan, R.M. and Grolnick, W.S. (1986) "Origins and pawns in the classroom: Self-report and projective assessments of individual differences in children's perceptions," *Journal of Personality and Social Psychology*, 50: 550–558.

Sallis, J., Prochaska, J., Taylor, W., Hill, J., and Geraci, J. (1999) "Correlates of physical activity in a national sample of girls and boys in grades four through twelve," *Health Psychology*, 18: 410–415.

Shah, J. (2003) "A motivational looking glass: How significant others implicitly affect goal appraisals," *Journal of Personality and Social Psychology*, 85: 424–439.

Siedentop, D. (1994) *Sport Education: Quality PE through positive sport experiences*, Champaign, IL: Human Kinetics.

Siedentop, D. (1998) "What is Sport Education and how does it work?" *Journal of Physical Education, Recreation and Dance*, 69(4): 18–20.

Siedentop, D., Hastie, P., and Van der Mars, H. (2004) *Complete guide to Sport Education*, Champaign, IL: Human Kinetics.

Sinelnikov, O.A. and Hastie, P. (2010) "A motivational analysis of a season of Sport Education," *Physical Education and Sport Pedagogy*, 15: 55–69. doi:10.1080/17408980902729362

Sinelnikov, O.A., Hastie, P., and Prusak, K.A. (2007) "Situational motivation in a season of Sport Education," *ICHPER-SD Research Journal*, 2: 43–47.

Spittle, M. and Byrne, K. (2009) "The influence of Sport Education on student motivation in physical education," *Physical Education and Sport Pedagogy*, 14: 253–266. doi:10.1080/17408980801995239

Standage, M., Duda, J.L., and Ntoumanis, N. (2003) "A model of contextual motivation in physical education: Using constructs from self-determination and achievement goal theories to predict physical activity intentions," *Journal of Educational Psychology*, 95: 97–110.

Trost, S., Pate, R., Saunders, T., Ward, M., Dowda, W., and Felton, G. (1997) "A prospective study of the determinants of physical activity in rural fifth-grade children," *Preventive Medicine*, 26: 257–263.

Vallerand, R.J. (2001) "A hierarchical model of intrinsic motivation sport and exercise," in G.C. Roberts (ed.) *Advances in motivation in sport and exercise*, Champaign, IL: Human Kinetics.

Vallerand, R.J. and Ratelle, C. (2002) "Intrinsic and extrinsic motivation: A hierarchical model," in E.L. Deci and R.M. Ryan (eds.) *Handbook of self-determination research* (pp. 37–63), Rochester, NY: University of Rochester Press.

Wallhead, T.L. Hagger, M., and Smith, D.T. (2010) "Sport Education and extra-curricular sport participation: An examination using the trans-contextual model of motivation," *Research Quarterly in Exercise and Sport*, 81: 442–455.

Wallhead, T.L. and Ntoumanis, N. (2004) "Effects of a Sport Education intervention on students' motivational responses in physical education," *Journal of Teaching in Physical Education*, 23: 4–18.

Wallhead, T.L. and O'Sullivan, M. (2005) "Sport Education: Physical education for the new millennium?" *Physical Education and Sport Pedagogy*, 10: 181–210. doi:10.1080/17408980500105098

Wallhead, T.L. and O'Sullivan, M. (2007) "A didactic analysis of content development during the peer teaching tasks of a Sport Education season," *Physical Education and Sport Pedagogy*, 12: 225–243. doi:10.1080/17408980701610177

Walling, M.D. and Duda, J.L. (1995) "Goals and their associations with beliefs about success and perceptions of the purposes of physical education," *Journal of Teaching in Physical Education*, 14: 150–156.

Wang, C.K.J., Biddle, S.J.H., and Elliot, A.J. (2007) "The 2 × 2 achievement goal framework in a physical education context," *Psychology of Sport and Exercise*, 8: 147–168.

Warburton, V.E. and Spray, C.M. (2009) "Antecedents of approach–avoidance achievement goal adoption in physical education: A longitudinal perspective," *Journal of Teaching in Physical Education*, 28: 214–232.

Xiang, P. and Lee, A. (2002) "Achievement goals, perceived motivational climate, and students' self-reported mastery behaviors," *Research Quarterly for Exercise and Sport*, 73: 58–65.

PART III

Professional development
for Sport Education

11

PREPARING PRESERVICE PHYSICAL EDUCATION TEACHERS TO TEACH SPORT EDUCATION

Matthew D. Curtner-Smith

In the earlier chapters of this book, you would have noted that there is a significant amount of research available which describes the impact of Sport Education on pupils and their teachers. By comparison, the body of work examining Sport Education physical education teacher education (SE-PETE) is not nearly as well developed, still in its infancy, and has included the programs at only a very few universities and colleges within very few countries. Nevertheless, the studies of SE-PETE that have been carried out to date, combined with theories drawn from other lines of sport pedagogy inquiry and some logical extrapolation from the research of the model as delivered by inservice teachers in schools, does provide some fairly solid clues as to how to go about preparing teachers to teach this relatively new and exciting form of physical education.

The primary goal of this chapter, then, is to explore this research and these theories in order to provide sport pedagogy faculty working in universities and colleges with some sound advice on how to train the preservice teachers in their charge to successfully employ the Sport Education pedagogical model. To this end, I begin by explaining why Sport Education is a model that is relatively easy to sell to most preservice teachers and how to go about doing so. In the second section of the chapter, I outline the conditions which are a prerequisite for successful SE-PETE and the various models and strategies that sport pedagogy faculty can employ in their methods and content courses, as well as early field experiences and student teaching, in order to give them the best chance of producing effective teachers of Sport Education. Third, I describe preservice teachers' interpretations and misconceptions of the model together with the problems that they have had implementing it during early field experiences and their culminating student teaching experience. Finally, I conclude the chapter by examining the potential for preservice teachers to employ the model once they graduate and move into the workforce.

Selling Sport Education to preservice teachers

Sociological advantages of Sport Education

The notion that PETE faculty have to "sell" good models of instruction to the preservice teachers in their programs and convince them to use these pedagogies on graduation must seem very strange to most interested parties outside of teacher education. Such is the power of preservice teachers' acculturation (i.e., pre-PETE socialization), however, that anyone who has taught a methods course will attest to the difficulty of changing the beliefs and values about practice with which their charges enter PETE. During this acculturation period, the primary socialization agents and contexts are preservice teachers' parents, siblings, teachers, coaches, their own schooling, particularly extracurricular sport and PE, and participation in sport outside of school (see Curtner-Smith, 2001, 2009; Lawson, 1983a, 1983b; Stran and Curtner-Smith, 2009a). Lawson (1983a, 1983b) was the first to observe that, collectively, these influences appear to produce two types of PETE recruits: those with coaching orientations and those with teaching orientations.

Coaching-oriented recruits are mainly attracted to a career in physical education by the opportunity to work with extracurricular school teams and view teaching curricular physical education as a "career contingency." They are more likely to be male, to have attended schools that prioritize extracurricular sport over physical education, and been successful in school sport themselves.

Teaching-oriented recruits, by contrast, are attracted to the profession by the prospect of teaching curricular physical education and view coaching extracurricular teams as a career contingency. They are more likely to be female, to have been pupils in schools that prioritized physical education over extracurricular sport, and to have participated in nontraditional forms of physical activity.

Teaching-oriented recruits are much more likely to take on the beliefs and practices espoused and modeled by PETE faculty than coaching-oriented recruits. Recruits with "moderate-coaching orientations" (Curtner-Smith *et al.*, 2008; Sofo and Curtner-Smith, 2010; Stran and Curtner-Smith, 2009a) who are not totally committed to sport can be convinced to change their beliefs and values regarding physical education, at least partially (Sofo and Curtner-Smith, 2010). The evidence, however, is that most recruits who are particularly successful in school sport themselves, and so develop "hard core coaching orientations" (Curtner-Smith *et al.*, 2008), are extremely difficult if not impossible to turn (Sofo and Curtner-Smith, 2010).

Faced with this scenario, it seems logical to suggest that PETE faculty will have more success in influencing the beliefs, values, and pedagogies of the majority of preservice teachers in their programs if they attempt to teach them models of instruction that are at least somewhat compatible with their acculturation. Sport Education is one such model (Collier, 1998; Curtner-Smith and Sofo, 2004b; Curtner-Smith *et al.*, 2007, 2008; Stran and Curtner-Smith, 2009a). It is innovative, yet its focus on authentic sport and its similarity to extracurricular sport make it more appealing to teaching and moderately coaching-oriented preservice teachers and, perhaps, to some recruits with hard core coaching orientations, than traditional multiactivity focused teaching, other innovative forms of instruction, or nonteaching (Curtner-Smith and Sofo, 2004b; Curtner-Smith *et al.*, 2007). Moreover, it will not be lost on recruits that, of all the innovative models they are taught during PETE, Sport Education is most likely to appeal to the teachers who will be their colleagues on graduation and so meet relatively less resistance and gain more support if they attempt to implement it. These sociological advantages Sport Education has over other curricular models, then, mean that selling it to preservice teachers should be a relatively easy task with a comparatively greater chance of success. They are also the reason for suggesting that the model might play a key role in breaking the "cycle of non-teaching physical education teachers" in the United States (Curtner-Smith, 2009; Curtner-Smith and Sofo, 2004b).

Structural advantages of Sport Education

As well as emphasizing the similarity of Sport Education with good-quality extra-curricular sport and other "real" sporting forms, a second key strategy that PETE faculty can use to sell the model to preservice teachers is to emphasize and highlight its structural advantages over traditional multiactivity teaching which even teaching-oriented recruits are likely to favor. Moreover, the results of several studies (e.g., Curtner-Smith and Sofo, 2004b; McCaughtry *et al.*, 2004; Sofo and Curtner-Smith, 2010) indicate that it is also important to make comparisons of Sport Education with both good-quality traditional instruction and the kind of noneducational low-quality interpretation of the traditional model that is taught in many American secondary schools (see Curtner-Smith, 2009; Ennis, 1999; Locke, 1992). This can be done during class discussions and by requiring preservice teachers to teach high-quality Sport Education seasons and traditional units to similar classes so that they experience the advantages for themselves (see Curtner-Smith and Sofo, 2004b, for an example of this strategy).

Alexander *et al.* (1996) provided an overview of the main structural advantages of Sport Education over traditional teaching. These authors emphasized that teachers instructing through Sport Education are "off center-stage" because the model is largely driven by pupil activity and decision-making. This provides more time for teachers to reflect on their practice which, in turn, serves to reduce stress and creates space for professional renewal. In contrast, Alexander *et al.* explained that traditional multiactivity teaching is relatively labor-intensive because the teacher is constantly having to drive the model and is always "center-stage." Additionally, and based on the work of Macdonald (1999) and Seashore-Louis and Smith (1990), Alexander and Luckman (2001) suggested that Sport Education is more appealing to teachers than the traditional multiactivity model because it is relatively empowering and more professionally satisfying due to the improved relationships with pupils facilitated by its structure.

Hastie (2003) came to similar conclusions following a synthesis of the ecological work he had conducted on the model with a number of others (Carlson and

Hastie, 1997; Hastie and Pickwell, 1996; Hastie and Siedentop, 1999). Specifically, he pointed out that, during traditional multiactivity instruction, teachers are constantly required to refocus pupils as they attempt to socialize with each other. Conversely, during Sport Education this kind of intervention is not often necessary since the model incorporates the pupil social system without compromising instructional effectiveness. Consequently, the teacher does not take on the role of "ringmaster," manages less, instructs more, and is not forced to negotiate a reduction in accountability with pupils in exchange for their compliance.

Examining Sport Education from a slightly different perspective, Ennis (1999) described how the model creates positive forces which make the teacher's life more comfortable by promoting "positive social relations" and a "sense of community" among pupils and teachers. In addition, she observed that dominant boys taught through Sport Education are unable to undermine the teacher since ownership and authority are shared by all members of a class.

By comparison, Ennis (1999) noted that the "curricular scaffolding" of the traditional multiactivity model leads to the production of "negative forces" and is of little help to teachers. Consequently, even well-taught traditional multiactivity units require a significant commitment of time and energy by the teacher to make sure pupils are not overly competitive, aid those pupils with less skill, encourage positive social interactions between pupils, and ensure pupils are on-task. Ennis went on to suggest that the stress the traditional multiactivity model puts on the teacher may well cause burnout, emotional fatigue, "instructional neglect," and ultimately lead to a move out of physical education.

Finally, sport pedagogy faculty attempting to convince preservice teachers that Sport Education is a model that they should employ can draw on some of the research which strongly suggests that the structural advantages of Sport Education lead to improved outcomes for pupils. For example, Browne *et al.* (2004) found that pupils taught through both Sport Education and traditional multiactivity units improved their knowledge of key concepts to a similar degree but noted that pupils taught through Sport Education gained a greater understanding of game play. Similarly, Hastie and Trost (2002) discovered that pupils taught within a Sport Education season engaged in levels of health-promoting moderate to vigorous physical activity (MVPA) that exceeded those which had been observed in studies of traditional multiactivity teaching (e.g., Curtner-Smith *et al.*, 1995, 1996). Moreover, two studies (Spittle and Byrne, 2009; Wallhead and Ntoumanis, 2004) suggested that pupils taught through Sport Education gained more than those taught through traditional multiactivity instruction in terms of the effort they thought they gave, enjoyment, and their perceptions of competence.

Cultural advantages of Sport Education

A third strategy that PETE faculty might employ when marketing the Sport Education model to incoming recruits is to focus on its cultural advantages over traditional forms of instruction. Specifically, the goal is to help preservice teachers see the increased cultural relevance Sport Education has for pupils when compared to traditional multiactivity teaching which has largely been unearthed by research and thinking from a critical perspective.

Building on the opinions of Kirk and Almond (1999) and Lave and Wenger's (1991) concepts of "legitimate peripheral participation" in "communities of practice" and "situated learning," Alexander and Luckman (2001) made the cultural relevance case succinctly. These authors noted that Sport Education was more culturally relevant for pupils because it necessitated their taking part in authentic learning activities which were similar to sporting experiences they might engage in outside of school. In addition, and based on Tinning and Fitzclarence's (1992) work, Alexander *et al.* (1996) suggested that Sport Education was more compatible with postmodern youth culture than traditional instruction.

Conditions, models, and methods for SE-PETE

Prerequisite conditions

Regardless of the specific methods faculty use in an attempt to prepare their charges to employ the Sport Education model, the literature and research concerned with the effectiveness of PETE indicates that, for the best chance of success, a number of key conditions should exist within programs (see Lawson, 1983a, 1983b; Stran and Curtner-Smith, 2009a).

Professional socialization through PETE normally exerts least influence on physical education teachers as it cannot overcome the combined power of acculturation and organizational socialization (i.e., the influence of the school culture on newly graduated teachers). Many PETE programs have little or no impact on preservice teachers and instead serve to affirm and solidify the misconceived ideas with which coaching-oriented recruits enter and to deter teaching-oriented recruits from progressing into the profession. Those PETE programs that do have a positive influence on preservice teachers are generally staffed by credible specialist sport pedagogists with innovative orientations to the subject who directly challenge preservice teachers' faulty beliefs and ideas about practice and provide tight supervision of early field experiences and student teaching. Moreover, faculty in high-quality PETE programs tend to agree on a professional ideology and what Lortie (1975) referred to as a "shared technical culture" (i.e., the knowledge and pedagogical skills required to teach physical education).

Organizational considerations

As well as examining their PETE programs for the presence and absence of favorable conditions, sport pedagogy faculty may contemplate and consider different organizational approaches they might take in order to gain optimal results in terms of preservice teachers learning how to deliver Sport Education effectively. More traditional PETE programs might take a *foundational approach* when training preservice teachers to employ Sport Education and other curricular models. My own university's PETE program is an example of such an approach (Curtner-Smith et al., 2009). In this program, my colleagues and I teach a series of secondary, elementary, and advanced methods and content courses and supervise a series of early field experiences in which we begin by emphasizing key pedagogies and pedagogical concepts and theories which are foundational to all the curricular models we focus on later in the program (these are Sport Education, traditional multiactivity, teaching games for understanding, health-related fitness, and the skill themes approach). For us, these foundational pedagogies and pedagogical concepts and theories include the effectiveness literature (see Graham and Heimerer, 1981; Silverman, 1991), Mosston's spectrum of teaching styles (see Mosston and Ashworth, 2008), critical approaches to physical education (see Curtner-Smith and Sofo, 2004a), constructivism, classroom ecology (see Hastie and Siedentop, 1999), knowledge types (see Shulman, 1987), and value orientations (see Jewett, 1994).

An alternative to this more traditional organizational approach, which is congruent with what could be termed more recent thinking (e.g., see Metzler, 2005), is a *models-based approach*. This involves teaching self-contained methods courses and early field experiences for each curricular model the program faculty decide their preservice teachers should learn to deliver, including Sport Education. A key difference of this models-based approach from the foundational approach is that pedagogies and pedagogical concepts and theories are not taught in isolation but if, as, and when they are relevant to the understanding and delivery of each model. A downside of utilizing the models-based approach might be that it does not allow for the infusion of Sport Education (or other models) throughout a PETE program, a strategy that gives preservice teachers time to assimilate and comprehend the model and increase the likelihood that they will be able to deliver it successfully (Collier, 1998; Jenkins, 2004; McCaughtry et al., 2004; Stran and Curtner-Smith, 2009a).

Pedagogical packages

Those few SE-PETE programs which have been investigated or described to date have employed various pedagogical strategies as a package in an attempt to prepare preservice teachers to use the model. For example, the three programs examined by Curtner-Smith et al. (2008) and the programs outlined by Jenkins (2004) and Collier (1998) employed the pedagogical packages described in Table 11.1.

The strategies and methods that comprise the various pedagogical packages of SE-PETE as shown in Table 11.1 can be classified as university based (e.g., discussions, participating in a Sport Education season, reading articles), field based (i.e., teaching mini- and full Sport Education seasons to school children), or those which fall somewhere in between (e.g., watching a film of Sport Education and peer teaching). All these strategies and methods appear to have a positive effect on preservice teachers but are more effective when part of the overall package (Curtner-Smith et al., 2008; Stran and Curtner-Smith, 2009a). Moreover, it seems reasonable

TABLE 11.1 Pedagogical packages employed in five SE–PETE programs

SE–PETE program 1 (Curtner-Smith *et al.*, 2008)
- Class discussions of SE with a sport pedagogy faculty member
- Reading articles about SE
- Watching a film of SE being taught at a local school
- Guest lecture by a teacher from a local school who employed the SE model
- Observing at a local school where the SE model was employed
- Participating in a season of SE taught by a sport pedagogy faculty member

SE–PETE program 2 (Curtner-Smith *et al.*, 2008)
- Class discussions of SE with a sport pedagogy faculty member
- Reading articles about SE
- Reading sample lesson plans from an SE unit
- Participating in sample lessons of SE taught by a sport pedagogy faculty member
- Teaching one full season of SE during the culminating student teaching practice

SE–PETE program 3 (Curtner-Smith *et al.*, 2008)
- Class discussions of SE with a sport pedagogy faculty member
- Reading Siedentop's (1994) text on SE
- Teaching two 10-lesson miniseasons of SE during early field experiences
- Teaching three full seasons of SE during the culminating student teaching practice

SE–PETE program 4 (Jenkins, 2004)
- Class discussions of SE with a sport pedagogy faculty member
- Reading Siedentop's (1994) text on SE
- Participating in a season of SE taught by a sport pedagogy faculty member
- Formal reflection assignment on own participation in a SE season
- Group presentations of alternative SE seasons
- Teaching full SE seasons to university students enrolled in activity courses
- Teaching full SE seasons in early field experiences and/or the culminating student teaching practice

SE–PETE program 5 (Collier, 1998)
- Participating in a season of SE taught by a sport pedagogy faculty member
- Observing at a local school where the SE model was employed
- Watching a film of SE being taught at a local school
- Reading articles about SE
- Class discussions of SE with a sport pedagogy faculty member
- Workshop for PTs and inservice teachers
- Teaching SE to peers
- Teaching full SE seasons in early field experiences and/or the culminating student teaching practice

to suggest that the more of these strategies and methods employed, the more potent the package.

Initially, preservice teachers are more likely to gain a thorough understanding of the model if sport pedagogy faculty employ university-based strategies and methods. Away from the pressures of teaching, where practical and pragmatic issues naturally come to the fore, preservice teachers have space to contemplate and consider the theoretical underpinnings of the model in more depth (Jenkins, 2004; Sofo and Curtner-Smith, 2010).

Some research also suggests that, during the early stages of SE-PETE, faculty should give priority to preservice teachers gaining curricular knowledge (Stran and Curtner-Smith, 2010) as well as mastering indirect teaching styles (Parker and Curtner-Smith, 2009) and pedagogies linked with the construction of a task-involving motivational climate (Parker and Curtner-Smith, 2010) and pupils engaging in high levels of MVPA (Parker and Curtner-Smith, 2005). In addition, faculty should be careful not to give preservice teachers the impression that merely employing the Sport Education model is a guarantee that masculine bias and sexism in physical education is rejected and combated (Parker and Curtner-Smith, in press).

Of key importance, however, is the opportunity for preservice teachers to teach a progressive series of mini- and full seasons of Sport Education during early field experiences and student teaching (Curtner-Smith *et al.*, 2008; Jenkins, 2004; Stran and Curtner-Smith, 2009a). This should occur within favorable conditions, in terms of teacher support and supervision and pupil behavior and readiness, and while being closely supervised by faculty members who are well versed in the Sport Education model and hold preservice teachers accountable for following the model faithfully.

Gradually giving preservice teachers more autonomy to plan their Sport Education seasons and lessons also seems to be important (Collier, 1998; Curtner-Smith *et al.*, 2008; Stran and Curtner-Smith, 2009a). Preservice teachers' initial attempts to teach the model are more successful when they are provided with a season plan written by a faculty member from which they write lesson plans. This strategy ensures that preservice teachers include all elements of Sport Education and allows them to experience the model's structural advantages. Even within early field experiences, the strategy can result in preservice teachers focusing on the outcomes of their teaching and on the effects of the various components of Sport Education on pupils as opposed to being consumed with their own actions and management and discipline as they are when at the same stage of learning to employ other models (Curtner-Smith and Sofo, 2004b; Curtner-Smith *et al.*, 2007). During the teaching of subsequent seasons, requiring preservice teachers to base their own season plans on the original template also helps before giving them license to experiment with their own versions and ideas about implementing the model.

As well as progressing from university-based to field-based strategies and methods and faculty-planned to preservice teacher-planned Sport Education seasons, sport pedagogy faculty might consider following the sequence of progressions based on Sport Education concepts and content suggested by Collier (1998). The sequence begins by focusing on management issues unique to Sport Education, teaching preservice teachers how to organize teams and initiate sporting rituals, and examining authentic competitive formats. The second stage involves preservice teachers learning to develop content within the Sport Education framework so as to maximize pupil learning and skill development. The final stage is devoted to teaching preservice teachers how to assess pupils authentically through portfolios and using the statistics and records that are collected within Sport Education seasons.

Interpretations and misconceptions of Sport Education

Both inservice teachers and preservice teachers can "read" pedagogies differently and so produce varying interpretations of the same curricular frameworks and models (Gore, 1990). Providing these interpretations adhere to the spirit of a model and include all its elements, they can be considered as legitimate. If they do not, they can be classified as misconceptions. Importantly, for most models, including Sport Education, this means that the existence of a range of legitimate interpretations is possible and probable.

Knowledge of the limited amount of research on preservice teachers' interpretations and misconceptions of Sport Education, then, should help PETE faculty to assess whether their own preservice teachers' interpretations of the model are legitimate or misconceived. Such knowledge should also aid faculty to avoid their preservice teachers' misconceiving Sport Education in the first place or work to rectify misconceptions once they are detected.

Broad interpretations of Sport Education

Three broad ways in which preservice teachers and inservice teachers interpret and deliver Sport Education have been identified (Curtner-Smith *et al.*, 2008). Those delivering the *full version* of the model follow the spirit conveyed and include all the elements described and explained in the most widely read Sport Education texts (i.e., Siedentop, 1994; Siedentop *et al.*, 2004).

Those delivering a *watered-down* version of the model organize units of instruction around formal competition because it is a good management strategy, but stop short of including many of the other elements of the model which serve to make the sporting experience authentic. Often, this means that teachers will not allow pupils to take on different roles (particularly those less directly associated with participation in game play) and more responsibility or keep and post statistics and records. In addition, they may make little effort to create a festive atmosphere or include a culminating event. Alternatively, teachers who water Sport Education down may pervert elements of the model. For example, they may assign peripheral roles (e.g., scorekeeper, board member) to less able pupils while reserving central roles (e.g., captain, coach) for those who are athletically gifted.

Teachers who adopt a *cafeteria approach* to Sport Education pick and choose elements of the model to include within what is essentially traditional multiactivity instruction. They often fail to comprehend the structural and cultural advantages of employing the full version of the model, and, ironically given Sport Education's potential to ease management and disciplinary issues, are loath to relinquish control of their classes.

Higher quality SE-PETE, as described in the preceding section of this chapter, is likely to lead to preservice teachers employing the full version of Sport Education during early field experiences and student teaching more often and watering the model down or taking a cafeteria approach to it during these experiences less often. Moreover, sport pedagogy faculty should realize that the potential for preservice teachers to water down Sport Education or take a cafeteria approach to it will be increased if they enter PETE with moderate or strong coaching orientations. Conversely, preservice teachers who enter their programs with teaching orientations and are provided with high-quality SE-PETE are unlikely to attempt anything but the full version of the model.

Other legitimate interpretations of Sport Education

A number of studies have shown that it is possible for inservice teachers to deliver the full version of Sport Education while emphasizing different deep-rooted beliefs about the purpose of schooling or value orientations (Jewett, 1994). For example, teachers in Alexander and Luckman's (2001) study emphasized affective goals, Hastie and Buchanan (2000) focused on self-responsibility, Hastie and Curtner-Smith (2006) featured a combination of skill learning and learning how to learn, and Kinchin (1997, 1998) used the model in an attempt to facilitate social change. These foci led to slightly different but legitimate interpretations of the model.

The only study directly investigating the influence of preservice teachers' value orientations on their interpretation and delivery of Sport Education was completed by Stran and Curtner-Smith (2009b). One preservice teacher in this study had a moderate-coaching orientation and the other had a teaching orientation. Not surprisingly, both prioritized the disciplinary mastery perspective. This priority led to them delivering a conservative form of Sport Education during their student teaching practice in which they emphasized the learning of skills and strategies and showed great concern for the type of game forms in which they asked their pupils to participate. The priority also meant that, although present, some elements of the model were given less emphasis including the provision of opportunities for pupils to take on more responsibility. In addition, pupils' competency was given priority over their literacy and enthusiasm. Furthermore, during the course of the study, it became apparent that Sport Education was a good model through which preservice teachers could explore and consider different value perspectives. Toward the end of their seasons, the two preservice teachers began to use pedagogies that were consistent with the social reconstruction, self-responsibility, and self-actualization value orientations. Although their socialization dictates that most preservice teachers will interpret Sport Education conservatively and have a focus consistent with the disciplinary mastery value orientation, these findings suggest that faculty need to be ready to support and nurture preservice teachers with different emphases and hence different interpretations of Sport Education.

Other misconceptions of and problems with implementing Sport Education

The obvious and greatest danger of teaching Sport Education to preservice teachers with hard core coaching orientations is that they misunderstand the model altogether and use it to justify employing the nonteaching "model" many hope Sport Education will replace (see Alexander and Luckman, 2001; Alexander *et al.*, 1996; Curtner-Smith *et al.*, 2008). Aside from this major concern, four key misconceptions that have led to preservice teachers delivering the watered-down version of Sport Education or taking a cafeteria approach to the model are concerned with teaching within competitive games, the role of skill development in Sport Education, components of the model thought not central to encouraging pupil participation in activity, and length of seasons (Curtner-Smith and Sofo, 2004b; Curtner-Smith *et al.*, 2008; McCaughtry *et al.*, 2004).

Preservice teachers, who have themselves been taught through a series of progressive but isolated decontextualized skill practices and drills before playing games and participated in competitive sport that is largely coach controlled, tend not to have a well-developed understanding of tactics and strategies or the use of small-sided and conditioned games and so struggle to teach pupils once they are engaged in the competitive game play phases of a Sport Education season. Moreover, their frustration with the lack of skill displayed by their pupils during games leads them to retreat to what is safe and what they believe works—teaching through isolated skill practices and drills.

Again, mirroring the skill-to-game method by which they were taught as pupils during low-quality traditional multiactivity instruction, the conviction that skill development should come before game play, and if left to their own devices, means some preservice teachers will abandon the authentic sporting organizational formats (e.g., preseason, regular season, postseason) which full-version Sport Education calls for and revert to providing a series of lessons in which skills are taught in isolation before adding a tournament in which little or no instruction takes place.

Despite the strong research evidence to the contrary, some preservice teachers also believe that pupils do not enjoy taking on roles other than player during Sport Education seasons and are not capable of doing so. Consequently, they make little effort to teach these roles in the first place or to provide ongoing support for pupils who take them on. Furthermore, they are not convinced that pupils are motivated by being given more responsibility, a festive environment, or the recording and posting of statistics. In addition, they believe that these elements detract from their central mission which is engaging pupils in physical activity and skill learning. Moreover, they consider the effort needed to incorporate these elements to be unreasonably great and are concerned that it will be impossible to give once they graduate. Consequently, they suggest that, once free to make their own curricular decisions, they intend to water the model down by stripping away all of these components.

Another common preservice teacher misunderstanding is that pupils will tire of seasons that are much lengthier than traditional multiactivity units. This, they suggest, will result in boredom, counter efforts at skill teaching, and lead to managerial and disciplinary issues.

Ironically, all four of the key misconceptions described in the preceding paragraphs are partially the result of preservice teachers having a strong disciplinary mastery focus. To help counter them, faculty need to channel this focus in a more productive direction. This can be done by ensuring preservice teachers understand the model's goals before they attempt to employ it. In addition, these misconceptions indicate that, within high-quality SE-PETE, sport pedagogy faculty should give particular attention to helping preservice teachers learn how to teach within game play, teach roles, and support pupils who take these roles on. Furthermore, these misconceptions highlight the need for preservice teachers to teach full Sport Education seasons before graduating, fully comprehend Sport Education's structural advantages over more traditional models of teaching, and for tight supervision of early field experiences and student teaching. Finally, following Collier (1998), these misconceptions show how important it is for faculty to avoid placing preservice teachers with inservice teachers who claim to teach through Sport Education, but, in actuality, have the same misunderstandings of the model themselves.

Beginning teachers' implementation of the Sport Education model

Once preservice teachers graduate and move into the workforce, what is the likelihood that they will use the Sport Education model and in what form might they employ it? Curtner-Smith *et al.* (2008) predicted that beginning teachers who enter the workforce with teaching orientations and received high-quality SE-PETE will attempt to use the model in one of two forms. Those who face particularly conservative, adverse, or hostile conditions will either be forced to water Sport Education down or may fight to employ the full version of the model. Those who are fortunate enough to gain employment in schools with supportive cultures will employ the full version of Sport Education with very few difficulties.

Curtner-Smith *et al.* (2008) also theorized that beginning teachers who received high-quality SE-PETE yet enter the workforce with moderate-coaching orientations may well attempt to employ the full version of the model if their working conditions are supportive. Faced with less favorable conditions, however, this type of beginning teacher is more likely to take a cafeteria approach to the model or implement it in a watered-down form.

Finally, Curtner-Smith *et al.* (2008) hypothesized that beginning teachers who enter the workforce with hard core coaching orientations intact are unlikely to try Sport Education even if they received high-quality SE-PETE and encounter potentially nurturing school cultures. Similarly, beginning teachers who enter the workforce with teaching orientations or moderate-coaching orientations but who received low-quality SE-PETE are also unlikely to implement the model regardless of the school conditions they encounter.

References

Alexander, K. and Luckman, J. (2001) "Australian teachers' perceptions and uses of the Sport Education curriculum model," *European Physical Education Review*, 7: 243–267. doi:10.1177/1356336X01007300

Alexander, K., Taggart, A., and Thorpe, S.T. (1996) "A spring in their steps? Possibilities for professional renewal through Sport Education in Australian schools," *Sport, Education and Society*, 1: 23–46. doi:10.1080/1357332960010102

Browne, T.B.J., Carlson, T.B., and Hastie, P.A. (2004) "A comparison of rugby seasons presented in traditional and Sport Education formats," *European Physical Education Review*, 10: 199–214. doi:10.1177/1356336X04044071

Carlson, T.B. and Hastie, P.A. (1997) "The student social system within Sport Education," *Journal of Teaching in Physical Education*, 17: 176–195.

Collier, C. (1998) "Sport Education and preservice education," *Journal of Physical Education, Recreation and Dance*, 69(5): 44–45.

Curtner-Smith, M.D. (2001) "The occupational socialization of a first-year physical education teacher with a teaching orientation," *Sport, Education and Society*, 6: 81–105. doi:10.1080/713696040

Curtner-Smith, M.D. (2009) "Breaking the cycle of non-teaching physical education teachers: Lessons to be learned from the occupational socialization literature," in D.L. Housner, M.W. Metzler, P.G. Schempp, and T.J. Templin (eds.) *Historic traditions and future directions of research on teaching and teacher education in physical education* (pp. 221–226), Morgantown, WV: Fitness Information Technology.

Curtner-Smith, M.D., Chen, W., and Kerr, I.G. (1995) "Health-related fitness in secondary school physical education: A descriptive-analytic study," *Educational Studies*, 21: 55–66.

Curtner-Smith, M.D., Hastie, P.A., and Kinchin, G.D. (2008) "Influence of occupational socialization on beginning teachers' interpretation and delivery of Sport Education," *Sport, Education and Society*, 13: 97–117. doi:10.1080/13573320701780779

Curtner-Smith, M.D., Kerr, I.G., and Clapp, A.J. (1996) "The impact of national curriculum physical education on the teaching of health-related fitness: A case study in one English town," *European Journal of Physical Education*, 1(1): 66–83.

Curtner-Smith, M.D., Sinelnikov, O., and Woodruff, E. (2009, October) "One university's attempt at doing research-based PETE—The good, the bad, and the ugly," NASPE Conference on PETE, Myrtle Beach, SC.

Curtner-Smith, M.D. and Sofo, S. (2004a) "Influence of a critically oriented methods course and early field experience on preservice teachers' conceptions of teaching," *Sport, Education and Society*, 9: 115–142. doi:10.1080/1357332042000175845

Curtner-Smith, M. and Sofo, S. (2004b) "Preservice teachers' conceptions of teaching within Sport Education and multi-activity units," *Sport, Education and Society*, 9: 347–377. doi:10.1080/13573320412331302430

Curtner-Smith, M.D., Woodruff, E.A., Stran, M.E., Zmudy, M., Oh, J.I., and Zengaro, F. (2007, March) "Preservice teachers' conceptions of teaching within skill theme, games for understanding, and Sport Education units," National AAHPERD conference, Baltimore, MD.

Ennis, C.D. (1999) "Creating a culturally relevant curriculum for disengaged girls," *Sport, Education and Society*, 4: 31–49.

Gore, J. (1990) "Pedagogy as text in physical education teacher education: Beyond the preferred reading," in D. Kirk and R. Tinning (eds.) *Physical education, curriculum and culture: Critical issues in the contemporary crisis* (pp. 101–138), London: Falmer Press.

Graham, G. and Heimerer, E. (1981) "Research on teacher effectiveness: A summary with implications for teaching," *Quest*, 33: 14–25.

Hastie, P.A. (2003) *Teaching for lifetime physical activity through quality high school physical education*, San Francisco, CA: Benjamin Cummings.

Hastie, P.A. and Buchanan, A.M. (2000) "Teaching responsibility through Sport Education: Prospects of a coalition," *Research Quarterly for Exercise and Sport*, 71: 25–35.

Hastie, P.A. and Curtner-Smith, M. (2006) "Influence of a hybrid Sport Education–Teaching games for understanding unit on one teacher and his students," *Physical Education and Sport Pedagogy*, 11: 1–27. doi:10.1080/17408980500466813

Hastie, P.A. and Pickwell, A. (1996) "A description of a student social system in a secondary school dance class," *Journal of Teaching in Physical Education*, 15: 171–187.

Hastie, P.A and Siedentop, D. (1999) "An ecological perspective on physical education," *European Physical Education Review*, 5: 9–29.

Hastie, P.A. and Trost, S.G. (2002) "Student physical activity levels during a Sport Education season," *Pediatric Exercise Science*, 14: 64–74.

Jenkins, J.M. (2004) "Sport Education in a PETE program," *Journal of Physical Education, Recreation and Dance*, 75(5): 31–36.

Jewett, A.E. (1994) "Curriculum theory and research in sport pedagogy," *Sport Science Review*, 3: 56–72.

Kinchin, G.D. (1997) "High school students' perceptions of and responses to curriculum change in physical education," unpublished doctoral dissertation, The Ohio State University, Columbus.

Kinchin, G.D. (1998) "Secondary students' responses to issues of gender in sport and physical activity," *Journal of Sport Pedagogy*, 4(1): 29–42.

Kirk, D. and Almond, L. (1999, April) "Sport Education as situated learning in physical education: Making links to citizenship, leadership, and critical consumerism," paper presented at the AIESEP International Congress, Besancon, France.

Lave, J. and Wenger, E. (1991) *Situated learning: Legitimate peripheral participation*, New York: Cambridge University Press.

Lawson, H.A. (1983a) "Toward a model of teacher socialization in physical education: The subjective warrant, recruitment, and teacher education (part 1)," *Journal of Teaching in Physical Education*, 2: 3–16.

Lawson, H.A. (1983b) "Toward a model of teacher socialization in physical education: Entry into schools, teachers' role orientations, and longevity in teaching (part 2)," *Journal of Teaching in Physical Education*, 3: 3–15.

Locke, L.F. (1992) "Changing secondary school physical education," *Quest*, 44: 361–372.

Lortie, D. (1975) *Schoolteacher: A sociological study*, Chicago: University of Chicago Press.

McCaughtry, N., Sofo, S., Rovegno, I., and Curtner-Smith, M. (2004) "Learning to teach Sport Education: Misunderstandings, pedagogical difficulties, and resistance," *European Physical Education Review*, 10: 135–155. doi:10.1177/1356336X04044068

Macdonald, D. (1999) "The professional work of experienced physical education teachers," *Research Quarterly for Exercise and Sport*, 70: 41–55.

Metzler, M.W. (2005) *Instructional models for physical education* (2nd ed.), Scottsdale, AZ: Holcomb Hathaway.

Mosston, M. and Ashworth, S. (2008) *Teaching physical education*. Available HTTP: http://www.spectrumofteachingstyles.org/ebook (accessed January 14, 2011).

Parker, M. and Curtner-Smith, M.D. (2005) "Health-related fitness in Sport Education and multi-activity teaching," *Physical Education and Sport Pedagogy*, 10: 1–18. doi:10.1080/1740898042000334872

Parker, M. and Curtner-Smith, M.D. (2009, October) "Preservice teachers' use of productive and reproductive teaching styles within multi-activity and Sport Education units," NASPE conference on PETE, Myrtle Beach, SC.

Parker, M. and Curtner-Smith, M.D. (2010) "A comparison of the motivational climates created during multi-activity instruction and Sport Education," manuscript submitted for publication.

Parker, M. and Curtner-Smith, M.D. (in press) "Sport Education: A panacea for hegemonic masculinity in physical education or more of the same?," *Sport, Education and Society.*

Seashore-Louis, K. and Smith, B. (1990) "Teacher working conditions," in P. Reyes (ed.) *Teachers and their workplace: Commitment, performance and productivity,* Newbury Park, CA: Sage.

Shulman, L.S. (1987) "Knowledge and teaching: Foundations of the new reform," *Harvard Educational Review,* 57: 1–22.

Siedentop, D. (1994) *Sport Education: Quality PE through positive sport experiences,* Champaign, IL: Human Kinetics.

Siedentop, D., Hastie, P.A., and van der Mars, H. (2004) *Complete guide to Sport Education,* Champaign, IL: Human Kinetics.

Silverman, S. (1991) "Research on teaching in physical education," *Research Quarterly for Exercise and Sport,* 62: 352–365.

Sofo, S. and Curtner-Smith, M.D. (2010) "Development of preservice teachers' value orientations during a secondary methods course and early field experience," *Sport, Education and Society,* 15: 347–365.

Spittle, M. and Byrne, K. (2009) "The influence of Sport Education on student motivation in physical education," *Physical Education and Sport Pedagogy,* 14: 253–266. doi:10.1080/17408980801995239

Stran, M. and Curtner-Smith, M.D. (2009a) "Influence of occupational socialization on two preservice teachers' interpretation and delivery of the Sport Education model," *Journal of Teaching in Physical Education,* 28: 38–53.

Stran, M. and Curtner-Smith, M.D. (2009b) "Influence of two preservice teachers' value orientations on their interpretation and delivery of Sport Education," *Sport, Education and Society,* 14: 339–352. doi:10.1080/13573320903037846

Stran, M. and Curtner-Smith, M.D. (2010) "Impact of different types of knowledge on two preservice teachers' ability to learn and deliver the Sport Education model," *Physical Education and Sport Pedagogy,* 15: 243–256. doi:10.1080/17408980903273147

Tinning, R. and Fitzclarence, L. (1992) "Postmodern youth culture and the crisis in Australian secondary school physical education," *Quest,* 44: 287–303.

Wallhead, T.L. and Ntoumanis, N. (2004) "Effects of a Sport Education intervention on students' motivational responses in physical education," *Journal of Teaching in Physical Education,* 23: 4–18.

12

LEARNING SPORT EDUCATION THROUGH REFLECTIVE INQUIRY

Four case studies

Gary D. Kinchin

As seen in previous writing (e.g., Collier, 1998; Kinchin *et al.*, 2005), as well as in this book (see Chapters 5 and 11), Sport Education is now warranting attention within the higher education setting and specifically within teacher preparation. In these instances, a range of progressive experiences with the model is outlined including lectures, guest speakers, practical work delivered using the model, and observation of Sport Education being taught within public schools. For those of us working within initial teacher education, one indication of the model's appeal is the extent to which student teachers then seek to include this approach within their periods of student teaching.

As a contribution to this international reader, this chapter provides some examples of project work in Sport Education undertaken by physical education (PE) student teachers as a part of their program of initial teacher education. The work represents the student's first opportunity to "do the model for real" with pupils. The projects described in this chapter were completed by student teachers who were undertaking a 1-year Postgraduate Certificate of Education (PGCE) in secondary PE at a large university in England. Students who gain entry to the PGCE have already completed an undergraduate degree normally within a sport studies, sport science, or equivalent area. The PGCE award also includes a recommendation for Qualified Teacher Status which is subject to students meeting a set of prescribed standards during their year of study.

The PGCE is a 36-week course. The division of time is specified in that 24 weeks must be spent within the school setting and 12 weeks spent at the university. For the particular course set out within this chapter, student teachers complete two periods of student teaching lasting 6 and 12 weeks, respectively. The first period of student teaching takes place between early November and ends the week before Christmas and the second period of student teaching occurs between the middle of February and the end of May.

A particular feature of the PGCE is the opportunity for student teachers to gain some initial credits toward a master's degree, known as M-level PGCE. Students on the M-level PGCE set out within this chapter can gain up to 60 credits, which is the equivalent to half of a taught masters. Students are then able to accredit this prior learning if they seek to enroll for further academic study. Credit is earned through successful completion of two 6,000-word assignments at a minimum of a C-level grade, both of which are marked using masters' assignment assessment criteria. One of those assignments lies within the specified curriculum area, and which is known as the Curriculum Subject Assignment (CSA); the other examines a whole-school professional issue, and which is known as the Special Study Assignment (SSA).

The purpose of the CSA is for the student teacher to examine a particular pedagogical issue within PE within their school placement context, formulate a research plan, gather some data/evidence, and consider this issue with due attention to both the academic and professional literature and their existing and future teaching. The CSA assignments are conceptualized as a piece of reflective inquiry and will normally include an introduction, review of relevant literature, a methodology/description of procedures, a discussion of the findings, a concluding section, and a suitable set of references. Assessment criteria focus on knowledge of the professional and empirical literature, the integration of theory and practice, description and justification of the methodology, attention given to matters of ethics, appropriate use of referencing, and overall presentation and level of writing evident within the work.

To assist students in working toward achievement of master's credit, there are taught sessions for student teachers at the university on how to begin to write at master's level and how to use research to both inform and lead teaching. While implementation of the CSA normally occurs during the second period of student teaching, student teachers are encouraged to give early consideration to potential topics which will typically emerge from reading they might undertake, individual tutorials with teacher education faculty, conversations with their mentors in schools, and sessions delivered at the university. The rationale for this early development is the known workload experienced by student teachers in both attempting to complete two substantial pieces of work and meeting the expectations for extended periods of student teaching.

Of relevance to this chapter is that, before the first period of student teaching, the PGCE PE course gives early practical attention to Sport Education followed by a half-day workshop. Here, student teachers continue to learn about the features of the model, receive guidance on how seasons are planned, and develop their understanding of the research and development to date. While many of the local schools include Sport Education within their PE curriculum, not all student teachers will see the model while on their first placement. The descriptions of the following projects, however, are those of four secondary PE student teachers who *did* experience the model during their PGCE course.

Why Sport Education as a topic for the CSA?

The student teachers provided a number of reasons why they had selected Sport Education as the topic of their CSA assignment. However, they all pointed to the attention given to the model within lectures and seminars as part of their initial teacher education, and in particular a feeling that at the conclusion of this input they had "a real grasp and understanding of the concept." A belief that pupils would be more motivated and interested to learn within Sport Education lessons was also apparent. One of the student teachers offered the following explanation:

> I chose to do Sport Education for my CSA as I took a real interest in the subject after having lectures on it. I really felt it would help to motivate some of my classes, and help with the behavior in lessons. I also feel that it is really important for students to learn the value of teamwork. This is linked very strongly with Sport Education.

For another student teacher Sport Education was potentially "different and interesting . . . There is also the added benefit that the segregation between higher and lower ability pupils disappears and pupils work as a team as opposed to an individual in the spotlight."

The possibilities for Sport Education were further reinforced during the first period of their student teaching. One student states:

> Whilst at my first placement school, I taught a group of pupils with special educational needs and after observing a few lessons and what pupils struggled with I was convinced that Sport Education would be beneficial to their learning and ultimately the enjoyment of the lesson.

The following sections outline a summary of four CSAs which were completed by the student teachers. The descriptions include the focus of the work, the context of the investigation, what was learned, and what issues emerged for the respective student teachers. It should be remembered that these case examples are not dissertations and so should be read with that in mind. They are primarily reflective assignments intended to serve as a range of illustrations of the lines of inquiry followed by student teachers in relation to Sport Education, how they have gone about addressing the question during their full-time student teacher placements, and how and what they have learned has in their view contributed to their professional development and understanding of the model. All case examples described below sought and received the necessary ethical approval by the institution and by the respective secondary schools.

Case 1. Sport Education and children with special educational needs

This CSA investigated the introduction of Sport Education to a class of 18 pupils with a range of special educational needs, which included Asperger's and both mild and more severe behavioral conditions, some of which required statements which had been identified through the local educational authority. The pupils were all in Year 8 (aged 12/13 years) and attended a large mainstream secondary school in the south of England. There were 14 boys and 4 girls in the class. No in-class learning support was available.

Pupils participated in a season of table tennis lasting a total of 400 minutes in lessons taught over a 4-week period (see Table 12.1). Based upon the pupils' prior knowledge and experience with table tennis, the student teacher divided pupils into four teams (the United States, the United Kingdom, Japan, and France) with individuals taking on the following roles: equipment manager, captain, coach, official, and scorekeeper/statistician. Teams received points for changing quickly, wearing the correct kit, displaying positive sport-like behavior, and completing role-related tasks. During the festival, teams all played each other on a round-robin basis and had a member of a different country umpiring each game. Results were based on all the points accumulated through the other lessons and the points from the tournament. Certificates were presented to the pupils by the Director of Sport at the school.

This CSA was particularly interested in these pupils' perceptions of Sport Education and the ways in which they engaged with the model. Data were collected via an exit survey developed by Tannehill (2004), lesson evaluations completed by the cooperating teacher, an interview with the PE cooperating teacher (experienced in teaching children with special educational needs), and the student teacher's field notes, which were completed after each lesson had been taught. The reading age for some pupils was reported as being quite low; therefore, some learners needed some assistance to complete the questionnaire.

The findings from the questionnaires revealed that all pupils had enjoyed having a role during the season and over 90 percent had enjoyed being a member of a team. Almost all pupils claimed to prefer Sport Education to their previous curriculum time in PE. Although many pupils claimed not to have a particular liking for table tennis, this did not detract from their overall enjoyment of the lessons.

TABLE 12.1 Table tennis season plan

Week	Content	Teacher's role	Student's role
1	Introduction	Present teams	Participant
	Ball and bat coordination	Discuss roles	Learn team roles
2	Service shot	Discuss fair play	Coaches, players
	Progression of forehand	Head coach	
	Backhand shots		
3	Rules of play	Referee advisor	Coaches, players
	Playing tactics	Head coach	Team roles
4	Olympic festival	Program manager	Coaches, players
			Team roles

Observations undertaken by the cooperating teacher described pupils responding positively to being on a team and "feeling a part of their countries" (Observation 1), being motivated by the opportunity to gain points which were displayed on a daily basis, and supporting the expected routines. Field notes also pointed to pupils being able to manage their own games, support each other during practice, and take their participation in the Olympic culminating festival "very seriously" (Field note, Lesson 4) while being excited by the pending ceremony where prizes would be awarded.

At interview, the cooperating teacher highlighted the benefits of "clear routines" and the persistence of team membership as particular characteristics of Sport Education highly suited to the learners in this study, believing that these pupils felt more secure in knowing what to expect on a daily basis. The cooperating teacher also held the view that Sport Education promoted high levels of enthusiasm among the pupils and was an appropriate teaching and learning model for working with pupils who have additional learning and support needs.

Within the discussion section of the CSA, the student teacher focused on documentation on teaching students who are included published by the Department for Children, Schools and Families (2010). In particular, the discussion sought to demonstrate some linkages between teaching techniques that promote routine and which help pupils learn to help themselves and others, as well as the pedagogy of Sport Education. The student teacher acknowledged some of the curricular design challenges within the setting that make the adoption of lengthier seasons quite problematic, and at the same time calls for more empirical work which might examine pupils with more acute additional needs learning under the Sport Education framework. The perceived benefits of the project work were outlined with a specific focus on how the assignment added to their knowledge and understanding of specific learning needs and what pedagogies might be suitable to include such learners.

Case 2. Sport Education and perceived role suitability for boys and girls in health-related exercise, netball, and soccer

This CSA broadly sought to investigate the degree to which Sport Education and in particular the use of nonplaying roles could promote a more gender-inclusive learning environment for boys and girls. The setting for this project was a large secondary school in the south of England. The school has over 1,400 pupils on roll with nearly all of White-British background.

One mixed gender class of children in Year 7 (aged 11/12 years) participated in the project. There were 13 boys and 14 girls in the class. The pupils participated in a health-related exercise (HRE) unit which consisted of 4 × 100-minute lessons taught over a period of 4 weeks. Following an introduction to Sport Education provided by the student teacher, pupils self-selected teams of either five or six which would persist for the entire teaching period. Five teams emerged who then determined their team name. The student teacher explained the nonplaying roles, and without teacher input pupils allocated the roles within their teams.

The principal method of data collection was a questionnaire administered pre- and postseason. The questionnaire included a mixture of open-ended and closed questions, multiple choice, and Likert-style items which collectively sought to investigate pupils' perceptions of role suitability in relation to using Sport Education within a HRE context. The students were also asked to respond to these same prompts if they were to participate in other Sport Education seasons such as soccer and netball (not taught in the study, but common within the school). The questionnaire also included some items where pupils rated perceived skill level for both genders within both netball and soccer.

The findings revealed that, prior to the season, while two-thirds of the boys and three-quarters of girls indicated that all Sport Education roles were suitable for both genders in an HRE context, almost one-third of boys were of the opinion that the major leadership roles were for boys only. Notably, following the HRE unit, there was an increase in the belief that *all* of the Sport Education roles offered in this activity were suitable for either boys or girls.

When turning to perceptions of ability in soccer and netball, the vast majority of boys and girls strongly agreed with the statement "Girls are better than boys at netball." However, before the HRE Sport Education season, around half of the boys were of the view that roles in netball were suitable for both genders while one-third of boys indicated that all roles in netball were for girls only, with the exception of the warm-up coach. Girls were mostly of the view that only the equipment manager was more suitable for boys in netball. After the Sport Education HRE season, data indicated that roles in netball continued to be seen as predominantly female, with only a slight increase (6 percent from the boys and 4 percent from the girls) that the roles could be taken on by either gender.

Around half the boys in the class strongly agreed with the statement "Boys are better at soccer than girls," whereas two-thirds of girls strongly disagreed with the same statement. In relation to a Sport Education season in soccer only one of the boys thought any role in such a season would be suitable for girls only. Almost two-thirds of the girls held the view that roles in a soccer Sport Education season should be for both boys and girls. The questionnaires from both boys and girls identified three roles—statistician, motivator, and health and safety officer—as being potentially female-only roles.

The greater perceived suitability for roles taken on by either boys or girls in HRE was partly attributed to the nongender-specific nature of this activity. Offering a season of HRE seemed to permit more inclusive perceptions of role suitability among both boys and girls. The student teacher concluded that for these pupils there appeared to be a leaning in netball by both boys and girls toward more female-held roles and at the same time a shared perception that boys were not better than girls in this activity. Of note, the reverse was apparent for soccer; however, girls in the class seemed more inclined to challenge taken-for-granted assumptions about skill and ability in soccer. This was not apparent for this class in netball where both boys and girls perceived girls to be better in terms of skill and ability in this activity. Interestingly only girls felt inclined to offer responses to open-ended items which addressed role opportunities for girls and boys and perceived ability in sports, with the following illustrative:

"I think girls and boys are equal at sports," Year 7 female
"It doesn't matter whether you are male or female," Year 7 female

This CSA claims that Sport Education offers a suitable model of instruction to address apparent gendered perceptions of role suitability and states that both boys and girls should be permitted the opportunity to take on a full range of roles within both of these invasion games. The student teacher viewed the CSA as furthering their professional development through the incorporation of Sport Education into their teaching. They added that the CSA prompted reflection on their teaching and the choice of activities they might teach within the curriculum. More specifically, the CSA experience led to much thinking about how to make lessons more inclusive and as a teacher not be influenced by stereotypes and beliefs concerning the abilities and roles learners might take on in a range of Sport Education seasons.

Case 3. Examining pupil motivation in classes taught using Sport Education and a more traditional teaching approach

This CSA examined pupil motivation in two basketball classes, one taught using Sport Education and the other through a more traditional teaching and learning approach. Forty-two Year 8 girls (aged 12–13 years) from a large mixed inner city comprehensive school within a major city in the south of England participated in the study. Twenty participants were taught basketball under the Sport Education condition and 22 participants using the traditional approach across four lessons each lasting 100 minutes. Within the Sport Education class, teams were selected by the student teacher. Four teams of five pupils were chosen and each took on one of four team names with associated shirt colors: Kelly Holmes (blue), Paula Radcliffe (yellow), Beth Tweddle (red), and Kelly Smith (green). Pupils also took on one of five nonplaying roles which included captain, warm-up coach, skills coach, equipment monitor, and scorer. Additional points were awarded for wearing kit in line with school policy, attendance, acceptable behavior, and demonstrating a positive work ethic.

Within the Sport Education classes, lessons tended to include a student-led warm-up, some teacher-directed skill practice, student-led activities and progressions either determined by the teacher or by team leaders, and a modified games phase overseen by teams. This allowed pupils to take some control of their own learning and at the same time promoted a sense of affiliation within teams. A small presentation was carried out at the end of the fourth lesson to congratulate the class on their enthusiasm and participation. Lessons taught using the more traditional approach were teacher directed with all instructional decisions made by the teacher with minimal pupil input. A typical lesson included an aerobic warm-up with stretches, a skill phase including a variety of isolated drills implemented solely by the teacher, and a game at the end. No specific roles were given to the pupils and any team combinations were changed each week.

In terms of data collection, intrinsic motivation for sport and PE in both classes was measured using the Intrinsic Motivation Inventory (IMI) (Ryan, 1982) that had been reworded by Deci *et al.* (1994) to make it more applicable to the current study. Participants in both classes responded to 14 items which assessed three underlying dimensions of intrinsic motivation: value/usefulness, interest/enjoyment, and perceived choice. Participants responded on a seven-point scale from 1 (not at all true) to 7 (very true). The IMI has been found to have adequate validity and reliability when used with adolescents in PE (Goudas and Biddle, 1994; Mitchell, 1996), and has also been used in research on Sport Education (Spittle and Byrne, 2009). In addition to the required lesson evaluations, the student teacher also made written observation notes after each lesson recalling significant events and anything pupils may have said. The time which pupils took to change for each class and be present in the teaching space was also collected.

Questionnaires were analyzed and means were recorded pre- and post-test of each teaching approach. The range and standard deviation was then calculated (see Table 12.2). The student teacher suggested that these data showed that Sport Education was slightly more successful in maintaining levels of motivation than the traditional teaching approach, given that motivation levels in Sport Education increased by 1.1 compared with only a 0.32 increase for the traditional group.

Data from written notes indicated that pupils taught through the Sport Education approach generally displayed greater enthusiasm before each lesson. Notes also indicated that these pupils paid attention when the teacher asked for silence, and behavior in the class improved, as the following note illustrated: "There is a lot of excitement in the air as the pupils get changed, they are a lot quicker than usual and can't wait to get started. Their behavior has also improved dramatically compared to normal."

Students in the Sport Education class were typically changed and were ready for instruction over 2 minutes sooner than those in the traditional class.

Data gathered through observation notes suggested that the increased responsibility given to pupils in the Sport Education class may have been a factor in raising enthusiasm in addition to opportunities for greater decision-making and developing team affiliation. The student teacher concluded, though somewhat tentatively,

TABLE 12.2 Pre- and post-test questionnaire results

Test	Teaching approach	Pre-test	Post-test	Difference
Mean results	Traditional	60.36	60.68	+0.32
	Sport Education	58.95	60.05	+1.1
Standard deviation	Traditional	9.68	9.95	+0.27
	Sport Education	9.86	9.92	+0.06

that for these specific pupils it would appear that Sport Education can be linked to slightly increased motivation levels within PE classes. In looking forward, the student teacher was of the view that, through the knowledge gained from completing this CSA study through results and personal observations, they plan to ensure greater use of Sport Education in their teaching and aim to try to encourage their work colleagues to do the same.

Case 4. Using the Task and Ego Orientation in Sport Questionnaire as a predictor of the degree of interest in participation within a Sport Education unit

The setting for this CSA was a large secondary school in the south of England. The school was located within an area of low socioeconomic status with approximately 750 pupils on roll. The participants in the study were 42 pupils: 21 were in Year 7 (aged 11/12 years) and 21 in Year 10 (aged 14/15 years). Pupils completed the Task and Ego Orientation in Sport Questionnaire (TEOSQ) (Duda and Nicholls, 1992) which determined whether they were either task motivated or ego oriented. The TEOSQ is a 13-item questionnaire whereby subjects indicate their degree of agreement with each of the items which are measured on a five-point Likert-type scale. Due to circumstances beyond their control, the student teacher was not able to implement a practical season of Sport Education. Instead, following completion of the questionnaire, the student teacher taught a classroom-based lesson to the pupils on Sport Education where pupils were introduced to the objectives and features of Sport Education and given an insight into what both pupils and teachers do across a season of work. Immediately following this classroom-based session, the student teacher used a set of open-ended statements which asked pupils to set out what they perceived as the potential benefits and drawbacks for them as learners if they were to experience Sport Education within their PE program.

Using information gained from analysis of the TEOSQ (whether an individual was predominantly task or ego oriented), the student teacher then sought to identify any patterns in relation to the open-ended responses to Sport Education. Pupils were allocated a number which they wrote on both instruments. Results indicated that almost two-thirds of pupils in Year 7 were task oriented with the remaining students ego oriented. In Year 10, 70 percent of pupils were predominantly ego oriented and 30 percent were predominantly task oriented. From reading comments on the open-ended statements, 70 percent of the pupils identified as predominantly task oriented were positive about Sport Education. Very few ego-oriented pupils were positive in their comments. In Year 10, over 80 percent of the pupils who were identified as mostly task-oriented pupils were generally enthused in their writing by Sport Education.

From reading the comments from the pupils, the student teacher looked for recurring items. The following references to Sport Education were illustrative of the positive comments across both year groups: opportunities for increased responsibility in class and how this might transfer to other parts of their life, having a sense of more control in the lesson, the potential for taking on roles in class (particularly the coach), and having more involvement in their own learning and the learning of others. Less supportive comments which appeared in both year groups pointed to concerns over possible arguments within teams, becoming frustrated with teammates who may not try or contribute, letting down a teammate, and a preference to want to work alone and rely just on themselves for improvement. Negative comments from some Year 10 pupils also pointed to a preference for more "recreational PE" and that Sport Education was, as one wrote, "Too much effort." The student teacher is careful about drawing any firm conclusions but did observe that for these two classes task-oriented pupils tended to write more supportive comments concerning processes within and potential benefits of Sport Education, with less supportive remarks more often made by ego-oriented pupils. The student teacher indicated that as a function of the CSA they were now more aware of the potential attractions for Sport Education but, equally important, mindful of some sources of possible dissent among learners which, in their view, will be of help when being in a position to deliver the model "for real" and in doing so attempt to meet the needs of pupils with different orientations.

Conclusion

Communications with the student teachers following completion of their PGCE course enabled some evaluation of the current status of Sport Education within their teaching. The students also reflected on what they had learned as a consequence of attempting Sport Education for the first time as a student teacher. For some there was a feeling that attempting the model had both positively contributed to an enhancement of subject knowledge and an improved confidence in the management of pupil in-class behavior. Student teachers reflected upon the benefits in relation to student-centered learning while reporting continued interest in the model:

> Sport Education is a great way to help with teamwork, behavior, and motivation. I now use it within my teaching across all my Year 7 classes and into my Year 9 classes. Sport Education helps to give pupils a sense of ownership for what they are doing and contributes to the teaching of life skills. I think it is vital within PE to not only develop the physical skills in sport but also to teach social skills that the students can use in all aspects of their life.

Another student teacher reported what they had seen in pupils and how an interest in the model had also been sustained: "I learned that pupils like to have specific roles and responsibilities within the lesson . . . Since completing my CSA I have ensured to implement a greater use of Sport Education within my teaching."

It is particularly pleasing to see how Sport Education became such a key feature within the initial teacher education of these new teachers and how an opportunity to examine some aspect of the model has then carried forward into teaching beyond the preservice stage. These practitioners have seen first-hand many of the benefits of Sport Education for both learners and themselves as developing professionals which have been consistently reported within the international literature, and long may this continue for them.

Acknowledgment

My thanks go to the four physical education student teachers for their many contributions to this chapter, and for their continued interest in Sport Education.

References

Collier, C. (1998) "Sport Education and pre-service education," *Journal of Physical Education, Recreation and Dance*, 69(5): 44–45.

Deci, E.L., Eghrari, H., Patrick, B.C., and Leone, D. (1994) "Facilitating internalization: The self-determination theory perspective," *Journal of Personality*, 62: 119–142.

Department for Children, Schools and Families (2010) *How to help with special educational needs and slow learners engage with the framework*. Available HTTP: http://nationalstrategies. standards.dcsf.gov.uk/node/195346 (accessed April 15, 2010).

Duda, J.L. and Nicholls, J. (1992) "Dimensions of achievement motivation in schoolwork and sport," *Journal of Educational Psychology*, 84: 1–10.

Goudas, M. and Biddle, S.J.H. (1994) "Perceived motivational climate and intrinsic motivation in school physical education classes," *European Journal of Psychology of Education*, 9: 241–250.

Kinchin, G.D., Penney, D., and Clarke, G. (2005) "Sport Education in teacher education," in D. Penney, G. Clarke, M. Quill, and G.D. Kinchin (eds.) *Sport Education in physical education: Research-based practice* (pp. 217–228), London: Routledge.

Mitchell, S. (1996) "Relationships between perceived learning environment and intrinsic motivation in middle school physical education," *Journal of Teaching in Physical Education*, 15: 368–383.

Ryan, R.M. (1982) "Control and information in the intrapersonal sphere: An extension of cognitive evaluation theory," *Journal of Personality and Social Psychology*, 43: 450–461.

Spittle, M. and Byrne, K. (2009) "The influence of Sport Education on student motivation in physical education," *Physical Education and Sport Pedagogy*, 14: 253–266. doi:10.1080/17408980801995239

Tannehill, D. (2004) "Implementing a Sport Education season," University of Limerick. Available HTTP: http://www.peai.org/download.aspx?f=Sport + Education + Season + Project.doc (accessed October 13, 2009).

13

PROFESSIONAL LEARNING OF PRIMARY GENERALIST TEACHERS IN IRELAND

Modelling Sport Education

Ann MacPhail and Deborah Tannehill

Sport Education is a new experience for the teacher who plans and delivers physical education using this approach and for the learner who takes on new and extended learning roles. Teachers face numerous challenges when attempting to implement the student-led instructional approach encouraged by Sport Education. Siedentop *et al.* (2004) describe a new role for the teacher as an 'instructional engineer' who teaches, facilitates and assesses learning, and shares both the teaching and managerial tasks with learners. This shift from the more traditional teacher-led approach to one where the learner takes centre stage with responsibility for their own learning can be difficult for both the teacher and the learner (Penney *et al.*, 2005). As this process evolves, learners become active in assuming leadership, making decisions, cooperating effectively with their team, and developing skills beyond that of a player.

Professional development and teacher learning

The study reported in this chapter is contextualised within (continuing) professional development and teacher learning. While we support the preference for the use of 'professional'/'teacher learning' to the notion of 'professional development', which suggests teacher passivity (Armour and Yelling, 2004b), not all literature makes that distinction and uses both terms interchangeably. There is however a consensus that professional/teacher learning is promoted through effective professional development opportunities. There is a growing recognition of the importance of providing teachers with professional development opportunities where learning is aligned, coherent and sustained (Armour and Duncombe, 2004; Armour and Yelling, 2004a; Cochran-Smith and Lytle, 1999; Finley *et al.*, 2000). A number of reviews comprehensively report the types of effective physical education professional development and influencing factors of physical education teacher development (Armour, 2006; Armour and Yelling, 2004a, 2004b; Bechtel and O'Sullivan, 2006; Li, 2010; Petrie, 2009; Wang and Ha, 2008).

While professional development initiatives for practising teachers are not new, less is known about what constitutes effective practice for primary/elementary physical education. Primary teachers in Armour and Duncombe's (2004) study suggest that professional development must be closely linked to practice, school-based with the teacher's own pupils, and realistic. Petrie's (2009) work evaluates the impact of a professional development programme on knowledge associated with teaching physical education, and the complexity of subject-specific knowledge development for generalist teachers. Unlike imposed professional development opportunities, the two generalist primary teachers in the study reported in this chapter were proactive in seeking a professional development opportunity through inviting the second author, Deborah, to the school to deliver Sport Education. Both teachers were willing to be involved in professional learning, being positively disposed to making conceptual changes to their teaching of physical education. Factors that facilitated professional learning, and also acted as criteria for the selection of modelling of Sport Education in particular as a collaborative learning strategy, included the emphasis placed on sport in Irish primary schools, students eager to be involved in sport experiences, for one teacher their previous experience with the model and for the other teacher the novelty of transferring responsibility from the teacher to student, and Deborah's experience in teaching and researching Sport Education.

Consensus has been reached that 'collaborative learning' (including organisation partnership, small group models, and informal networks) is an effective method of physical education teacher development (Armour, 2006; Armour and Yelling, 2007; McCaughtry et al., 2005; Wang and Ha, 2008). In response to the recommendation that more studies are needed to examine how to efficiently put collaborative learning into practice (Duncombe and Armour, 2004; Wang and Ha, 2008), this research set out to examine whether a professional development initiative, using modelling of Sport Education, would provide primary teachers with sufficient knowledge, skill and confidence to plan and deliver a Sport Education season. Teacher modelling as an effective teaching strategy has been discussed in the context of a teacher demonstrating a concept for a student (Haston, 2007). In this instance, the primary teachers might be considered the students and the second author viewed as the teacher. Modelling took the form of Deborah demonstrating the teaching behaviours and strategies that reflect those supported by the Sport Education model. This modelling provided a sample of 'how to do Sport Education' for adaptation and application to the design of their own season. It was anticipated that modelling a Sport Education season would reduce the limitations in professional development experienced by teachers of 'one-shot' design professional development programmes (Armour and Yelling, 2002; Ward and Doutis, 1999) that tend to be part of national continuing professional development (CPD) physical education programmes (see Armour and Duncombe, 2004; Atencio et al., 2009; Petrie, 2009). The Sport Education season would encourage the two teachers to learn together, as well as interact and collaborate with those who have expertise in Sport Education pedagogy.

The improvement in the quality of teachers' instruction (and learning), and students' learning, is to some extent reliant upon improvements in the quality of teachers' professional learning (Armour and Yelling, 2007; Borko, 2004; Cohen and Hill, 1998). As Petrie (2009) succinctly points out, little is known about the extent to which a shift in teachers' physical education rhetoric translates into changes in the practice of physical education lessons and the associated (effective) teaching and learning of physical education in primary schools. Similar to Ko *et al.*'s (2006) analysis of identifying the components of a Sport Education professional development workshop that teachers plan to use in their lessons, we asked teachers to analyse professional learning through modelling and its *potential* to enhance their students' learning. Unfortunately, being unable to commit time and resources to follow the two teachers as they extended the athletics season into an orienteering season resulted in no attempt to evaluate the direct impact of teacher learning on pupil learning.

Context of elementary education in Ireland

In Ireland, primary teachers are responsible for teaching the six curriculum areas of language, mathematics, social environmental and scientific education, arts education, social personal and health education, and physical education. The Irish National Teachers Organisation policy is that primary class teachers deliver all curriculum areas and consequently there is limited scope for the employment of primary physical education specialists. Primary teachers are encouraged to pursue the revised primary school curriculum in physical education (Department of Education and Science/National Council for Curriculum and Assessment, 1999a) and the corresponding teacher guidelines (Department of Education and Science/National Council for Curriculum and Assessment, 1999b). There is no compulsory level of physical education provision; however, the suggested minimum weekly time framework includes 1 hour per week for the subject. The quality and breadth of physical education provision varies and physical education is not provided in all primary schools. There is an increasing trend of National Governing Bodies providing coaches for particular sports within the school day and also providing resources and training to teachers (MacPhail *et al.*, 2008). Similar to international practice (Duncombe and Armour, 2004), primary teacher candidates in Ireland receive only limited training in physical education during their teacher training and thus often lack knowledge and confidence to teach this content.

The only other documented formal introduction of Sport Education to Irish primary schools was when four schools within the Munster region of Ireland were invited to deliver, with guidance from experts in the Sport Education field, a Sport Education season on an agreed generic activity that would allow the four schools to meet at the end of the season to participate in a shared culminating event (Kinchin *et al.*, 2009). The school referenced in this chapter was part of that Munster group, and one of the teachers, Aine, had been a participant.

Methodology

As the site of a previous Sport Education research project and teachers being interested in continuing the school's involvement not only with Sport Education but with university teacher educators, this study took place in a primary school in the Munster region of Ireland. A modelling approach was undertaken with the second author, Deborah, acting as lead instructor in the design and delivery of a Sport Education athletics season to 48 fourth class students (aged 8 and 9 years) across two physical education classes. Each class met weekly for physical education over 8 weeks in 45-minute sessions held in a large sports hall. In week 9, the two classes came together for a double period to participate in the culminating event. These students had not previously experienced Sport Education before undertaking the athletics season, although one of the teachers, Aine, had the previous year. The primary teachers observed and assisted with instruction, and informally interacted on the planning of the season which followed a structured format (Table 13.1). Following the athletics season, the primary teachers were responsible for designing and delivering an orienteering season in which the content and Sport Education framework would be extended.

TABLE 13.1 Sport Education season framework

- Design to include tools and materials to guide implementation
- Keep the pieces you like from the first season and adapt those you feel need revision
- Be prepared to talk about why you made the choices you did
  1 Context for season
     - Sport, time, days in season
  2 Teams
     - Number/size of teams, team selection process, building affiliation
  3 Roles
     - Determine/define roles, role selection procedure, strategies for teaching roles
  4 Class management
     - Fair play agreement, routines, rules
  5 Festivity
     - Awards, recognition, rituals and traditions
  6 Season design
     - Sport Education: season aspects, competitive schedule, culminating event
     - Content: skills and techniques
  7 Record keeping
     - Scoring, statistics, maintaining records

Sport Education athletics season

Content of the athletics season included running and field events. The 400-metre run, 60-metre sprint and a medley relay were taught and a standing start was taught for both distance and sprint events. Triple jump and shot put constituted the field events. Each student was expected to participate in one individual running event, one field event and the relay event. The season schedule is displayed in Table 13.2 and includes training (Weeks 2–6 training and trials), competition (Weeks 7–8 relay jamboree) and a culminating event (relay jamboree). The season was intended to be cooperative with all events run using a relay format so that individual performance was not the focus. Rather, all competitions were scored using a team average system regardless of number of competitors in an event so that each individual's performance counted towards the whole. For each event, scores were kept on a score sheet and final team scores posted. In addition, each team had their own portfolio of class materials and role task cards. The intent was that, while Deborah taught the initial season, the primary teachers would be designing an orienteering season using the Sport Education framework. As teacher educators, we were interested in identifying which pieces of the Sport Education season the primary teachers chose to keep, extend or refine in an attempt to sustain the Sport Education framework upon our departure from the school.

The intention of focusing on, developing and modelling the use of task cards in this study was to provide resources that help teachers integrate new curricula and instructional skills into their existing contexts without teachers becoming overly reliant on them (Ko *et al.*, 2006; Petrie, 2009). It was anticipated that task cards would act as a resource for teacher and student learning. Characteristics of Sport Education were added in a progressive fashion as the season unfolded and were applied within the athletics context. A detailed account of using the task cards to teach athletics with Sport Education is provided elsewhere (Tannehill and Collier, 2008).

In line with Sport Education, affiliation was created through the selection of teams. There were four teams of six students in each of the two physical education classes. These teams had their own designated team court in the sports hall for warm-up, practice and team meetings. Initially, captains were selected by the teachers based on their judgement of students as leaders who were respected by their peers, and organised. Captains sat with Deborah and selected 'equal' teams based on their knowledge of peers' abilities. To further build affiliation, teams selected team names, colours, uniforms and mascots, and designed a team poster.

In conjunction with the two teachers, it was determined that it would be most effective if the teachers could view several roles being taught to students and used by them throughout the season. The roles of captain, publicist, trainer, head throwing official, head jumping official and head track official were introduced. Role responsibilities were defined and adapted, as needed, as the season progressed. While the captains were appointed as previously noted, the remaining students reviewed the responsibilities of the various roles and applied for the one in which

TABLE 13.2 Sport Education athletics season schedule

Day/date	Sport Education	Content
Week 1	Name tags to start	Cooperation and getting acquainted
	Introduction to Sport Education Discussion	Group juggling
	• Teamwork	• Use names, encouragement, praise
	• Team experiences	In the woods
	• Competition/cooperation	• Mosquito, salmon and bears
	• Praise and encouragement	
	Design fair play agreement	
Post class	Captains pick teams	
Week 2	Captains announce teams	T teach warm-up
	Captains share responsibilities of captain role	T teach shot put technique and rules
	Teams sign captain's contract	Do all of this on court as part of demonstration
	Assign team courts	Teams go to home court to practise
Post class	Apply for festivity and/or trainer	
Week 3	Announce festivity coordinator Name, colour, mascot, task chosen	T teach running technique drills
	Announce trainer Trainers count as T lead warm-ups	Shot practice on team court
Week 4	Trainer-led warm-up on team courts	Team warm-ups Review running technique
	Festivity coordinator organises team photos	T teach standing sprint start and rules
		Practice starts with running technique
Week 5	Festivity coordinator gets ideas for team poster with picture	Team warm-ups
		Review sprint start and running technique
		Split class for triple jump (hop, step, jump) and distance running. Students go to both for ½ class
		T teach triple jump
		T teach rules of triple jump
		T teach distance running technique
Week 6	Students practise in teams taking responsibility for learning	Team warm-ups
		Half of class at each event for 20 minutes
		Practise shot put and/or triple jump

TABLE 13.2 (*continued*)

TABLE 13.2 (continued)

Post class	Captain-led event sign ups	
	Announce event competitor	
	Apply for sprint, distance, shot or triple jump judge	
Week 7	Announce officials	Team warm-ups
		Performance practice
	Shot and sprint officials practise with time trials	Go to participation event or officiating event
		Shot and/or sprints
Week 8	Triple jump and distance officials practise with time/distance trials	Team warm-ups
		Performance practice
		Go to participation event or officiating event
		Triple jump and/or distance running
Week 9	Relay festival	Team warm-ups
	Duty roles	Relay festival
	Awards ceremony with combined classes	Sprint, shot, distance and triple jump

they were most interested. Decisions were made by the captain in conjunction with Deborah and the primary class teacher. Task cards were developed to guide students in learning their role responsibilities. Students in charge of the various roles from each team met to discuss their responsibilities, after which they shared their understanding with the rest of the class. Deborah provided guidance and feedback on how they were progressing.

Learning to be fair players is a critical aspect of Sport Education and one that is facilitated in part by the classroom management system. A 'fair play agreement' was developed by students following cooperative discussion and activities on the first day. Once developed, teams signed the fair play agreement and, to maintain their commitment to it, assessed their individual and/or team achievement of goals set in the agreement on a weekly basis.

Festivity is a key aspect of sport at all levels and one that Sport Education attempts to support and foster. To achieve this goal, an awards and recognition programme was developed and implemented. Each day students were recognised for fair play behaviour, strong role performance and athletic achievement. This became a significant aspect of each class session along with consistent praise and encouragement being expected from all participants.

Data collection and analysis

Data collection occurred during and following the modelling period and involved journaling, teacher interviews and student surveys.

Throughout delivery of the Sport Education athletics season, Deborah kept a journal on how she perceived the season progressed, noting students' reactions to the tasks, task cards and teaching methods as well as noting informal comments made or questions asked by the primary teachers. Analysis of the journaling involved reading and rereading journal entries, identifying any themes and patterns.

At the conclusion of the Sport Education athletics season, and as teachers were designing a Sport Education orienteering season, a semi-structured one-on-one interview was conducted with each teacher by the first author, Ann. The focus of the interview was to determine whether modelling was viewed as facilitating teachers' design and delivery of a Sport Education season, what might have been missing from the modelling and which aspects of Sport Education teachers intended to pursue for the subsequent orienteering season. Interview data were analysed through continuous reading and rereading of the data sources, identifying similarities and differences, themes and patterns through inductive analysis (Strauss and Corbin, 1998).

Following delivery of the athletics season, students completed a survey to inform which aspects of the season were most effective, enjoyable and worthwhile from their perspective. The first part of the survey included 12 statements to which the student could choose a 'smiley face', 'neutral face' or 'frowning face' to reflect their perception of the statement. These data were analysed descriptively to report frequency. The second part of the survey provided open-ended questions to which the pupils responded relative to their likes/dislikes, learning they felt occurred, areas of improvement, problems they encountered and how instruction might be delivered differently. Survey qualitative data were uploaded to the ATLAS/ti 5.0 for Windows as a means of organising the responses but not to analyse the data. Similar to the analysis of the journaling, themes and patterns across responses were noted. Qualitative comments reported in the chapter are presented as students wrote them and are denoted to particular students by a reference number.

Reactions to Sport Education and the modelling experience

Data collection allows us to comment on the extent to which the Sport Education unit was perceived to be effective by the students, teachers and Deborah. While any success of Sport Education in facilitating students' learning in Sport Education cannot be attributed to the generalist teachers' learning in this instance, as Deborah was responsible for the organisation and delivery of the season, it does provide the two teachers with an insight into how their professional learning has the potential to enhance their students' learning. What teachers perceive as worthwhile student learning experiences from the Sport Education season, as well as instructional formats that they have been exposed to and are attracted to pursuing through the Sport Education modelling experience, are likely to inform their level of intention to implement Sport Education in the future. This also allows us to comment on the extent to which teachers would attribute their disposition towards teaching Sport Education in the future to their confidence in delivering Sport Education and/or the students' responses to the Sport Education that they have witnessed.

Consequently, we present the findings in two parts – (1) successful attributes of a Sport Education unit: shared perspectives, and (2) putting learning into practice: teachers' perspectives on future implementation of Sport Education.

Successful attributes of a Sport Education unit: shared perspectives

Students reported similar experiences and responses to Sport Education to that reported in previous Sport Education studies and summarised by Kinchin (2006).

Student learning through Sport Education

Students recorded enjoying learning about athletics (shot put and triple jump were identified most frequently by students as being something new they had experienced and learned about) and reported increased knowledge and understanding of athletics following the Sport Education season, expressing a desire to learn more about athletics in the future. Students reported feeling good about themselves as 'players' in athletics, as well as learning about teamwork ('I learned that working as a team is easier than working by yourself', S23), cooperation and fair play ('I learned to help and let people join in at games', S8). Students also valued the use of task/information cards in helping them learn their roles and in learning the different events in the athletics season.

Team affiliation, roles and responsibilities

If Sport Education is to be successful, students must learn both their player and non-player roles and come to respect and value the contribution of each player, and their respective roles, towards their team's achievements (Tannehill and Collier, 2008). Team affiliation was an attractive feature of the Sport Education season for students: 'I liked it [being on a team] because I had extra people on my side and more help and support' (S12), 'I liked the team of players because we worked well' (S18) and 'I like being on a team because I got to know people better than before' (S44). One major aspect of Sport Education that this season attempted to foster was that of working cooperatively to achieve team goals. Deborah made note of student progress in this area:

> One team was struggling but using FVC [full value contract] seemed to help. They held a team discussion and made plans on what they needed to do differently. Not a lot of finger pointing and blaming, just what might be done to solve issues.

At the close of each day when students were involved in self-assessment of team or individual effort, Deborah noted 'they [students] were quiet and appeared to be considering events that occurred seriously'.

Both teachers and Deborah were surprised by the students' response to taking on leadership within their teams, with every student applying for a role. The Festivity Coordinator role was a role that seemed to evolve by group consensus, as Deborah noted: 'FC [Festivity Coordinator] was a role that many seemed to know who would be best (. . .) "She is very creative" or "He likes that stuff" were comments overheard during team discussions.' In other instances, Deborah reflected that students provided 'detailed reasons for why they wanted a role and why they would be good at it', which suggested their willingness to take responsibility for a portion of the athletics season. Nicola (teacher) talked about the roles the students took on as being an effective element of the Sport Education season from the students' perspective:

> Definitely being their own trainer, that was brilliant, they all took it on board and they loved it and you could see everybody doing it. I loved it, it was excellent . . . they were a lot more positive towards each other, by the end of it. It took a while for some of them to get into it, but they were egging each other on, it was all good, it was all nice things and I felt like they improved their confidence, they gained confidence from it, and there were students patting each other on the back, it was all positive reinforcement.

As students took on these roles, their behaviour was noticed in Deborah's journal comments:

> Excited group of captains as they picked teams. Came in with notepads and met in the corner before I even had things ready . . . [they] took task of choosing teams seriously (. . .) intense and talked through problems about those who may not get along.

It was also noted by Deborah that the captains did not seem to focus on selecting their friends but rather developing even-skilled teams and the focus of the trainers as they came into class daily, immediately picking up their trainer task cards, and moving to team courts for warm-ups with minimal prompting.

Use of task cards

Task cards were reported by students as being useful in explaining their role in the athletic season and in being able to do the skills and follow the rules of each athletic event. Using task cards was noted by Deborah in several instances as a positive aspect of season delivery, whether for management of the Sport Education season or guiding student learning of athletics events:

> Pupils focused on task cards and technique throughout practice tasks . . . gave each other corrective points [practice tasks] . . . captains used task cards to lead practice of shot and/or running on team courts. They kept peers to the task with little conflict [role responsibility].

An appreciation for the attributes of the teacher

The majority of students noted an appreciation of the teaching attributes of Deborah and how it facilitated student learning. Students conveyed an appreciation for clear explanations that aided understanding ('I liked the way the teachers explained clearly and nicely, it helped a lot', S12; 'I liked the way athletics was taught because it was easy to understand', S21), an opportunity for clarification ('I think it was good because we could ask questions and it was taught in an easy way', S19; 'I like the way you taught me because you explained it clearly and helped us through the way', S43) and teaching strategies that were conducive to gaining students' attention ('I liked when Miss T [Deborah] got us to sit down to tell us what to do because she explained it good', S17; 'Nobody rushed you and they showed you very well how. Because nobody gave out to you', S28; 'You were kind to us because we listened', S38).

Maximising the effectiveness of Sport Education

For the Sport Education season to maximise its effectiveness for all students, dislikes reported by some students such as an overemphasis on the technicality of athletic events, problems with teammates ('When team members disagreed with each other', S1; 'The unfiare [unfair] teams', S24), reinforcing fair play ('Nothing was wrong with the way athletics was taught, but some people didn't go by the fair play agreement and that caused problems', S27) and the pacing of the lessons need to be addressed. The latter issue received mixed responses, with some students wanting to spend more time on the events they had covered ('Have it a bit longer. Do new things every maybe two weeks', S28) and others wanting to be introduced to other athletic events ('There could be more events for a longer time', S22). The techniques promoted for the triple jump and shot put were problematic for some students and it is imperative that an opportunity to achieve success in all events is accommodated. For students who recorded problems arising with team members, they accredited this to work rate ('When people in the team weren't working hard' S19) or confusion over roles ('The only problem was one person on the team was acting like they had my role,' S12).

Putting learning into practice: teachers' perspectives on future implementation of Sport Education

Team affiliation and roles and responsibilities

When commenting on aspects of Sport Education that the teachers believed to be most effective, and that they were likely to continue to pursue in the Sport Education orienteering season they planned to deliver, Aine noted:

> . . . team affiliations and roles and the responsibilities were very important . . . the roles and responsibilities and encouraging their teammates and their

classmates was beneficial and they did enjoy it and they saw the importance of it within a classroom situation. So, they did improve as time went on and the modelling was good and especially the team affiliations. I think they did learn something from it and they enjoyed it.

Deborah noted throughout the Sport Education season that teachers were impressed by the students' response to teamwork: 'Teachers impressed by student response to activity and teamwork. Nicola indicated that this was much more cooperative than they typically are even though they do get along [as a class of students].' Nicola felt that the entire notion of Sport Education was helpful and exciting for her students:

> The kids were more involved in it, the kids took more leadership in it, you know, they were the leaders, they were doing the training, they were doing the scoring, all that was brilliant, it was great . . .

Teachers' appreciation of the students' independence from the teacher was noted by Deborah: 'Teachers surprised by the response from students to leadership . . . Teachers pleased to see that students could lead much of the lesson themselves and it would be productive.'

Festivity and culminating event

Both teachers planned to maintain the festivity created in the Sport Education athletics season. Nicola proposed that one way to do this is through the awards and recognition aspect:

> We're going to have a notice board in the hallway, in the hall there, and it'll be (. . .) every week there'll be one person from the team up with their name, their (. . .) details about the team. That'll change then every three weeks, so that over the nine weeks everybody gets a turn of being on the notice board.

Managerial and instructional task cards

Use of task cards for various aspects of the season was discussed and Aine noted her reaction to the managerial task cards:

> They were good, they got them focussed. Because often times you tell kids 'Okay lads, this is the warm-up, this is how it's done. I want ye to run around first, I want ye to do jumping jacks second, blah, blah, blah, whatever.' So it kind of focussed them and they were able to kind of refer to it if they got stuck, so it was kind of a crutch for them.

When it came to using instructional task cards, Aine noted their worth but that she would not develop them further:

> Again, you'll always have some that do [read them] and some that don't. I'd say it was fifty-fifty, some read it, some didn't read it. Some wanted kind of feedback from their own classmates more than actually reading it. So you'll always have one that'll read and one that won't read it, so I wouldn't bring in any more task cards as such because by fourth [class], they should be better able to read, but some of them are reluctant and when they see reading involved in PE they say 'Oh', they turn off.

Aine did note that using task cards was attractive to her as a teacher: 'Student response to them [was positive] and having a task card and having to complete that task card within a PE lesson. They wouldn't have been used to that kind of structure before.' Nicola was less intrigued by their use:

> Every now and then they'd glance at them, but they never actually looked at it and if they were doing anything incorrectly, they didn't look at it to figure out how to do it. Like, that was even when they were, let's say, they were learning how to do the long jump – the task card was there in front of them, but nobody read it. You know, you'd see them doing it [a skill] and they'd be doing it all wrong, but they won't bother looking at it [task card]. I think they should be more drawn to it, 'Well here you go, now look at the task card and see what you're supposed to be doing.' And even stuck up on the wall, as opposed to down on the floor, so that they were stuck up on the wall and they couldn't move.

While the teachers found the task cards problematic, they planned to continue using them to see if they could be more effective, with Nicola stating: 'I still think it's a good idea to use it, yeah, just maybe in a different way or maybe put more focus onto it.'

Transferability (or not) of modelling

The notion of modelling was new to both teachers and this impacted the extent to which the teachers engaged with the intervention, not fully aware of how to make the best of such an opportunity. For example, Nicola admitted to at times 'switching off' and this could perhaps be attributed to Deborah modelling the classes with no active role for the teachers. Nicola had also intended to write notes at the end of each class to remember the intricacies of the lesson but this never materialised. In discussing how modelling may affect the teachers' planning of the orienteering Sport Education season, Nicola appreciated the Sport Education framework:

> I liked the layout. We had ten weeks, a ten week structure, and you knew what you were supposed to do every week, so I could see myself definitely

doing that next year, and saying 'This week I'm going to talk about captains, next week I'm going to talk about trainers', so I liked that. I liked the way she [Deborah] did the training at the beginning . . . she was very clear how to train and how to do their stretches, so that was good.

However, Nicola reported that the transferability of the Sport Education framework was somewhat limited when designing the orienteering season:

We were changing our orienteering from week to week, let's say we were spending three weeks on photo orienteering, three weeks on using the compass and three weeks on . . . something else . . . symbols or something, so I think it was hard to tie it in with the way she [Deborah] did it.

Aine and Nicola admitted that, while modelling of the season, use of task cards (for management of the Sport Education season and instruction) and developing student roles had been useful, they were not confident in their ability to transfer this to another area within the physical education curriculum, as hinted in the previous quote. This was particularly true for Nicola whose limited experience and knowledge of physical activity opportunities in physical education did result in a lack of confidence and subsequently clouded her perception on the extent to which she could benefit from the modelling intervention:

. . . at some level, yeah [modelling had been helpful] but I'm not too sure how it's going to work with our one, because it's so different. I can see myself doing this next year, doing the athletics one next year, and I'd have no problem with it, but having to change it to suit the orienteering, I think, would be [difficult].

Finding space to invest in professional learning

Whether Aine and Nicola are prepared, and able, to continue using Sport Education is also dependent on the students in their classes and time constraints around which they must plan. Aine relayed her concern that she would not have, or was not prepared to make available, the same amount of time that Deborah had invested in planning for the Sport Education unit:

. . . she [Deborah] was very organised and she had all her sheets and she was . . . like, she knew where she was going, she knew what her aims were. She was very organised from the point of view of paperwork and that kind of thing. I don't know if we'd get as much time to do what she did . . . I liked her awards, the little stickers, I thought they were nice and they were very creative. Do you know, if we'd have time to cut them in the nice shapes and put all those stickers on them . . . I would have had to make out the task cards and laminate the task cards and . . . so a lot of it is to do with time as well. I don't think, as I said earlier, we would have had the time to do out the task cards that Deborah did out.

Nicola indicated that continuing to have debriefing sessions each week to link what had just happened with their own orienteering season might have clarified for them how to progress in their planning. However, she admitted that the initial plan to meet with Deborah on a weekly basis after each week's athletic class to parallel plan the orienteering season based on what Deborah had modelled that particular week did not occur because the teachers were unable to find the time in their day to give to such a weekly activity:

> We had them [debriefing] at the beginning, but I didn't think there was a need to continue, once we could see what they [students] were doing with it. I suppose what we could have done was maybe talked about it in relation to our one [orienteering season], what we were going to do if we wanted to parallel plan it, which was the idea at the start but it just didn't work, because we didn't take it on. It's our own fault, you know. I suppose it was just the time constraints, there was just so much to do.

The demands placed on primary teachers to emphasise other subject areas and get students ready for exams rarely allows time to consider alternative delivery methods for physical education and the related planning and preparation, as Nicola shared:

> With a different class I might need to work harder on them and you mightn't let them have so much time. Like, we're supposed to have, let's say, the hour of PE during the week, so I felt like it takes, it does take up a lot of time. You know, you're under a lot of pressure . . . I worked around it, but that's one of my worries, like, let's say, we have tests now coming up and you, kind of, want to make sure they get on well enough, that they've learned enough in English and maths, let's say. Now I know how important PE is and I know we should have it more often, but the curriculum doesn't allow for it . . . I don't want other subjects to suffer.

In spite of these issues, Nicola noted that maintaining a connection with Ann or Deborah to seek assistance would help her feel confident to continue with Sport Education:

> Yeah, maybe a check-in, yeah, definitely, because you'd forget things. You know, maybe a check-in, say 'How did you do that again?' . . . definitely a kind of a reference or somebody that . . . maybe I could email Deborah or whatever.

Points for consideration

It was evident that the lack of appropriate and adequate content knowledge and subsequent confidence in delivering physical education (Armour and Duncombe, 2004; Petrie, 2009; Rovegno and Bandhauer, 1997) appeared to be the weak link in the teachers' dispositions to develop Sport Education across other activity areas.

Regardless, they felt that the modelling provided them with a useful example to replicate Sport Education. We believe that modelling can be extended to the primary setting and professional learning of primary teachers in physical education by drawing on the work of O'Sullivan and Deglau (2006). In a longitudinal professional development project, they provide a set of principles for the design of professional development programmes that include allowing teachers to form their own interpretations of educational issues as a result of their participation, providing teachers the opportunity to take ownership of programme initiatives, situating professional development in teaching practice, focusing on design and delivery of physical education content, developing means of sustaining teacher interaction and dialogue, conducting professional development in the actual teaching and learning context of schools and working to meet teachers' needs while striving towards larger programme goals. Through modelling of curricular initiatives and physical activity content in the school setting, working collaboratively with teachers to design and deliver their own units of instruction and being available for continued support, collaboration and dialogue, primary teachers can develop their skill and expertise in teaching physical education for learning to children.

Improving the quality of teachers' career-long professional learning is pivotal to raising the standards of physical education (Armour, 2006; Armour and Yelling, 2004b), and school-based, collaborative and informal learning, in which teachers engage voluntarily, are continually supported as the tenets of effective professional learning (Armour and Yelling, 2004b; Deglau and O'Sullivan, 2006). Teachers need to be supported continuously to overcome the inhibitors of professional learning concerning their practical teaching problems (Li, 2010) and this is where the authors, in the absence of other professional learning opportunities related to Sport Education for the two teachers, failed. Supporting Armour and Yelling (2007), we are conscious that the informal network the two teachers in this study form(ed) could benefit from appropriate input, including ourselves in the role as teacher educators.

Supporting the notion that students' learning outcome is an important measure index for the effectiveness of a professional development programme (Deglau and O'Sullivan, 2006), while there is evidence from the students of the effectiveness of their Sport Education venture, more could have been done to examine how much of this was attributed to the novelty of the Sport Education discourse and how much to Deborah's delivery. If professional development is to be validated as an effective instructional strategy, there is a need to link effective physical education teacher development with student achievement and growth (Wang and Ha, 2008).

In suggesting an alternative to the traditional model of CPD (i.e. off-site, with minimal follow-up or support to enable teachers to integrate new learning with practice), Armour and Yelling (2004b) refer to Garet et al.'s (2001) 'reform'-type activities: '"Reform" types of CPD typically take place within the school day, involve collective participation of teachers from the same school or group of schools, and are integrated into practice in the form of study groups, mentoring and coaching' (p. 86).

The modelling approach to professional learning in this instance did reduce a number of concerns that (physical education) teachers have raised previously, including time and location (Armour and Yelling, 2004b). Modelling the Sport Education unit with the teacher's own class of students did not take teachers' time from the school day or their own time and allowed professional learning to take place in the context in which teachers were being asked to reproduce the practice. However, the investment of time the teacher educators involved in the study gave to working with the primary teachers was in addition to their contractual teaching and research remit, resulting in it not being feasible for both to continue involvement with the teachers as they embarked on the orienteering season. We believe that teacher educators should be involved in providing professional learning opportunities for teachers in schools, that this should be acknowledged as a legitimate professional responsibility and hence be reflected in the remit of those working in teacher education.

References

Armour, K.M. (2006) 'Physical education teachers as career-long learners: A compelling research agenda', *Physical Education and Sport Pedagogy*, 11: 203–207. doi:10.1080/17408980600986231

Armour, K.M. and Duncombe, R. (2004) 'Teachers' continuing professional development in primary physical education: Lessons from present and past to inform the future', *Physical Education and Sport Pedagogy*, 9: 3–21. doi:10.1080/1740898042000208098

Armour, K.M. and Yelling, M.R. (2002) '"Talk and chalk" or learning from "doing": Continuing professional development for physical education teachers', *British Journal of Teaching Physical Education*, 33(4): 40–42.

Armour, K.M. and Yelling, M.R. (2004a) 'Continuing professional development for experienced physical education teachers: Towards effective provision', *Sport, Education and Society*, 9: 95–114. doi:10.1080/1357332042000175836

Armour, K.M. and Yelling, M.R. (2004b) 'Professional "development" and professional "learning": Bridging the gap for experienced physical education teachers', *European Physical Education Review*, 10: 71–74. doi:10.1177/1356336X04040622

Armour, K.M. and Yelling, M.R. (2007) 'Effective professional development for physical education teachers: The role of informal, collaborative learning', *Journal of Teaching in Physical Education*, 26: 177–200.

Atencio, M., Jess, M. and Dewar, K. (2009) 'Implementing a complex continuing professional development agenda', *Scottish Physical Education Complexity Conference*, University of Aberdeen, 12–13 January. Available HTTP: http://www.abdn.ac.uk/stne/uploads/files/MJ10JA_1.DOC (accessed 14 January 2011).

Bechtel, P.A. and O'Sullivan, M. (2006) 'Effective professional development – What we now know', *Journal of Teaching in Physical Education*, 25: 363–378.

Borko, H. (2004) 'Professional development and teacher learning: Mapping the terrain', *Educational Researcher*, 31(8): 18–20.

Cochran-Smith, M. and Lytle, L.S. (1999) 'Relationship of knowledge and practice: Teacher learning in communities', *Review of Educational Research*, 24: 249–306.

Cohen, D.K. and Hill, H.C. (1998) *Instruction, capacity, and improvement*, Philadelphia, PA: Consortium for Policy Research in Education, University of Pennsylvania (CPRE RR-43).

Deglau, D. and O'Sullivan, M. (2006) 'The effects of a long-term professional development program on the beliefs and practices of experienced teachers', *Journal of Teaching in Physical Education*, 25: 379–396.

Department of Education and Science/National Council for Curriculum and Assessment (1999a) *Primary school curriculum physical education*, Dublin: Government Publications.

Department of Education and Science/National Council for Curriculum and Assessment (1999b) *Primary school curriculum physical education: Teacher guidelines*, Dublin: Government Publications.

Duncombe, R. and Armour, K.M. (2004) 'Collaborative professional learning: From theory to practice', *Journal of In-service Education*, 30: 141–161. doi:10.1080/13674580400200230

Finley, S.J., Marble, S.T., Copeland, G. and Ferguson, C. (2000) 'Professional development and teachers' construction of coherent instructional practices: A synthesis of experiences in five sites', paper presented at the Annual Meeting of the American Educational Research Association, New Orleans, LA, 24–28 April.

Garet, S.M., Porter, C.A., Desimone, L., Birman, B.F. and Suk Yoon, K. (2001) 'What makes professional development effective? Results from a national sample of teachers', *American Educational Research Journal*, 38: 915–945.

Haston, W. (2007) 'Teacher modeling as an effective teaching strategy', *Music Educators Journal*, 93(4): 26–30.

Kinchin, G.D. (2006) 'Sport Education: A view of the research', in D. Kirk, D. Macdonald and M. O'Sullivan (eds) *Handbook of physical education* (pp. 596–609), London: Sage.

Kinchin, G.D., MacPhail, A. and Ni Chroinin, D. (2009) 'Pupils' and teachers' perceptions of a culminating festival within a Sport Education season in Irish primary schools', *Physical Education and Sport Pedagogy*, 14: 391–406. doi:10.1080/17408980802584982

Ko, B., Wallhead, T. and Ward, P. (2006) 'Professional development workshops: What do teachers learn and use?' *Journal of Teaching in Physical Education*, 25: 397–412.

Li, C. (2010) 'Serving PE teachers' professional learning experiences in social circus', *New Horizons in Education*, 58(1): 108–119.

McCaughtry, N., Hodges-Kulinna, P., Cothran, D., Martin, J. and Faust, R. (2005) 'Teachers mentoring teachers: A view over time', *Journal of Teaching in Physical Education*, 24: 326–343.

MacPhail, A., O'Sullivan, M. and Halbert, J. (2008) 'Physical education and education through sport in Ireland', in G. Klein and K. Hardman (eds) *Physical education and Sport Education in the European Union* (volume 2, pp. 188–201), Paris: Editions Revue EPS.

O'Sullivan, M. and Deglau, D. (2006) 'Principles of professional development', *Journal of Teaching in Physical Education*, 25: 441–449.

Penney, D., Clarke, G., Quill, M. and Kinchin, G. (2005) *Sport Education in physical education: Research based practice*, New York: Routledge.

Petrie, K. (2009) 'Teaching physical education: Primary school teachers as learners', unpublished thesis, The University of Waikato, New Zealand.

Rovegno, I. and Bandhauer, D. (1997) 'Psychological dispositions that facilitated and sustained the development of knowledge of a constructivist approach to physical education', *Journal of Teaching in Physical Education*, 16: 136–154.

Siedentop, D., Hastie, P.A. and van der Mars, H. (2004) *Complete guide to Sport Education*, Champaign, IL: Human Kinetics.

Strauss, A. and Corbin, J. (1998) *Basics of qualitative research: Grounded theory, procedures and techniques*, Newbury Park, CA: Sage.

Tannehill, D. and Collier, C. (2008) 'Using task cards to teach athletics with Sport Education', *Physical Education Matters*, 3(2): 16–21.

Wang, C. and Ha, A. (2008) 'The teacher development in physical education: A review of the literature', *Asian Social Science*, 4(12): 3–18.

Ward, P. and Doutis, P. (1999) 'Toward a consolidation of the knowledge base for reform in physical education', *Journal of Teaching in Physical Education*, 18: 382–402.

14

WITHIN SCHOOL, IN-DEPTH PROFESSIONAL DEVELOPMENT FOR SPORT EDUCATION

A Russian model

Oleg Sinelnikov

> The easier it is for the teacher to teach, the more difficult it is for students to learn.
>
> *(Lev Tolstoy)*

Sport Education has become a truly international curriculum, a strong supporting evidence of which is presented in this book. The purpose of this chapter is to describe and provide an account of Sport Education implementation into the physical education curriculum at a Russian school. This experience required physical education teachers and in some cases principals to reconceptualize physical education as a subject matter and its place in the school. In addition, it also required physical education teachers to move beyond what is known as a command style multiactivity approach to instruction (Metzler, 2000).

Physical education in Russia

The command style multiactivity approach to instruction is alive and well in Russian schools. Physical educators in Russia continue using outdated methods and styles of teaching, sometimes not necessarily by choice, but often as a result of a lack of appropriate information and resources. Physical education teachers do not have an opportunity for curricular freedom as the physical education program is relatively rigid and prescriptive. In addition, the teaching itself in many cases is "old school" and many lessons directly conflict with developmentally appropriate practices (Sinelnikov and Hastie, 2008). During a typical physical education lesson in a Russian school, for example, students spend a considerable amount of time waiting for their turn, as equipment is very limited. Teams for game play are often chosen by captains, and fitness and other testing is conducted one by one while other students watch the performance. The equipment or rules of adult games are rarely modified and full field games are the norm.

Moreover, the current school of thought in Russian academia on the place of physical education in the public schools centers on the idea of using physical education as the scouting and training grounds for elite athletes. For example, Balsevich (1999), a well-respected Russian academician, has suggested a complete elimination of physical education during regular school time, instead opening the doors to "training interest clubs" outside of regular school hours. Students would be offered a choice between three and four sports for the semester. Once a sport is chosen, the student would then participate in a rigorous training for this particular sport. The "training clubs" would be school based but the teaching would resemble and be in accord with coaching principles. In fact, it is also suggested that coaches from different sports and not physical education teachers would be the ones providing instructions and training for students.

The premise of Sport Education contradicts Balsevich's (1999) vision for Russian physical education. Nevertheless, there have been initial attempts to implement Sport Education into the Russian physical education curriculum. For example, Hastie and Sinelnikov (2006) were the first ones to describe Russian students' participation in and perceptions of a season of Sport Education. Similar to Western research in Sport Education, Russian students enjoy their participation: their intrinsic levels of motivation increase and levels of amotivation decrease (Sinelnikov et al., 2007). In addition, Russian students significantly improve their skill and tactical competencies (Hastie et al., 2009) and have a deeper understanding of sports as a result of participation in multiple seasons of Sport Education (Sinelnikov and Hastie, 2010b).

How to teach Sport Education

The following description of Sport Education in a Russian school is meant to be provided through the lens of professional development, as it is evident that, in order for students to experience a "full-on" and not "watered-down" Sport Education (Curtner-Smith et al., 2008), there is a need to properly train physical education teachers to first understand and then to deliver the instructional model in accord with its major tenets. Educational literature suggests that the implementation of any new pedagogical approach is time-consuming and highly labor intensive (Fullan, 1999). More specifically, acquiring pedagogical content knowledge and learning to teach within a model-based instruction framework, such as the case of Sport Education, seems to be an intricate and a dynamic process (Lund et al., 2008) that is sometimes met with resistance (McCaughtry et al., 2004). Specifically, McCaughtry et al. found that preservice teachers learning the Sport Education model struggled with the novel-to-them focus on tactical (vs. skill) instruction, and misunderstood the different approaches to skill development.

One of the reasons for this process being so challenging is explained by the necessity on the part of physical education teachers to attend to several key factors simultaneously rather than learn them as a set of deconstructed pieces of knowledge (e.g., management, content, and student characteristics) (Lund *et al.*, 2008). This presents a challenge to all educators learning to use model-based instruction, and specifically Sport Education.

One way of reducing that burden is to prepare the teachers to deliver Sport Education during teacher professional development. However, not every professional development opportunity is created equal. In the United States, the Consortium for Policy Research in Education published Policy Briefs (Corcoran, 1995) that provided starting points for several approaches to teacher professional development. These included: (a) joint work and job enrichment, (b) teacher networks, (c) collaboration between schools and colleges, (d) professional development schools, (e) national board certification, and (f) teachers as researchers. Regardless of the approach, however, the following three core features of professional development activities have significant positive effect on teachers' increases in knowledge and skills and, more importantly, in changes in classroom practice: focus on content knowledge, opportunities for active learning, and coherence with other learning activities. In addition, teacher learning is significantly affected by the form of the activity (workshop vs. study group), collective participation of teachers from the same school, grade, or subject, and the duration of the activity (Garet *et al.*, 2001).

However, professional development is still thought of almost exclusively in terms of formal education activities, such as courses or workshops. These "in-service" programs may or may not be relevant to teachers' professional development needs, and often there is little guidance about how to manage and improve efforts in the area of professional development (Corcoran, 1995). While the ideas that contribute to enhancing professional development are available, very few professional development programs follow them (Guskey, 1991).

There is an agreement in the literature about the ineffective practice in professional development for teachers, and evidence exists suggesting that sporadic "one-off" professional development activities are unlikely to have lasting impact upon teachers' practice (Armour and Yelling, 2004; Connelly and James, 1998). In the field of physical education, teachers' experiences in such programs are said to lack coherence and relevance (Armour and Yelling, 2004), as well as appropriate progression (Ward and Doutis, 1999). This seems to be also true in the case of professional development for physical education teachers in Russia.

Professional development for physical education teachers in Russia

The term that is most frequently used in Russian literature for different forms of professional development for teachers is "Additional Professional Education." The Additional Professional Education (professional development) systemic model for physical education teachers in Russia is typically lecture based and theory driven.

More specifically, to satisfy professional development requirements, physical education teachers attend a series of compulsory lectures in three major areas: sport specialization, methods of teaching physical education, and a thematic course from a local university or a well-known specialist (Loktev *et al.*, 2001). Sport specialization lectures focus on providing in-depth knowledge or current trends of a specific sport, while lectures on methods of teaching physical education mostly reiterate the information provided during university studies for physical education majors. More often than not, that information is rooted in the physical education literature from the Soviet period and is very outdated.

The content of the so-called thematic lecture courses varies. In addition, the type and content of thematic courses are often determined by the specialty and interests of the university faculty assigned to deliver instruction. For example, in places with more progressive university faculty, teachers may take "organization and methods of teaching students with disabilities" courses, while in others teachers participate in "social service and tourism."

While there is little to no information available on the effectiveness of professional development for Russian physical education teachers, these known features of professional development in a current system of education are reminiscent of those that have been criticized in educational literature. It is suggested that such forms of professional development are decontextualized, detached from the realities of teaching, provide little account for the individual school contexts, and are ultimately less effective (Guskey, 2002; NPEAT, 1999). The state and local government seldom provide the necessary funds for professional development in Russia as "the financing of professional development, especially for physical education teachers working in schools, colleges, and universities, is not considered a priority" (Loktev *et al.*, 2001, p. 50).

For these reasons, we therefore decided to avoid the typical Additional Professional Education (professional development) available in Russia and instead put into action a professional development program that is research and evidence based and which is rooted in effective professional development practices. While realizing the significant limitation in terms of the reach, we decided to focus on just one specific Russian school in which we intended to make a difference.

Previously, common avenues for teaching Sport Education to physical education teachers elsewhere included one or several of the following approaches: (1) the use of printed materials such as books or guides (Grant *et al.*, 1992; Siedentop, 1994; Siedentop *et al.*, 2004); (2) the development of teaching material (e.g., printed guides and videos) and its distribution to teachers (Alexander and Taggart, 1995); (3) the integration of key features of the model throughout the physical education teacher education curriculum and teaching preservice teachers how to teach Sport Education (Curtner-Smith and Sofo, 2004; Jenkins, 2004; McCaughtry *et al.*, 2004); (4) the presentation of Sport Education at conferences (Siedentop, 2002); and (5) the introduction to the model through workshops and seminars (Ko *et al.*, 2006).

While the effectiveness of each of these approaches can be questioned, by combining the practices from the educational literature on effective professional development and specific past experiences of different approaches of teaching Sport Education to others discussed above, we created the following professional development program for implementation in a single Russian school.

Sport Education professional development program

The plan for Sport Education professional development was to provide resources for physical education teachers who were unfamiliar with Sport Education, to teach them the model, to have them implement it in their school, and to gauge its effectiveness. This plan included following the consequential phases listed below.

Phase I—establishing a point of entry

First, we had to recruit physical education teachers who taught upper-level grades and would be willing to participate in the program. There are many teachers in Russia who are still enthusiastic about their profession, their work, their discipline, and about working with students. We decided to use a ground-up approach; that is, to first find the teachers willing to participate in the program and then ask the principal and local educational authorities for permission. The top-down approach might have been just as effective. To establish a point of entry to the schools, we contacted a local university in the Russian Central Chernozem region, explained our program, and asked for faculty recommendation. The faculty at the university recommended several local schools in which physical education teachers had various teaching experiences.

Phase II—recognizing the stakeholders and decision makers

It was important for us to understand who the stakeholders and decision makers were in the targeted school, so we visited several schools to meet with teachers, students, and the administration. We had to identify the individuals and groups that were likely to affect or to be affected by our program, and sort them according to their impact on it and the impact the program would have on them. While our stakeholders included the students, parents, and teachers, the decision makers were members of the administration, so our focus was on them during our preliminary school visits. We highly recommend gaining an understanding of stakeholders before embarking on any significant project. It is here where we learned more about physical education teachers and their administration.

Decision makers

The typical decision makers in the school administration in Russia include the school principal and assistant principal for the educational process. Out of five schools that we visited, only the administrations in three schools were open to the possibility of a professional development program for their physical education teachers. The reasons given by decision makers in those schools which refused professional development were superficial (one principal stated the impossibility of anything happening in physical education in his school because the roof in the gymnasium was leaking), but regardless of securing key stakeholders' support, professional development would be ineffective. Ultimately, based on meetings with primary stakeholders and visits to the school, we chose one school as the site for teachers learning how to implement Sport Education in their teaching. The school had a total enrollment of nearly 600 students in the first through 11th grade. It was located in a small rural city (population 30,000) in the central part of Russia.

Primary stakeholders

At the school two physical education teachers were mainly responsible for physical education instruction to upper-grade students. Both teachers were male: one teacher had 27 years of teaching experience and the other one had 3 years of teaching experience. According to the skill acquisition model (Dreyfus and Dreyfus, 1986), the first teacher is considered an expert and the other one is classified as an advanced beginner. Below is a brief sketch of each teacher's background.

Expert teacher

The expert teacher had taught physical education for 27 years and was considered one of the premier physical education teachers in Russia. Indeed, he held the title of an "Honor Teacher of the Russian Federation," which is the highest teaching honor awarded by the government. For the last 16 years, he had worked in the same school where the study took place. Of particular note was that he had been employed in this school since its opening in 1990 and was instrumental in designing the layout of facilities used for physical education for the school.

Advanced beginner teacher

The advanced beginner had 3 years of experience teaching physical education at the same school. He was a graduate student at the local state university and, in addition to teaching physical education classes at this school, the advanced beginner teacher also coached basketball and gymnastics.

Phase III—selling Sport Education

It is recognized that teachers' beliefs and attitudes have a powerful impact on the process of implementing curricula and instructional innovation (Borko and Putnam, 1995; Fullan, 1993). Our first step then was to "sell Sport Education" and convince physical education teachers to participate in the professional development program and have them "buy into the program." As we found out, the best way of selling the program was to focus on the potential benefits to the students. As we met with teachers and explained Sport Education and its main characteristics, we showed artifacts of student involvement, level of enthusiasm, and student learning in Sport Education seasons in other schools (photos and short videos). This seemed to have an impact on teachers' initial interest in the program.

However, there were some concerns. During the initial conversation, physical education teachers were initially apprehensive about: (a) allowing others in their professional space and (b) any potential changes in their program. Both concerns needed to be addressed before any progress could be made. Initially, an expert teacher seemed to be more apprehensive about the prospects of change while his less experienced colleague seemed more apt to embrace an innovative curriculum.

A good strategy at that point was for us to listen and learn from the teachers about their physical education program and outline the potential for innovation in their current teaching practices. Again, the main selling point of Sport Education seemed to be the potential benefits of the model for the students. Moreover, in addition to discussing physical education teachers' current program, we searched for ways in which Sport Education would fit and benefit *their* curriculum, *their* program, and most importantly *their* students. This was consistent with Fullan *et al.*'s (2006) summary of a process of a teacher change in which "the vast majority of teachers are motivated by moral purpose when ideas for activating it are evident" (p. 88).

Phase IV—providing printed materials

There is a Russian proverb, "what is written with a feather cannot be destroyed by an axe," which is similar to the English saying "the pen is mightier than the sword." The written word can be powerful. Therefore, first to help convince physical education teachers to participate in the program and second to familiarize teachers with Sport Education, we provided them with written materials and guides to Sport Education in the Russian language.

This phase was similar to the way Australian educators advanced with a national implementation of the model in which a group of researchers developed the *Sport Education in Physical Education Program (SEPEP)* manual for Australian teachers to use. This manual was published by the Australian Sports Commission (Alexander and Taggart, 1995). The teachers' manual progressed through 14 modules: understanding of Sport Education, teacher's role, student's role, programming, game modifications, selection, competition formats, publicity, end-of-season event, school community links, equity, assessment, making use of available resources, and troubleshooting. Teachers were invited to read through the modules and implement a season of Sport Education in their schools.

We based our materials on the most recent book about Sport Education available at the time (Siedentop *et al.*, 2004). In addition, we provided several articles published in Russian journals that described the model in detail (see Sinelnikov and Hastie, 2004, 2005; Sinelnikov *et al.*, 2004). We asked teachers to read the provided materials and, while the materials were practitioner oriented and easy to read, we nonetheless asked teachers to keep track of confusing points so that we could clarify them at our next meeting.

Phase V—securing teachers' agreement and staying in contact

We contacted the physical education teachers shortly after the initial meeting to gauge their interest in learning more about Sport Education. It was during this contact we were able to secure their agreement to participate in the program. Staying in contact, having lines of communications available, and being open and flexible is critical in this phase. We were able to maintain constant contact with the physical education teachers via telephone and e-mail. It was during this phase teachers were able to provide more details about their schools, facilities, and schedules, and they also became more comfortable and open with us. Physical education teachers also began to be enthusiastic about the upcoming Sport Education season. This communication helped us shape the direction of the project, and allowed teachers and researchers to jointly work out the necessary managerial issues: timeframe, schedule, activity taught, and classes.

Phase VI—Sport Education workshop

The more meaningful features that characterize the processes that occur during professional development include content, active learning, and coherence (Birman *et al.*, 2000; Steyn, 2005). Therefore, a 2-day Sport Education group study was designed upon these previously identified features of high-quality professional development. Professional development is more effective when it focuses on the content as well as on how students learn the specific content, rather than general noncontent-based teaching strategies (Cohen and Hill, 1998; Fennema *et al.*, 1996; Kennedy, 1998). In addition, when participants engage in active learning, such as interacting with other participants, leading exercises, simulating practice, and obtaining feedback, they learn more and changes in teacher practice are more likely (Carey and Frechtling, 1997; Darling-Hammond, 1997; Lieberman, 1996; Schifter, 1996).

The arrangement was for the researchers and teachers to meet at the school during the spring break, a week prior to the beginning of the academic quarter in which implementation of Sport Education commenced. The structure of the workshop was similar to the one described by Ko *et al.* (2006) with its three-part organization. The first part of the workshop was content specific and focused on the key features of Sport Education: its key structural characteristics and its dissimilarities with traditional teaching. An essential element present in all descriptions was the student-centered nature of the model, and researchers led this part of the workshop.

The second part provided active learning opportunities in which the physical education teachers and the researchers jointly designed a Sport Education season outline and wrote sample lesson plans representative of all parts of the season. The focus of this part was not on how to teach a sport, but rather on lesson and season structures specific to Sport Education as well as common to the model pedagogical problems. In addition, since teachers can influence the motivational climate of Sport Education (Sinelnikov and Hastie, 2010a), careful consideration was given to the structures of Sport Education that contribute to the mastery climate and performance climate. For example, issues of student-directed team selections, facilitating peer teaching, implementing graded competition, game modifications, and role selection and compliance were addressed. The purpose of this phase was "for the teachers to problematize the teaching methodologies required to deliver a student-centered curriculum such as Sport Education" (Ko *et al.*, 2006, p. 399).

The final part of the workshop was a summary and reflective group discussion about teaching and the model. During that time, physical education teachers were able to share their beliefs about teaching, thoughts of the model, and potential for its implementation. It is fair to say that the concepts of student-centered learning and peer teaching were most problematic in the views of the teachers. Arguably, this is due to the fact that most schooling in Russia is teacher driven and performance based.

Cothran *et al.* (2006) demonstrated that sometimes when teachers attend professional development workshops they grow excited about educational innovations and are eager to integrate them into their classrooms. However, when teachers return to their schools, they report feeling confused and frustrated as they forget what they learned or have difficulty integrating what they learned into their specific classrooms. Therefore, the next step was crucial for the success of our professional development program.

Phase VII—immersive and extensive on-site professional development

The final, and most time-consuming, portion of the professional development program was the immersive and extensive on-site professional development. Little and Houston (2003) have demonstrated that continued support was one of the required key variables in the process of teachers altering their teaching in a meaningful way through professional development. In addition, almost all of the literature on effective professional development calls for professional development to be sustained over time. In our case, there were three critical elements of this continued support: (1) *sustainability*—professional development was available and sustained throughout the entire school year; (2) *immediacy*—feedback, briefing, and debriefing was available to the teachers immediately before and after their teaching; and (3) *situated*—professional development took place at the teachers' workplace, in their gym, and in their offices. Therefore, it was critical for the person delivering the professional development to be present at the school for much of the implementation of the model.

In order to accomplish this, we observed physical education teachers teaching two of the three lessons each week, and conducted briefing and debriefing sessions with the teachers each time. The briefing and debriefing sessions were designed as an attempt at a positive connection of the theory (Sport Education curriculum) to practice (actual teaching) using a reflective framework for teaching in physical education suggested by Tsangaridou and O'Sullivan (1994). The framework for debriefing divides the reflective process into three categories of focus: technical, situational, and sensitizing. A technical focus includes instructional or managerial aspects of teaching; contextual issues of teaching are characterized as situational reflection; and sensitizing reflection deals with the social, moral, ethical, or political aspects of teaching (Tsangaridou and O'Sullivan, 1994). Although devised for pre-service teachers, the framework was deemed appropriate for use as a debriefing guide to focus teachers' comments after the lessons, and in retrospect it provided valuable structure for the sessions.

Both physical education teachers involved in the project taught separate sixth-grade classes at the time and both teachers were familiar with their respective sixth-grade classes, as they had taught them for the previous three-quarters of the academic year. Following Siedentop *et al.*'s (2004) recommendations to consider the existing school environment and advice to choose a familiar sport for an initial Sport Education season, both teachers chose basketball. The expert teacher taught a class consisting of 20 students and the advanced beginner teacher class was 17. The relatively smaller classes were typical for the rural school in which the program took place. Both classes were coeducational and met three times a week over a period of 6 weeks. This period of time corresponds to one full academic quarter in Russian schools, so the season of Sport Education, therefore, took place over an entire academic quarter.

Effectiveness of the Sport Education professional development program based on its implementation

To gauge the degree of effectiveness of the Sport Education professional development we documented teacher and student behaviors and the demonstration of Sport Education-specific pedagogical behaviors by the physical education teachers during the season.

Sport Education-specific teacher behaviors

The Sport Education benchmark observational instrument (Ko *et al.*, 2006) was used to discriminate teacher pedagogical behaviors necessary for the delivery of a "typical" Sport Education season. The instrument allowed an observer to code specific teacher behaviors that sufficiently reflect a pedagogy that emphasized each of the core principles of the Sport Education model, such as season, affiliation, student responsibility, formal competition, and record keeping. We coded Sport

Education-specific teacher pedagogical behaviors from the video records as they occurred in all of the recorded lessons. Intraobserver reliability was conducted on two representative lessons from each of the phases of the Sport Education season for each teacher. The intraobserver reliability equaled 98 percent, indicating acceptable levels of agreement suggested by van der Mars (1989).

The results are provided in Table 14.1. In addition to the existing elements of the instrument, the categories of festivity and culminating event were also added to provide for the inclusion of all key features of Sport Education.

Both teachers exhibited the greater majority of the Sport Education-specific pedagogical behaviors considered the benchmark elements of the Sport Education model. Although the teachers did not provide task sheets for coaches to complete with the team, both teachers did provide verbal instructions to team coaches as to what activities to perform. They also demonstrated the activity to the coaches when necessary.

Actual teacher behaviors across the Sport Education phases

During the Sport Education season, the patterns and time allocation of teacher behaviors and patterns of student lesson participation should change (Hastie, 1998). To document the change, the amount of time spent on selected teacher behaviors such as management, instruction, and observation as well as the amount of time students spent during the lesson participating in skill practice, practice games, and competition games during the three phases of the Sport Education season (preseason, practice competition, and formal competition) were collected following real-time recording principles and using the Behavioral Evaluation Strategies and Taxonomies software developed by Sharpe and Koperwas (1999).

To record the duration of the selected teacher behaviors and student lesson participation, a specially designed configuration of the Behavioral Evaluation Strategies and Taxonomies software was used. The category descriptions of the selected teacher behaviors and the student lesson participation and its assigned computer keyboard keys used in the analysis are presented in Table 14.2.

Mean, standard deviation (SD), and percent values of teachers' behaviors across the Sport Education season phases are presented in Table 14.3, while Figure 14.1 provides the visual representation of the observed teachers' behavior patterns across the Sport Education season phases. As can be seen in Table 14.3, as the Sport Education season progressed from preseason to practice competition and to formal competition, there was a decline in the expert teacher's total time spent during the lesson on management behaviors (Mep = 997.9; Mepc = 698; Mefc = 495.9) and instructional behaviors (Mep = 385.6; Mepc = 280.7; Mefc = 58.1). On the other hand, the percentage of lesson time the expert teacher exhibited observing behaviors more than quadrupled from 16 percent in preseason to 73 percent in the formal competition phases of the Sport Education season.

The advanced beginner teacher also exhibited an expected pattern of observed behaviors consistent with the Sport Education model (Hastie, 1998), with the

TABLE 14.1 Demonstration of Sport Education-specific pedagogical behaviors during the season

The benchmark element		Expert		Advanced beginner	
		Planned	Actual	Planned	Actual
The teacher plans the unit around the principle of a "**season**"	Management/organizational phase	✓	✓	✓	✓
	Team selection phase	✓	✓	✓	✓
	Preseason scrimmage phase	✓	✓	✓	✓
	Regular season phase	✓	✓	✓	✓
	End of season event	✓	✓	✓	✓
The teacher promotes the "**affiliation**" concept	Students involved in the process of team selection	✓	✓	✓	✓
	Persisting teams for duration of unit	✓	✓	✓	✓
Teacher promotes students taking "**responsibility**"	Incorporates student duty roles within lessons	✓	✓	✓	✓
	Establishes contract and/or accountability for student performance in roles	✓	✓	✓	✓
	Teacher holds student accountable	✓	✓	✓	✓
	Teacher provides training for referees	✓	✓	✓	✓
	Teacher utilizes tasks to train students on effective verbal communication and feedback	✓	✓	✓	✓
	Teacher provides task sheets for coaches/captains	X	X	X	X
	Teacher adopts a facilitator approach during interactions with student groups	✓	✓	✓	✓
	Teacher encourages students to resolve conflict within groups	✓	✓	✓	✓
Teacher uses "**formal competition**" within unit plan	A formal schedule of competition is established	✓	✓	✓	✓
	Fair play and sportsman awards utilized	✓	✓	✓	✓
Teacher utilizes a form of "**record keeping**" within unit	Teacher provides rubrics for scorekeeper	✓	✓	✓	✓
	Incorporates peer assessment as part of record-keeping process	X	X	X	X
The following elements were added by the author:					
Teacher uses "**culminating event**" near the end of the season	Culminating event is festive in nature	✓	✓	✓	✓
	Teams are easily identifiable (team names, team colors, team T-shirts)	✓	✓	✓	✓
Teacher creates "**festivity**" within unit	Regular postings of team/individual performances	✓	✓	✓	✓
	Teacher emphasizes the celebration of fair play	✓	✓	✓	✓

TABLE 14.2 Category description of teacher behaviors and student lesson participation and keyboard layout

	Category description	Keyboard key
Teacher behaviors		
Instruction (94.6%)	Teacher's "specific intent to influence learning in a particular direction" (Rink, 2006, p. 23).	I
Management (96.8%)	"Everything a teacher does that is not directly related to the content to be taught" (Rink, 2006, p. 52).	M
Observation (98.2%)	An attentive visual examination of students and their activities by the teacher.	O
Student lesson participation		
Skill practice (95.4%)	Individual or team practice aimed at developing skills (techniques and tactics).	S
Practice games (100%)	Nonconsequential games used to learn protocols, rules, and student roles such as officiating in addition to developing technical and tactical skills.	P
Competition games (100%)	Games that matter in the formal competition and in league standings.	C

Note: Intrarater reliability scores are provided in parentheses.

decline of percentage lesson time spent managing the class from 48 percent in preseason to 16 percent in practice competition and 14 percent during formal competition. The lesson time percentage devoted to instructional behaviors by the advanced beginner teacher declined from 31 percent in preseason and 28 percent during practice competition to 6 percent during formal competition. The advanced beginner teacher's lesson time percentage of observing behaviors almost doubled from preseason (29 percent) to practice competition (56 percent), thereafter increasing to 79 percent during the formal competition phase of Sport Education.

Student lesson participation

The mean, SD, and percent values of lesson time allocated by the expert and advanced beginner teachers for student participation in skill practice, practice games, and competition games across the Sport Education season phases are presented in Table 14.4.

Figure 14.2 presents a visual representation of the percent lesson time allocated to skill practice, practice games, and competition games across the phases of the Sport Education season by the expert and advanced beginner teachers, respectively.

TABLE 14.3 Mean, SD, and percent values of teachers' behaviors across the Sport Education season phases

Behavioral category	Preseason			Practice competition			Formal competition		
	Mean	SD	Percent	Mean	SD	Percent	Mean	SD	Percent
Expert									
Management	997.94	753.24	50.13	698.01	204.93	33.48	495.91	238.25	24.17
Instruction	385.57	545.23	21.09	280.65	73.13	13.46	58.06	3.06	2.98
Observation	295.52	417.92	16.17	1106	240.51	53.06	1436.62	206.94	72.85
Total	1679.03			2084.66			1990.59		
Advanced beginner									
Management	743.21	410.29	48.03	311.82	19.78	15.67	172.85	126.87	14.44
Instruction	482.91	341.47	31.19	563.82	234.93	28.37	73.97	11.24	6.18
Observation	448.84	634.75	29.08	1115.08	273.18	55.95	950.04	120.51	79.38
Total	1674.96			1990.72			1196.86		

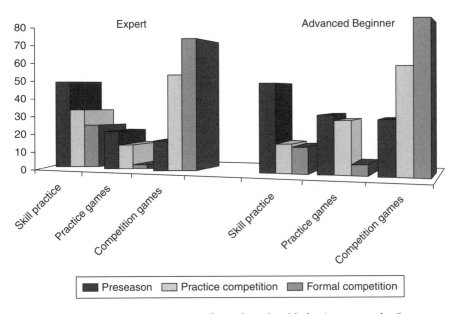

FIGURE 14.1   Lesson time percentage of actual teachers' behaviors across the Sport Education season phases

As can be seen in Figure 14.2, the percentage of lesson time allocated to skill practice by the expert teacher declined from 61 percent in preseason to 40 percent during practice competition, with a further decline to 11 percent during formal competition. The practice games were only evident during the practice competition phase of Sport Education, taking up 49 percent of lesson time, with competition games ensuing only during the formal competition phase, accounting for 55 percent of lesson time.

Likewise, there was a decline in the advanced beginner teacher's time allocation to student skill practice during the season, with 60 percent during skill practice and less than half of that (28 percent) during practice games. Moreover, when formal competition began, the students in the advanced beginner teacher's class did not participate in skill practices. Similar to the expert teacher's time allocation, the advanced beginner teacher allocated time for practice games (58 percent) only during practice competition, and only during formal competition did students participate in competition games for an average of 61 percent of the total lesson time.

The qualitative results of this professional development are described by Sinelnikov (2009) and include the need for sample lesson observance by the teachers in the training phase, model congruency validation, difficulties of "letting go of control," and the establishment of the new partnership relationships between teachers and students. Nevertheless, the current chapter provides a description of the Sport Education professional development program for Russian physical education teachers and the empirical support of its effectiveness. We understand that, if

TABLE 14.4 Time allocations to practice and games across the Sport Education season phases

Season phase	Preseason			Practice competition			Formal competition		
	Mean	*SD*	*Percent*	*Mean*	*SD*	*Percent*	*Mean*	*SD*	*Percent*
Expert									
Skill practice	994.84	108.74	60.55	752.37	493.11	39.57	213.77	61.45	10.57
Practice games	0	0	0	922.38	203.99	48.5	0	0	0
Competition games	0	0	0	0	0	0	1,124.88	313.67	54.66
Advanced beginner									
Skill practice	996.78	192.74	59.79	576.88	232.03	27.89	0	0	0
Practice games	0	0	0	1,110.95	381.83	57.62	0	0	0
Competition games	0	0	0	0	0	0	726.47	413.82	60.71

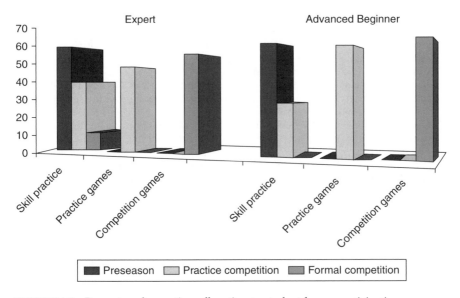

FIGURE 14.2 Percentage lesson time allocation to student lesson participation across the Sport Education season

professional development takes place over an extended period of time and is continuous (Fullan, 1995, 1999; Fullan *et al.*, 2006) and school based (NPEAT, 1999), as well as contextualized in teaching practices (Lave and Wenger, 1991; Sparks, 1997), physical education teachers in Russia can effectively implement a novel curriculum in their teaching.

References

Alexander, K. and Taggart, A. (1995) *Sport Education in Physical Education Program (SEPEP)*. Belconnen, Australia: Australian Sport Commission.

Armour, K.M. and Yelling, M.R. (2004) "Professional development and professional learning: Bridging the gap for experienced physical education teachers," *European Physical Education Review*, 10: 71–94. doi:10.1177/1356336X04040622

Balsevich, B.K. (1999) "Prospects of development for general theory and technologies of sports training and physical education," *Teoriya i Praktika Fizicheskoi Kul'turi*, 4: 21–26, 39–40.

Birman, B.F., Desimone, L., Porter, A.C., and Garet, M.S. (2000) "Designing professional development that works," *Educational Leadership*, 57(8): 28–33.

Borko, H. and Putnam, R.T. (1995) "Expanding a teacher's knowledge base: A cognitive psychological perspective on professional development," in T. Guskey and M. Huberman (eds.) *Professional development in education: New paradigms and practices* (pp. 35–65), New York: Teachers College Press.

Carey, N. and Frechtling, J. (1997) *Best practice in action: Follow-up survey on teacher enhancement programs*, Arlington, VA: National Science Foundation.

Cohen, D.K. and Hill, H.C. (1998) *Instructional policy and classroom performance: The mathematics reform in California (RR-39)*, Philadelphia: Consortium for Policy Research in Education.

Connelly, U. and James, C. (1998) "Managing the school improvement journey: The role of continuing professional development," *Journal of In-Service Education*, 24: 271–282.

Corcoran, T. (1995) *Consortium for policy research in education policy brief. Helping teachers teach well: Transforming professional development.* Available HTTP: http://www.ed.gov/pubs/CPRE/t61/index.html#TOC (accessed January 14, 2011).

Cothran, D., McCaughtry, N., Kulinna, P., and Martin, J. (2006) "Top down public health curricular change: The experience of physical education teachers in the United States," *Journal of In-Service Education*, 32: 533–547. doi:10.1080/13674580601024556

Curtner-Smith, M., Hastie, P.A., and Kinchin, G.D. (2008) "Influence of occupational socialization on beginning teachers' interpretation and delivery of Sport Education," *Sport, Education and Society*, 13: 97–117. doi:10.1080/13573320701780779

Curtner-Smith, M. and Sofo, S. (2004) "Preservice teachers' conceptions of teaching within Sport Education and multi-activity units," *Sport, Education and Society*, 9: 347–377. doi:10.1080/13573320412331302430

Darling-Hammond, L. (1997) *The right to learn: A blueprint for creating schools that work*, San Francisco, CA: Jossey-Bass.

Dreyfus, H. and Dreyfus, S. (1986) *Mind over machine: The power of human intuition and expertise in the era of the computer*, New York: Free Press.

Fennema, E., Carpenter, T.P., Franke, M.L., Levi, L., Jacobs, V.R., and Empson, S.B. (1996) "A longitudinal study of learning to use children's thinking in mathematics instruction," *Journal for Research in Mathematics Education*, 27(4): 403–434.

Fullan, M. (1993) *Change forces: Probing the depths of educational reform*, London: Falmer Press.

Fullan, M. (1995) "The limits and the potential of professional development," in T. Guskey and M. Huberman (eds.) *Professional development in education: New paradigms and practices* (pp. 148–162), New York: Teachers College Press.

Fullan, M. (1999) *Change forces: The sequel*, London: Falmer Press.

Fullan, M., Hill, P., and Crevola, C. (2006) *Breakthrough*, Thousand Oaks, CA: Corwin Press.

Garet, M.S., Porter, A.C., Desimone, L., Birman, B.F., and Yoon, K.S. (2001) "What makes professional development effective? Results from a national sample of teachers," *American Educational Research Journal*, 38: 915–945.

Grant, B., Sharp, P., and Siedentop, D. (1992) *Sport Education in physical education: A teacher's guide*, Wellington, New Zealand: Hillary Commission.

Guskey, T.R. (1991) "Enhancing the effectiveness of professional development programs," *Journal of Educational and Psychological Consultation*, 2(3): 239–247.

Guskey, T.R. (2002) "Does it make a difference? Evaluating professional development," *Educational Leadership*, 59: 45–51.

Hastie, P.A. (1998) "Skill and tactical development during a Sport Education season," *Research Quarterly for Exercise and Sport*, 69: 368–379.

Hastie, P.A. and Sinelnikov, O.A. (2006) "Russian students' participation in and perceptions of a season of Sport Education," *European Physical Education Review*, 12: 131–150. doi:10.1177/1356336X06065166

Hastie, P.A., Sinelnikov, O.A., and Guarino, A.J. (2009) "The development of skill and tactical competencies during a season of badminton," *European Journal of Sport Science*, 9: 133–140. doi:10.1080/17461390802542564

Jenkins, J. (2004) "Sport Education in a PETE program," *Journal of Physical Education, Recreation and Dance*, 75(5): 31–36.

Kennedy, M.M. (1998) *Form and substance in in-service teacher education*, Arlington, VA: National Science Foundation.

Ko, B., Wallhead, T., and Ward, P. (2006) "Professional development workshops: What do teachers learn and use?" *Journal of Teaching in Physical Education*, 4: 397–412.

Lave, J. and Wenger, E. (1991) *Situated learning: Legitimate peripheral participation*, Cambridge: Cambridge University Press.

Lieberman, A. (1996) "Practices that support teacher development: Transforming conceptions of professional learning," in M.W. McLaughlin and I. Oberman (eds.) *Teacher learning: New policies, new practices* (pp. 185–201), New York: Teachers College Press.

Little, M.E. and Houston, D. (2003) "Research into practice through professional development," *Remedial and Special Education*, 24: 75–87.

Loktev, S., Chernyshenko, Y., and Yaroshenko, L. (2001) "Problems and prospects of development of additional education in the area of physical culture and sports," *Teoriya i Praktika Fizicheskoi Kul'turi*, 12: 49–53.

Lund, J., Metzler, M.W., and Gurvitch, R. (2008) "Pedagogical content knowing for model-based instruction in physical education and future directions for research," *Journal of Teaching in Physical Education*, 27: 580–589.

McCaughtry, N., Sofo, S., Rovegno, I., and Curtner-Smith, M. (2004) "Learning to teach Sport Education: Misunderstandings, pedagogical difficulties, and resistance," *European Physical Education Review*, 10: 135–155. doi:10.1177/1356336X04044068

Metzler, M. (2000) *Instructional models for physical education*, Boston: Allyn and Bacon.

National Partnership for Excellence and Accountability in Teaching (NPEAT) (1999) *Improving professional development: Research-based principles*, Washington, DC: National Partnership for Excellence and Accountability in Teaching.

Rink, J.E. (2006) *Teaching physical education for learning* (5th ed.), New York: McGraw-Hill.

Schifter, D. (1996) "A constructivist perspective on teaching and learning mathematics," *Phi Delta Kappan*, 77(7): 492–499.

Sharpe, T. and Koperwas, J. (1999) *BEST: Behavioral evaluation strategy and taxonomy software*, Thousand Oaks, CA: Sage.

Siedentop, D. (1994) *Sport Education: Quality PE through positive sport experiences*, Champaign, IL: Human Kinetics.

Siedentop, D. (2002) "Sport Education: A retrospective," *Journal of Teaching in Physical Education*, 21: 409–418.

Siedentop, D., Hastie, P., and van der Mars, H. (2004) *Complete guide to Sport Education*. Champaign, IL: Human Kinetics.

Sinelnikov, O.A. (2009) "Sport Education for teachers: Professional development when introducing a novel curriculum model," *European Physical Education Review*, 15: 91–114. doi:10.1177/1356336X09105213

Sinelnikov, O.A. and Hastie, P.A. (2004) "Sport-oriented physical culture," *Medico-Biological Aspects of Physical Education*, 5: 152–153.

Sinelnikov, O.A. and Hastie, P.A. (2005) "The importance of Sport Education in public schools in the USA," in E.M. Osmanov (ed.) *Physical education and sports: The basics for a healthy mode of life. Proceedings of the all-Russia scientific and practical conference* (pp. 137–141), Tambov, Russia: Tambov State University.

Sinelnikov, O.A. and Hastie, P.A. (2008) "Teaching Sport Education to Russian students: An ecological analysis," *European Physical Education Review*, 14: 203–222. doi:10.1177/1356336X08090706

Sinelnikov, O.A. and Hastie, P.A. (2010a) "A motivational analysis of a season of sport education," *Physical Education and Sport Pedagogy*, 15: 55–69. doi:10.1080/17408980902729362

Sinelnikov, O.A. and Hastie, P.A. (2010b) "Students' autobiographical memory of participation in multiple Sport Education seasons," *Journal of Teaching in Physical Education*, 29: 167–183.

Sinelnikov, O., Hastie, P., and Prusak, K.A. (2007) "Situational motivation in a season of Sport Education," *ICHPER-SD Research Journal*, 2(1): 43–47.

Sinelnikov, O.A., Hastie, P.A., and Sychev, A.V. (2004) "Sporting physical education at schools: Sport Education," *Fizicheskaya Kultura: Vospitane, Obrazovanie, Trenirovka*, 6: 22–26.

Sparks, D. (1997) "A new vision for staff development," *Principal*, 77: 20–22.

Steyn, G.M. (2005) "Exploring factors that influence the effective implementation of professional development programmes on invitational education," *Journal of Invitational Theory and Practice*, 11: 7–34.

Tsangaridou, N. and O'Sullivan, M. (1994) "Using pedagogical reflective strategies to enhance reflection among preservice physical education teachers," *Journal of Teaching in Physical Education*, 14: 13–33.

van der Mars, H. (1989) "Observer reliability: Issues and procedures," in P.W. Darst, D.B. Zakrajsek, and V.H. Mancini (eds.) *Analyzing physical education and sport instruction* (pp. 53–80), Champaign, IL: Human Kinetics.

Ward, P. and Doutis, P. (1999) "Toward a consolidation of the knowledge base for reform in physical education," *Journal of Teaching in Physical Education*, 18: 382–402.

Index

Taylor & Francis

eBooks

FOR LIBRARIES

ORDER YOUR FREE 30 DAY INSTITUTIONAL TRIAL TODAY!

Over 23,000 eBook titles in the Humanities, Social Sciences, STM and Law from some of the world's leading imprints.

Choose from a range of subject packages or create your own!

Benefits for you
▶ Free MARC records
▶ COUNTER-compliant usage statistics
▶ Flexible purchase and pricing options

Benefits for your user
▶ Off-site, anytime access via Athens or referring URL
▶ Print or copy pages or chapters
▶ Full content search
▶ Bookmark, highlight and annotate text
▶ Access to thousands of pages of quality research at the click of a button

For more information, pricing enquiries or to order a free trial, contact your local online sales team.

UK and Rest of World: **online.sales@tandf.co.uk**

US, Canada and Latin America:
e-reference@taylorandfrancis.com

www.ebooksubscriptions.com

ALPSP Award for BEST eBOOK PUBLISHER 2009 Finalist
sponsored by

Taylor & Francis eBooks
Taylor & Francis Group

A flexible and dynamic resource for teaching, learning and research.